Ambedkar and the Bhangis

Ambedkar and the Bhangis

Efforts for their Upliftment

SHYAM LAL

RAWAT PUBLICATIONS
Jaipur • New Delhi • Bangalore • Guwahati • Kolkata

ISBN 978-81-316-0898-2

Published by
Prem Rawat for **Rawat Publications**
Satyam Apts, Sector 3, Jawahar Nagar, Jaipur 302 004 (India)
Phone: 0141 265 1748 / 7006 Fax: 0141 265 1748
E-mail: info@rawatbooks.com
Website: www.rawatbooks.com

New Delhi Office
4858/24, Ansari Road, Daryaganj, New Delhi 110 002
Phone: 011 2326 3290

Also at *Bangalore, Guwahati* and *Kolkata*

Typeset by Rawat Computers, Jaipur
Printed at Nice Printing Press, New Delhi

To
the sacred memories of a well-known and
committed Ambedkarian scholar,
Bhagwan Das
Advocate, Supreme Court of India,
who, by his writings and speeches, fought against
untouchability, violation of human rights and brought
glory to Untouchables in general and the Bhangis in
particular, whom we lost in 2010.

Contents

Foreword

An eminent sociologist, Professor Shyam Lal has been the Vice-Chancellor of three universities, namely, J.N. Vyas University, Jodhpur; University of Rajasthan, Jaipur; and Patna University, Patna. He is the author of nearly two dozen books on the untouchable castes and tribes of Rajasthan. His books on Bhangi, Bairwa, Bhil, Raigar, Meghwal, converted Buddhists and Christians of Rajasthan are the products of his four decades of dedicated research in the field. I know of no other scholar in the said field who has published so many authentic works on the untouchable castes of Rajasthan. Professor Shyam Lal, therefore, may justly be styled as a pioneer in the field of sociological studies of the untouchable castes of Rajasthan.

Professor Shyam Lal himself comes from the Bhangi caste of untouchables. He has seen extremely unpleasant situations, suffered traumatic experiences and witnessed the travails of life. Having faced pains and indignities in life, Professor Shyam Lal acquired a first-hand knowledge of the toils and tribulations associated with the life of Bhangis. His close association with a well-known Ambedkarian scholar, Bhagwan Das, from 1988 to 2010, further enriched his thought process and inspired him to write on an interesting, but neglected theme, namely Ambedkar-Bhangi relationship.

Professor Shyam Lal's present work titled *Ambedkar and the Bhangis: Efforts for their Upliftment* is a major contribution in the field of sociological studies. It is indeed a novel study, because no one before him has undertaken such an intensive study of the work done by Dr B.R. Ambedkar for the upliftment and mobilization of Bhangis – the lowest of the low untouchable caste. No doubt there are a number of works written by scholars on Dr Ambedkar's social and political ideas, his contribution towards the abolition of untouchability, nation-building, framing of the Indian Constitution, conversion to Buddhism and the like, but what Dr Ambedkar did for the betterment of the Bhangis had only received a frail and a fragmentary attention of the scholars. Professor Shyam Lal's present work is quite different from anything known before; it is the first notable work of significance that attracts the attention on a particular theme of

Ambedkar-Bhangi relationship, exclusively and wholly. The purpose of his work is to highlight the truth and reality of Dr Ambedkar's contribution to the cause of Bhangis' emancipation, completely and totally.

Citing relevant documentary evidences, Professor Shyam Lal has shown that there arose a breed of scholars – in pre- and post-Independence era – who seriously tried to undermine or minimize the contribution of Dr Ambedkar towards the betterment of the Bhangis. Such has been the role of the Congress Party and the intellectuals associated with it, who have knowingly pleaded that the upliftment of the Bhangis was mainly the contribution of Mahatma Gandhi: and that is why the Bhangis during the said period have been more aligned with the Congress. They have argued that instead of Dr Ambedkar, Mahatma Gandhi was the real saviour of the Bhangis and the untouchables. They have made every possible effort to cut to size the stature of Dr Ambedkar, because giving him recognition for his work towards Bhangis' betterment would have been injurious to the reputation of Mahatma Gandhi and the Congress. The value of the present book lies in the fact that Professor Shyam Lal, by quoting extracts, both from primary and secondary sources, has demonstrated in a convincing manner that Dr Ambedkar, not Gandhi, had been the true or genuine messiah of the Bhangis – a fact which is not known to many even today.

In addition, Professor Shyam Lal has raised some significant questions. Why have Bhangis not produced a new breed of leaders? Why they had no political and bureaucratic access to government for more than 30 years since 1952? The main reason for this, according to the author, has been that the Bhangis for a long time from the pre-Independence to the post-Independence period – had been associated whole heartedly with the Gandhi Congress. Gandhi Congress and its supporters, 'who were mainly high-caste Hindus, felt threatened by Dr Ambedkar's rising influence over the untouchables, had started an anti-Ambedkar campaign, which, according to the author, was no more than a mischievous campaign to tarnish Ambedkar's image and to reduce his influence over the Dalits. Because of their alignment with the Gandhi Congress, the Bhangis remained aloof from the progressive movement of Ambedkar; and, as such, they could not develop a consciousness of their existence. This blocked their progress for three decades or so since the enactment of reservations law. In fact, Professor Shyam Lal argues, Dr Ambedkar had always been in the vanguard, a dauntless crusader, fighting and pleading ceaselessly the cause of the untouchables; he contributed far better than Gandhi towards the social upliftment of the depressed classes, including the Bhangis. Professor Shyam Lal has analysed in a wonderful way the negative mentality of the Gandhi Congress which prevented the betterment of the Bhangis.

I have no hesitation in saying that Professor Shyam Lal is an erudite scholar in the field of Ambedkar studies. His present book on Ambedkar-Bhangi relationship is a work of magnificent scholarship. The arguments are clearly expressed and easy to understand. The facts are systematically arranged and the arguments given in defence of Ambedkar's role towards the emancipation of

Bhangis are logical and reliable. It is, perhaps, the first exhaustive research on Ambedkar-Bhangi relationship. Indeed, for producing such an impressive and excellent work, I would like to convey my congratulations to Professor Shyam Lal. The book, I am sure, would be of great benefit to the researchers and general readers who wish to know more about Dr Ambedkar's contribution to the cause of Bhangis' betterment.

Professor L.S. Rathore
Emeritus Professor of Political Science,
and Former Vice-Chancellor, JN Vyas University, Jodhpur.

Preface

Over the last 34 years, I have written and published 21 books on untouchable castes and tribes of Rajasthan, including *The Bhangis: A Sweeper Caste, Untouchable Movement in India: The Bairwa, Untouchable Saints of India, The Raigar Movement, Studies in Social Protest (Meghwal), Tribal Leadership, Tribals and Christian Missionaries, Education Among Tribes, Ambedkar and Dalit Movements, Ambedkar and Nation-Building, From Higher Caste to Lower Caste: A Process of Asprasheekaran* and *Myth of Sanskritisation* and more than 50 articles on many socio-educational and occupational issues in national and international repute journals. My life has been confined to and dominated by Ambedkar and his socio-political thoughts. In Rajasthan, no other scholar has yet studied the untouchable castes as a whole.

My books on Bhangi, Bairwa, Bhil, Raigar, Meghwal and converted Buddhists and Christians of Rajasthan have brought to attention the castes/ tribes in a very significant way into the academic world. The present book on *Dr Ambedkar and the Bhangis* is in a sense, a continuation of such efforts. In this book I have examined the unfolding of the efforts of Dr B.R. Ambedkar, the architect of the Indian Constitution and legendary Dalit right activist, about teaching the Bhangis, the art of using political weapon for the upliftment of their conditions, their journey, their struggle and their courage in the face of many odds.

While much has been written on Ambedkar's contribution to nation-building and Dalit-welfare, the efforts of Ambedkar for the mobilization and upliftment of the lowest of the low untouchable castes have not been separately studied by any scholar, except in a fragment. There is a dearth of material. However, with respectable exception such as the work of Bhagwan Das, sociological and anthropological literature has paid little attention to this. In modern times the measures initiated by Ambedkar are particularly significant for the Bhangis and this book primarily deals with them.

Anyone attempting to write on Ambedkar and Bhangi relationship would agree that it is a tough job venturing into an analysis of this complex but important socio-political issue, particularly when writing about Ambedker's efforts for the upliftment of the marginalised and oppressed community – the Bhangis. For me, writing about Ambedkar and the Bhangis was an enormous challenge for two reasons. First, Ambedkar was not only a leader of downtrodden but of the country. He fought throughout his life for equality, liberty, fraternity, human rights, socio-economic democracy and state and minority. Secondly, Ambedkar through his writings and speeches, with particular reference to the Bhangis, often supported and advocated for their cause. The object of this book is to bring out his efforts for the upliftment of the Bhangis.

My search for information in this regard took me to state, central universities and public libraries and the Bhangi Basti, Panch Kuian Road, New Delhi, also the place where Gandhi stayed whenever he visited Delhi and the place where Gandhi used to meet several foreigners and Indian dignitaries.

It is such an important issue that one wonders why scholars did not pay attention to it. The present book is an outcome of four years of hard work. It can help to create a new field of research that has long been neglected. It will be a beacon to researchers for political reasons have remained out of research ambit. Now, time has come when these issues should be taken up by the researchers.

I had fruitful discussion on book with S.L. Verma, University of Rajasthan, Gopal Bhardwaj and K.S. Saxena, J.N. Vyas University, Jodhpur, and I am grateful to all of them for their valuable comments and encouragement. I must place on record my special thanks to my friends Daulal Mathur and Jagdish Roy who made extensive comments on the manuscript which led to the sharpening of focus.

I take the pleasure to acknowledge with gratitude all social workers, social activists, political elites, writers and masses of Samaj who shared their knowledge, their spirit and their feelings for the community with me and have extended their continued co-operation for over the years. I cannot adequately thank them for the insights they have given me into the dynamics of mass movement.

Shyam Lal

Introduction

Why this Study?

In 1982, while doing fieldwork on 'the Bhangis' in Jodhpur, Rajasthan, my relative O.P. Jawa gave me a book, 'मैं भंगी हूँ'[1] to read. It was written by Bhagwan Das and published by Bheem Patrika, Jalandhar. That was the first time I encountered the work of Bhagwan Das. From then on, I dug up a little more about Bhagwan Das and his works and wrote a few letters at his Delhi address to meet him personally. But it was only after a long interval, when I moved to Pali in 1988, that I met him for the first time. He was 61. Through the interactions that followed with him, I realized that Bhagwan Das had edited, compiled and produced books on Ambedkar and Dalits. It was, perhaps, the first professional effort to be published on the Bhangis.

Having first met Bhagwan Das in Pali, Rajasthan, in 1988 at the age of 61, I remained in touch with him till his death in 2010 at the latter's residence at Munirka, Delhi. I met Bhagwan Das several times and also spent several nights at his residence from 1988 to 2010 with an intention to know more about Ambedkar–Bhangis relationship, Bhangi leadership, Bhangis issues and their solutions – merely as an academic exercise. A mere reading of his writings was not enough, I wanted to see and hear Bhagwan Das. I had to fall in love with him and be charmed by him as I did. He had been a reservoir of insight and information. Our friendship had since then grown from strength to strength. Bhagwan Das and I knew the core issues and hurdles of Bhangi Samaj and both worked tirelessly to write more on Dalits in general and Bhangis in particular. Bhagwan Das not only encouraged me, but also admired my works.

On reading his book 'मैं भंगी हूँ' published in 1981, I procured all available books written and published by Bhagwan Das. In post-Independence India, we hardly have any record or published material on Ambedkar who especially played a key role in Bhangi Movements across the country. Several scholars, academicians and intellectuals, who have written and published volumes, talk about Ambedkar's contribution nation-building, but not about the Ambedkar–Bhangi relationship.

Bhagwan Das has produced scores of books on Dalits in general and Ambedkar's role in emancipation of Bhangis in particular. Forty years after Ambedkar's death, Bhagwan Das decided to write a book and to get it published. The title of the book is 'बाबा साहेब भीमराव अम्बेडकर और भंगी जातियाँ'.[2] On reading this slim book (61 pages) published in Hindi in 1996, I decided to write a detailed study. For me it is important that Ambedkar and Bhangi phenomenon be rendered to larger public. A mere voicing against Ambedkar is not enough, people want to know the truth and the reality. Like Bhagwan Das, I decided to write this book.

In India, as elsewhere, national figures tend to be seen largely through the lens of the party they are affiliated to or rough and humble of political debate. A book entitled, *Politics of the Untouchables: Congress and the Bhangis* (2016) and *Ambedkar and the Bhangis: Efforts for their Upliftment*, provides a different view, exploring the role of the two national figures, the saviours of the untouchables in general and Bhangis in particular. Written by the author, former Vice-Chancellor of Patna University, Patna, Bihar, the profiles are diverse, ranging from well known figures like Mahatma Gandhi and Dr Ambedkar to lesser known like Bhangis. The author, who has been working on this subject for the last few years found new facts to narrate the history. Some of the important issues have been left out of history/research because they were related to the Bhangis, the lowest of the low. Avoiding the role of Ambedkar or the Bhangis in Congress is a political game. Ambedkar is a part of a whole procession of giants who was not allowed to gain prominence amongst the Bhangis, all these years because of the fear that acknowledging Ambedkar's contribution towards the betterment of Bhangis would under-cut the Congress's narrative about the greatness of Gandhi. Gandhi and Congress ensured that Ambedkar, the saviour of untouchables, did not get his due particularly amongst the Bhangis during his life time.

I believe scholars and cultural historians must explore history and discuss new points of view even if it offends some people, so that all its aspects are out in the open. Today's youths are tomorrow's leaders and one wants to know vital and difficult issues that confront society today. I also acknowledged it during more than 33 years of my teaching and research at Government Colleges of Rajasthan and Department of Sociology, University of Rajasthan, Jaipur. As a University teacher, I also tried to understand the complexities of Gandhi-Ambedkar contribution for the upliftment of the Bhangis.

In an article, Rukmini Bhaya Nair ('Sanitation is My Birthright', *The Times of India*, Jaipur, Thursday, 7 January 2016) focused on an untouchable, who recounts a day in the life of a sweeper of the Bhangi caste, Bakha, who faces various humiliations as his day unfolds.

No doubt, we have come a long way since 1935. We only have to read E.M. Forster's Preface to Mulk Raj Anand's novel *Untouchable* to understand this. Forster wrote:

> Untouchable could only have been written by an Indian who observed from the outside. No Europeans, however sympathetic, could have created the character of Bakha, because he would not have known enough about his troubles. And no

untouchable could have written the book, because he would have been involved in indignation and self-pity.

It is noteworthy that discriminatory caste practices remain a social scourge. For instance, according to Rukmini Bhaya Nair's recent article, we no longer think or act as was decreed under colonialism. In the article, Rukmini Bhaya Nair wrote:

> Today, there are several powerful Dalit voices in literature and politics. Fierce arguments about 'reservation', notwithstanding a robust egalitarianism is the foundation of our national discourse. Untouchability was, of course, firmly 'abolished' in Article 17 of the Indian Constitution. But while all this is comforting – we have to admit that discriminatory caste prejudices remain a social scourge. We also know that the obvious answers to dealing with these endemic problems lie in eradicating poverty, improving living conditions and most importantly educating our youth.

Dominant SC communities in Rajasthan have achieved what Bhangis have been trying to achieve for the last 68 years. It was in 1970 when I first started writing on Bhangi Samaj. The Constitutional declaration of a caste-based reservation at the time of Independence was an attempt to address and eliminate horrific discrimination suffered by Dalits in general and Bhangis in particular. It was expected to be an exceptional and interim measure for social justice which has, however, been ever since mutated into a strategy for capturing political power among other communities.

I found many youths telling me that they were not getting jobs despite being educated. There were various exams for various recruitments in Government departments and the bargaining rates were lakhs of rupees. They also told me that collective future of the Samaj was at stake if other SCs were given access to education and government services. So I thought that though we had a reservation policy to protect our Samaj yet the current reservation policy was making our Samaj more hollow. No need to go far to seek demonstration of this fact. There has not been a single MLA in Rajasthan Assembly from Bhangi Samaj since 1985 till date and the only dominant SCs have had representation with a large number of MLAs. A new generation of leaders with Bhangi community has not been produced so far since 1952.

The children of Rajasthan's poor Bhangi families have had no political and bureaucratic access to government for more than 30 years. This is the reason why Bhangis, though lowest of the low untouchables, do not express themselves well. An entire generation has been denied entry into white collar jobs because of this. The children of the poor in Rajasthan cannot harbour a dream of social mobility because of this. I also found a large number of unemployed youths. People got good degrees but still had no jobs. That's why I have been studying our issues over the past three decades or so:

> My belief has become stronger and stronger and it has now turned into my conviction. In January 2016, I published for the first time the book entitled, *The*

Politics of Untouchables: Congress and the Bhangis after returning from Patna University, Patna, Bihar and.,was appreciated by scholars.

Over the last few decades, there has been a steady stream of outlandish statements made by upper caste Hindus and also Dalits. This has included questioning the contribution of Ambedkar in emancipation of Bhangis in particular. From the pre-Independence to the post-Independence, the Bhangis in particular across the country were with the Gandhi Congress. Subsequently, the Congress took direct control over the Bhangis. Thus, Congress and the Bhangis became inseparable and synonymous. This sparked anti-Ambedkar campaign in early 1930s. Gandhi Congress and its supporters felt threatened by Ambedkar and started anti-Ambedkar campaign, raising in their minds doubts of Ambedkar being anti-Dalit.

The Indian version holds that the Gandhi–Ambedkar imbroglio over Dalits began when Gandhi was declared the sole messiah of Dalits by the Congress in 1930. But many Ambedkarites, Dalit leaderships, including Bhagwan Das in his writings, argue that the anti-Ambedkar campaign was the first step in upending Ambedkar's influence. Bhagwan Das has written a first person account of the Bhangi tragedies in his book, 'बाबा साहेब अम्बेडकर और भंगी जातियाँ'.

Ambedkar and Bhangi phenomenon strongly encouraged me to concentrate on three policy issues.

First, a beginning of Ambedkar and Bhangi phenomenon was noticed after 1990 when Congressmen, caste Hindus, staunch supporters and followers of Gandhi kicked up a storm by questioning as to what Ambedkar had done for the Bhangis in particular. This led Ambedkar leadership, Ambedkarites and Ambedkar followers to criticize him bitterly. They latched onto the baseless statements calling the charges serious and grave. From thence began controversy on Ambedkar and Bhangi relationship. But now true Gandhi loyalists, that too the old faithful ones have started voicing their doubts. It is well said that 'to be great is to be misunderstood'. Unfortunately this is true about Ambedkar.

It was Ambedkar who fought for the most deprived section of India and therefore, he was rightly called Indian crusader for social justice. In his book 'बाबा साहेब अम्बेडकर और भंगी जातियाँ', Bhagwan Das[3] wrote:

> 'यह पुस्तक कुछ विशेष कारणों से एक विशेष जाति के लोगों को संबोधित करके लिखी जा रही है। एक कारण तो यह है कि जब बाबा साहेब के अनुयायी वाल्मीकि जाति के लोगों से बाबा साहेब के दिखाये रास्ते पर चलने की बात करते हैं तो उनमें से वे लोग जो कांग्रेस या भारतीय जनता पार्टी से जुड़े हुए हैं या कट्टर गांधीवादी या हिन्दू हैं, एक सवाल उठाते हैं कि डॉ. अम्बेडकर ने हमारे लिया क्या किया?' 'हमारे' से उनका तात्पर्य 'वाल्मीकि' कहलाने वाली जाति के लोगों से है। भंगियों की अन्य जातियां जैसे धानुक, हेला, बंसफोड, डोम, डोमर, रावत, हाड़ी, मादिया, पाकी, थोटी, मखियार आदि में जन्में लोग आमतौर पर ऐसे सवाल नहीं उठाते और न ही अन्य अनुसूचित जातियों के लोग बाबा साहेब के कार्य, सेवाओं, संघर्ष और त्याग पर उंगली उठाते हैं। परन्तु कुछ जातियों जैसे चमार, महार, नमोशूद, परईया, माला आदि के बारे में यह कहते सुना जाता है कि वे सब प्रकार के लाभ उठा रही हैं और आगे बढ़ गयी हैं।

'दूसरा कारण हिन्दू नेताओं का गलत और गुमराह कर देने वाला प्रचार है जो सवर्ण हिन्दू नेताओं की आदत है और जिसका खंडन करना जरूरी है।'

Even before Ambedkar and Bhangi phenomenon emerged in the post-Independent India, the Bhangis of Kanpur, UP had been the first to undertake an organized protest against Ambedkar during the British rule. Agnelal and Rahul Raj, former Professor and Assistant Professor respectively, in the Department of Ancient Indian History and Archaeology, Lucknow University, Lucknow, and Banaras Hindu University, Banaras, respectively, not only wrote a book on 'उत्तर प्रदेश में दलित आन्दोलन' (2011) but also narrated a significant incident in their book. To quote[4]:

> 'कानपुर के दलित सम्मान संघर्ष की एक दूसरी झलक दूसरे रूप में दिखाई देती है। एक बार जब बाबा साहेब डॉ. अम्बेडकर अपने सैलून से कानपुर होकर यात्रा कर रहे थे, उस समय किसी राजनैतिक पार्टी के लोगों के उकसाने पर सफाई कर्मचारी समाज के लोगों ने विरोध प्रदर्शित किया। उन्होंने कहा कि जब बाबा साहेब ने अपनी बिरादरी के लिये कार्य किया है, हम सफाई मजदूरों के लिये कोई कार्य नहीं किया। हमारे लिये तो कांग्रेस ही कार्य कर रही है। इस तरह से जो कुछ उन्हें बताया गया था, वह सब कुछ कहकर उन्होंने विरोध प्रदर्शित किया।'
>
> 'बाबा साहेब डॉ. अम्बेडकर भली-भांति यह समझ गये कि यह हवा कहीं से सफाई कर्मचारी समाज में भरी गयी है। अस्तु उन्होंने पूरे विरोध प्रदर्शन के बाद में प्रदर्शनकारियों के प्रमुख दो-तीन लोगों को आमंत्रित किया और उनसे वार्ता की। अन्त में उन्होंने कहा कि "जाओं और सैलून के कार्यालय भाग में जो लोग कार्य कर रहे हों, उन सभी के नाम और जाति लिखकर लाओ।" वे लोग गये और कार्यालय में कर्मचारियों की पूरी-सूची बनाकर ले आए। उसमें अधिकांशत: सफाई कर्मचारी ही थे। शायद एक अन्य अनुसूचित जाति का और दूसरा क्रिश्चियन था। कर्मचारियों की संख्या 20 से कम न थी। वे लोग यह देखकर बहुत शर्मिंदा हुए और बाबा साहेब के चरणों पर सिर रखकर कहा कि मुझे कांग्रेस नेताओं ने ऐसा करने को कहा, बाबा साहब, हम लोग अन्धकार में थे। आपने यह अन्धकार दूर कर दिया।'
>
> इस प्रकार समय-समय पर दलित सम्मान आंदोलन को तोड़ने या फूट डालने के लिये विरोधियों ने अनेक षड्यंत्र रचे, परन्तु दलित सम्मान आंदोलन रूका नहीं, आगे ही बढ़ता गया।'

Agnelal and Rahul Raj extended full support to the claims made by Bhagwan Das in his book. There was a deliberate effort by Congressmen to malign Ambedkar's reputation and tarnish his image as messiah of Dalits.

In order to understand the part played by high caste Hindu Congressmen in sending the fake signed telegrams of Bhangis to London, it is necessary to study another sabotage activity of the Congress. For instance, during the third decade of 20th century, when Round Table Conference (RTC) was going on in London (1932), some Gandhi Congressmen and Arya Samajis held a public meeting of Valmiki/Mehtar outside Lahori Gate in Lahore (undivided India). In this meeting more than 100 men and women assembled there. On this occasion Smt. Mata Rameshwari Devi was also present. They held socio-political discussion with men and women of Bhangi caste. Members of the Congress sent fake signed telegram of Bhangis to London informing that their leader was

Mahatma Gandhi, not Ambedkar and that Ambedkar had no right to speak on their behalf.

Many interpreted this as an official signal to knock down the most eminent leader of the untouchables. A smear campaign against Ambedkar was launched. The mainstream political parties were calling Ambedkar 'ब्रिटिश सरकार के भक्त, देशद्रोही, अम्बेडकर ने जो नफरत बोई थी उसी की पौध मायावती[5] है।'

It was unfortunate that untouchables were so gullible that they lapped up propaganda as fact. While there can be no doubt that Gandhi was an important figure in national movement, its impact had been such, untouchables unity was affected.

Sohan Lal Shastri says that for fighting untouchables' cause, Ambedkar did much better job as a hero than Gandhi. Ambedkar was inspired by Buddh, Kabir and Jyoti Rao Phule to build a society based on equality, liberty and fraternity without religious interference.

Sohan Lal Shastri[6], author of Ambedkar's writing 'बाबा साहेब डॉ. अम्बेडकर के सम्पर्क में पच्चीस वर्ष', points out that:

> 'गोलमेज कान्फ्रेन्स लंदन के समय, मैं सन् 1931 में श्री मद्दयानन्द महाविद्यालय लाहौर का विद्यार्थी था। परमपूज्य बाबा साहेब डा. बी.आर. अम्बेडकर का नाम पहले ही सुन चुका था। उनके नाम की पंजाब में विशेष करके लाहौर में बहुत चर्चा थी। उनके साईमन कमीशन के सामने गवाही देने के कारण तथा आर्यसमाज के गढ़ लाहौर में अछूतों की वकालत करने के कारण पंजाब का हिन्दू समाज और पंजाब के हिन्दू समाचार पत्र उन्हें बुरा भला कहने में सब प्रान्तों में आगे थे। मैं इन आलोचनाओं को बड़े ध्यानपूर्वक सुना और पढ़ा करता था। न जाने मुझे बाबा साहेब के नाम में इतना आकर्षण तथा हार्दिक खिंचाव क्यों प्रतीत होने लगा। 1932 में लाहौरी गेट के बाहर आर्यसमाजी तथा कांग्रेसी हिन्दू एक मीटिंग कर रहे थे जिसमें एक सौ के करीब वाल्मीकि या मेहतर भाई सम्मिलित थे। श्रीमती माता रामेश्वरी देवी भी उस जल्से में उपस्थित थीं। मैं अचानक ही वहां जा पहुंचा। जल्से में वाल्मीकि भाईयों के हाथों में चपातियां हिन्दुओं में बांटी जा रही थी। लाहौर के वाल्मीकि भाईयों की ओर से गोलमेज कान्फ्रैन्स लंदन में तार दिलवाए जा रहे थे कि हमारा नेता महात्मा गांधी है। डा. अम्बेडकर को गोलमेज कॉन्फ्रेन्स में हमारी तरफ से बोलने का कुछ भी अधिकार नहीं। मुझसे यह ढोंग न देखा गया। मैंने ऊंचे स्वर में कहा कि अछूतों के साथ यह ठगी क्यों बरती जा रही है। मुझे कई खद्दरपोशों ने खद्दरधारी कांग्रेसी नवयुवक समझा और कहा कि तुम कांग्रेसी होकर ऐसी बात क्यों मुंह से निकालते हो? अगर गोलमेज सम्मेलन कान्फ्रेन्स लंदन में डा. अम्बेडकर को भारत के अछूतों का लीडर मान लिया गया तो मिस्टर जिन्ना की तरह वह भी अपनी अछूत कोम के अधिकार जुटा करा लेगा। मैंने कहा कि इसमें हर्ज ही क्या है। अछूतों की हालत मुसलमानों से कहीं बदतर है अछूतों को तो हिन्दू धर्म तथा समाज ने अधमरा कर रखा है। मेरी इस प्रकार की बातचीत उन लोगों को अच्छी न लगी और उन्होंने यह ताना देते हुए मुझे प्लेटफार्म से परे धकेल दिया कि तुम नकली खद्दरधारी हो जो ऐसी बातें करते हो। मैंने कहा 'मैं भी तो जन्म से अछूत हूं इसलिये मुझे तुम्हारा यह पाखंड और फरेब बहुत बुरा लग रहा है – और मेरी दृष्टि में सचमुच अछूतों का यदि कोई सच्चा नेता है तो वे डॉक्टर अम्बेडकर ही हैं। यहां से मेरी बाबा साहेब के प्रति भक्ति और श्रद्धा का आरम्भ होता है। तबसे मेरी यह दृढ़ धारणा बन गई कि अछूतों का मसीहा और पैगम्बर यदि कोई हो सकता है तो वह डा. बाबा साहेब अम्बेडकर ही हो सकते हैं, क्योंकि वह अछूतों के गोश्त पोस्त है। वह कानून की ऊंची से ऊंची शिक्षा रखते हैं, वे एक निर्भीक एवं निडर सैनिक योद्धा हैं। उसी दिन से ही मेरी एक अमिट धारणा हो गई कि जिस महापुरूष की सहायता ओर सहानुभूति के लिये शताब्दियों से करोड़ों निरीह एवं पददलित अछूतों की दु:ख भरी निगाहें प्रतीक्षा कर रही थी, उसका अवतार हो चुका है। और वह है स्वनाम धन्य बाबा साहेब डॉ. भीमराव अम्बेडकर।'

The increasing consciousness amongst the Bhangi youths along with growth of education, has also raised a question mark over the hypocrisy of one and real concern for the other.

A few decades ago, when I went to my home-town Jodhpur, I also visited late N.D. Gujarati's[7] residence at Chopasani Housing Board Jodhpur. Gujarati was a freedom fighter and also old active Bhangi Congress worker from pre-Independence to post-Independence period. He was associated with Harijan Sewak Sangh too for years together. I asked him for his experiences with the Congress. Gujarati first evaded questions on this. But Gujarati said, 'अगर मैं कुछ कहूंगा तो कांग्रेस वाले मुझे मार डालेंगे'.

I wondered when Gujarati changed his stance from not telling to telling me. He called the Congress being 'more anti-Ambedkar' than others. Narrating an incident with the author, Gujarati claimed: Once a sammelan of Congress Dalit workers in Jodhpur was to be addressed by the then PM. The venue was stadium ground, Jodhpur. Gujarati was asked by local Congress netas to convene it. He replied in affirmative. A day earlier to the scheduled programme, Gujarati was wonder struck when Congress leaders asked him to speak against Ambedkar. According to Gujarati he was upset over Congress boss's directives to him. What particularly displeased Gujarati was Congress boss hinting that he must speak against Ambedkar. Other details were not divulged. This incident seems ominous when viewed in the backdrop of reminiscences about the darkest day of his life.

Gujarati says that Ambedkar was more concerned with the atrocities heaped on the untouchables even in 1920, Ambedkar had written extensively about the plight of untouchables. He was the saviour of the untouchables; at that time, the sole leader fighting about the untouchables' commitment to civil liberties. From pre-Independence to post-Independence the period methods through which the Congress tarnished Ambedkar's image have now undergone radical changes. The case of Gujarati illustrate the point. The Congress used untouchable workers to inform his audience about the negation of Ambedkar's leadership. The lesson that comes through clearly from accounts of that difficult period a few decades ago is that this is not the first time the Congress netas have tarnished the image of Ambedkar. Earlier also it had instigated Bhangis of Kanpur, UP for agitating against Ambedkar. Most Congressmen give little importance to such things. No wonder Congressmen and Congress netas in private conversation lamented against Ambedkar. What is equally lamentable is that even the first foreign educated Dalit messiah, who represented Dalits at the Round Table Conference (RTC), some 85 years ago, was criticized bitterly by the Congress. Gujarati argued that this is what the Congress expected from him as well. Refusing to speak against Ambedkar made him feel good. It was such a herculean task to say 'No' and for a Bhangi Congress worker, it was even more difficult. It was the biggest compliment to Ambedkar. What an achievement it was for Gujarati and his family. He has given Bhangi Samaj something to be proud about him.

Second, besides Congressmen, Bindeshwar Pathak, the founder of Sulabh International, also triggered contentious remarks against Ambedkar which appeared on 2 September 1995 in *Sarita,* one of the leading Hindi magazines published from Delhi. The remarks of Pathak were one sided. The remarks were worse. This shocked the Dalits. They had never heard of that. There was anger when Ambedkar supporters came to know it.

First, Bindeshwar Pathak[8] targetted Dalit leadership, saying: 'देखिए दलितों के नाम पर सिर्फ राजनीति करने वाले दलितों का भला कभी नहीं कर सकते।' But Pathak crossed all limits. This time he charged[9] 'सबसे ज्यादा आश्चर्यजनक बात तो यह है कि डॉ. भीमराव अम्बेडकर का भी स्कैंजरों की तरफ ध्यान नहीं गया।' Pathak's sarcastic remarks had raised eyebrows among Dalits in India.

Pathak, born in a Brahmin family, hails from Bihar. He is a staunch supporter of Gandhi. His career has gone through many ups and downs. After India achieved Independence, in 1947, Sulabh International came into existence and Pathak was the founder and there has been no looking back since then. He studied sociology and devoted his whole life to the cause of Bhangi upliftment, spearheading the agitation for social emancipation of this most deprived section of India and became messiah of Bhangis. Pathak was criticized by Bhagwan Das for making irresponsible statements about Ambedkar. This was the first time that the Gandhian supporter has dragged particularly Ambedkar's name in Bhangi welfare controversy. All Dalits read this statement in the press. Bhagwan Das alleged that Pathak in his individual capacity became messiah of Bhangis and he continued to play a negative role in exploiting the Bhangis in Sulabh International. His main objective is not to emancipate the Bhangis but to improve the sanitation. It is also true that Pathak either unfamiliar with Ambedkar's work and contribution or being a true Gandhian mis-interpreted the whole thing. Dalits not only protested against Pathak's remarks against Ambedkar, but also expressed their displeasure on unwanted remarks. Bhagwan Das and other Dalits were upset with Pathak's hardhitting remarks suggesting that Ambedkar did nothing for the Bhangis in particular.

Many academicians, former bureaucrats turned writers, etc. in north India nowadays are challenging these negative perceptions and views. In fact, according to a recent publication an overwhelming majority of Dalits negate such views. It is time for them to pay heed.

In 1996, following India-wide media attention, former IPS officer S.R. Darapuri[10] – also an Ambedkarite wrote the 'Prastavna' of the book 'बाबा साहेब भीमराव अम्बेडकर और भंगी जातियाँ'. In Prastavna, he bitterly criticized those who spread such negative views against each other and divide the Dalits. He replied to these views, thus:

> 'अनुसूचित जातियों में भंगी जातियां पेशे के हिसाब से वास्तव में सबसे अधिक अछूत हैं। शिक्षा का दर न्यूनतम होने के कारण सरकारी नौकरियों में आरक्षण का उचित लाभ नहीं उठा पा रही हैं। इस तथ्य को गलत ढंग से पेश करके कुछ राजनीतिक पार्टियां उन्हें अन्य दलित जातियों के विरूद्ध बरगला रही हैं कि उनका हिस्सा दूसरी बड़ी अनुसूचित जातियों द्वारा हड़पा जा रहा है तथा वे उनके लिए अलग आरक्षण की मांग को उठवा रही हैं। यह उनके भंगी जातियों के हितैषी होने का प्रतीक न होकर उन्हें गुमराह करने और दलित एकता को तोड़ने का एक प्रयास है। यह सर्वविदित है कि आरक्षण तथा अन्य सरकारी प्रोग्रामों का लाभ तभी उठाया जा सकता है, जब इन जातियों में शिक्षा के

प्रचार-प्रसार को बढ़ावा दिया जाए और अच्छी लीडरशिप उभरे परन्तु वास्तव में ऐसा तो कुछ नहीं किया जा रहा है। केवल इन जातियों को दूसरी दलित जातियों के विरूद्ध बरगला कर उनका भावनात्मक शोषण किया जा रहा है। यहां तक दुष्प्रचार किया जा रहा है कि दलितों के मसीहा बाबा साहेब भीमराव अम्बेडकर ने भी भंगी जातियों के उत्थान के लिए कोई विशेष कार्य नहीं किया है। वास्तव में यह दुष्प्रचार पूर्णतया भ्रामक है।'

'... अम्बेडकर आंदोलन के पुरोधा, समाज सेवी, प्रगतिशील विचारक एवं विद्वान लेखक श्री भगवान दास जी ने सवर्गों के भंगी जातियों के संबंध में किए जा रहे दुष्प्रचार का तथ्यात्मक एवं तार्किक उत्तर दिया है। उन्होंने भंगी जातियों को अपनी मूल समस्या को पहचानने तथा उसे दर करने हेतु अपने द्वारा सुझाए गए कारगर उपायों को अपनाने का अनुरोध किया है। उन्होंने ऐतिहासिक तथ्यों से यह भी स्थापित किया है कि बाबा साहेब इन जातियों के उत्थान के लिए कितने चिन्तित और समर्पित थे। इस संबंध में बाबा साहेब का अपने प्रमुख पत्र ''मूक नायक'' के संपादकीय में अंकित ''मूल खोजो विवाद मिटेगा'' का मूलमंत्र भी इन जातियों में पिछड़ेपन के कारणों के संबंध में पैदा किया जा रहे भ्रम को दूर करने में बहुत सहायक सिद्ध हो सकता है।'

Lastly, over the past few decades, there have been countless questions on Ambedkar's contribution in the emancipation of the Bhangis across the country. A few years ago, Congressmen, Bindeshwar Pathak and Bhangis too in 2001 in Delhi started voicing their doubt about Ambedkar. Case in point: Educated Bhangi youths. On the occasion of Ambedkar anniversary in 2001, BOMSEF organized a two-day national seminar on April 14–15 at Delhi on 'मूल निवासी बाल्मिकी जाति मुक्ति सम्मेलन'. The main speaker was D.D. Kalyani from Amritsar, Punjab. This incident was the third of the series that took place in April 2001.

Just when the speaker was about to speak, some educated Bhangi youths dared to stand up and ask certain questions to the speaker. What was the contribution of Ambedkar for the upliftment of the Bhangis in particular? And what Ambedkar has done for Bhangis? Bhangis are the lowest of the low in India. Bhangis are dismayed to learn that the benefit of protective discrimination policy is denied to them. There is growing sense of unease among them that they are being isolated slowly, but surely. The speaker faced a volley of questions from the audience, especially Bhangi youths. But in a democracy people's expectations are growing and they are getting impatient, some times fuelled beyond reasons by politicians. We have to guard against that.

In such an environment, it is important for Ambedkarites and Ambedkar leadership to take the charge and speak up. Disengaging with the ongoing dialogue only raises suspicion that this astonishing silence implies complicity. Ambedkarites and Ambedkar supporters should provide positive answer to the frequently asked question as to Ambedkar's contribution for the lowest of the low. By maintaining lofty distance, they allow critics to draw their own conclusion. If no attempts are made by scholars, researchers and writers, perhaps the Bhangis will believe that Ambedkar had not cared as much.

Whatever the reasons, the phenomenon was unprecedented. It has provoked sentiments among the Bhangis and shaken them. Ambedkar and Bhangi phenomenon that we are witnessing today is because of indifferent attitude of mainstream parties toward Bhangis across the country, which we have seen in last 67 years. The protective discrimination policy and subsequently the progress of certain dominant Dalit castes/communities have created a new socio-political consciousness – an impatience for better living. There are many more examples.

The speaker answered the questions as Ambedkar did lot for the Dalits in general and Bhangis in particular. Hitting back at youths, Kalyani[11] said:

> मैंने उनको उत्तर दिया कि मूल निवासी बहुजन समाज में से जिन जातियों ने बाबा साहेब अम्बेडकर की विचारधारा को पढ़ा और उस पर अमल किया, उन जातियों का ही उत्थान हुआ है। उदाहरणतया – पंजाब में अकेले होशियारपुर जनपद में से कम से कम एक सौ आईएएस अधिकारी चमार जाति में से ही बने। कौन से चमत्कार ने केवल एक जिले से ही एक जाति के 100 आईएएस अधिकारी बना दिए। कल तक जिनको किसी सरकारी कार्यालय में चपरासी तक बनने का अधिकार नहीं था, वो आज इतने ऊंचे पदों पर आसीन कैसे हो गए?
>
> जब मैंने इस उदाहरण का विश्लेषण करके देखा तो पता चला कि पंजाब में बाबा साहेब अम्बेडकर की विचारधारा का प्रचार और प्रसार जितना भी हुआ है, उसमें मुख्यतया देन चमार जाति के पढ़े-लिखे लोगों की है और आज यदि चमार जाति में से ज्यादा लोग पढ़-लिख कर उच्चाधिकारी बने हैं तो उसकी महज एक ही वजह है कि उन्होंने बाबा साहेब डा. अम्बेडकर जी को अपना रहबर और मसीहा माना और उनकी विचारधारा को ही अपने आचरण में ढाला।
>
> उस सम्मेलन में एक और प्रश्न भी पूछा गया कि वाल्मीकि जाति के लोग फुले, अम्बेडकर की विचारधारा से अभी भी आकर्षित क्यों नहीं हुए हैं तो मैंने उन्हें बताया कि वाल्मीकि जाति की स्थिति बंजर जमीन के समान है और बंजर जमीन पर सीधा बीज डालने से कोई फसल होने वाली नहीं है। इसलिए सर्व प्रथम वाल्मीकि जाति रूपी जमीन पर जागृति रूपी हल चलाकर फूले अम्बेडकरी विचारधारा का बीज डालना होगा तब कहीं जाकर क्रांति रूपी फसल पैदा होगी।
>
> परन्तु दु:ख की बात यह है कि वाल्मीकि जाति के लोग आज भी बाबा साहेब अम्बेडकर को अपना रहबर ही नहीं मानते। वे कहते हैं कि डॉ. अम्बेडकर तो चमार जाति से थे, उनका हमारे साथ में कोई संबंध नहीं है। उनकी ऐसी अज्ञानता और बेबसी पर तरस आता है कि उनको यह पता नहीं है कि बाबा साहेब अम्बेडकर कौन थे? इसके बारे में भी उनको थोड़ी सी जानकारी देना कोई अतिश्योक्ति न होगी।
>
> वाल्मीकि जाति के अलावा दूसरी जातियों के लोगों के दिमाग में अकस्मात यह प्रश्न आ सकता है कि क्या बाबा साहेब अम्बेडकर जी ने केवल सफाई का धंधा करने वाली जातियों के लिए ही सब कुछ किया। उनको बताना चाहते हैं कि बाबा साहेब की देन तो पूरे संसार की मानवता के प्रति है, किसी समाज या जाति विशेष के प्रति नहीं। परन्तु भारत की सामाजिक व्यवस्था ऐसी है जिसकी आधारशिला वर्ण व्यवस्था अर्थात् जात-पात है और इस व्यवस्था में असमानता ही नहीं क्रामिक असमानता है और इसी कारण से हर व्यक्ति अपनी जाति के प्रति ही सोचता है। इसी वजह से वाल्मीकि जाति के लोग भी समझते हैं कि हमारा भला तो कोई वाल्मीकि जाति का नेता ही कर सकता है।
>
> परन्तु जब वाल्मीकि जाति के लोगों की हम आस्था और विश्वास गांधी जी में देखते हैं तो विरोधाभास सा लगता है, गांधी जी तो बनिया जाति के थे लेकिन फिर भी इस जाति के लोगों ने गांधी के नेतृत्व को स्वीकार किया और बाबा साहेब अम्बेडकर जैसे महान मसीहा ने इस जाति के लिए क्या किया इसके बारे में सफाई का धंधा करने वाली जातियों को कोई जानकारी नहीं है। परिणामस्वरूप आज भी यह लोग पतन की ओर अग्रसर हो रहे हैं और दूसरी जाति के लोग फूले-अम्बेडकर विचारधारा को अपना रहे हैं और वे सभी क्षेत्रों में उन्नति कर रहे हैं।

हम चाहते हैं कि वाल्मीकि जातियों अर्थात् सफाई का धंधा करने वाली जातियों को भी पता चले कि बाबा साहेब अम्बेडकर ने उनके लिए क्या-क्या संघर्ष किया। यदि उनको इस विचारधारा की जानकारी हो जाएगी तो वे समझ सकेंगे कि केवल और केवल बाबा साहेब अम्बेडकर जी की विचारधारा ही उनके कल्याण और उत्थान का मार्क है।

The Ambedkar versus Bhangis equation is driven by myth-making rather than facts, say scholars.

Silencing a man or even a thousand men! women is easy. How does one silence an entire generation? The key question as asked by Bhangis at national seminar and Dalit summit was what Ambedkar had done for the lowest of the low. That's what Ambedkarite, Ambedkar followers, need to answer.

I attach great significance to Bhangi socio-political relations with Ambedkar and their enormous potential for the future. Therefore, it is important to place the fact on a reliable legal basis. It is a good opportunity to discuss the challenges that the Ambedkarites are facing at the moment.

Realizing the importance as stated earlier I started gathering more knowledge about it and discovered something startling. I then consulted with some of the top scholars and published materials. We do not have enough published material about the realities. Unfortunately none of the sources – official and non-official – is detailed enough to put together a comprehensive picture of Ambedkar-Bhangi relationship. However, I went through scattered sources and attempted to reconstruct the Ambedkar and Bhangi past. In a few years, I succeeded.

The factors that inspired me to write a book on Ambedkar and Bhangi phenomenon are:

(i) To understand the various efforts made by Ambedkar and action that he took on his own from early 20th century.
(ii) To study Ambedkar's early concerns regarding working conditions, education, recruitment and, of course, their interaction, participation and relationship with the contemporary socio-political movement.
(iii) To bring out many hidden facets about Ambedkar.
(iv) Its outcomes have settled an important debate.

I was awarded Ambedkar National fellowship for the year 2003–2004 and 2004–2005 by ICSSR, HRD Ministry, Government of India, New Delhi. I enjoy writing on Dalits. I am doing that more after my retirement from university. I read and spend time with my family. I write a lot but I need to write more.

I have done extensive research for the book which involved visiting various libraries for old manuscripts. There are many startling facts which I came across during my fieldwork.

In this book, I have endeavoured my best to place before the caste Hindus in general and Bhangi netas and educated Bhangi youths in particular, the thoughts, views and feelings of Ambedkar and also on their inter-relationship. While aiming to help the reader by placing before him all the relevant and important materials, I have not sought to impose my views on him. I have placed both sides of the issues dealt with in the book and have left it to the reader to form his own opinion.

I will discuss in details the major role played by Ambedkar in the emancipation of the Bhangis in the following chapters. In fact the Scavenging communities benefitted in varied ways under Ambedkar leadership. For instance, the First Commission for Safai Karamcharis during the British rule, organized the Bhangis: their organization was called Municipalities Kamgar Sangh (MKS), Ambedkar's anguish, love and affection for the Bhangis, the Bhangis and their participation in Scheduled Caste Federation (SCF), Samata Sainik Dal and Mobilization of Bhangis, Rift in SCF, recruitment of educated Bhangis to public services and strategies to protect their interest, imperative of education, Ambedkar's visit to Matang Samaj, 1937, Matang Conference, 1938 and Equality of Citizenship. Labour Ministry introduced a number of measures which benefitted to lower caste sections, including the Bhangis, besides introducing uniform Rules in Municipalities, Dalits (including Bhangis) participating in foreign universities for higher studies, ban on migration of the Bhangis from Pakistan to India, 1947. And the Congress instigates Bhangis and fans their resentment against Ambedkar, with emergence of Bhangi propagator of Buddhism.

Notes

1. भगवान दास, मैं भंगी हूं, जालंधर, भीम पत्रिका प्रकाशन, 1981.
2. भगवान दास, बाबा साहेब भीमराव अम्बेडकर और भंगी जातियां, लखनऊ, उत्तर प्रदेश, दलित टुडे प्रकाशन, 1998.
3. वही, पृ. 1.
4. अंगनेलाल एवं राहुल राज, उत्तर प्रदेश में दलित आन्दोलन, दिल्ली, गौतम बुक सेन्टर, 2011, पृ. 203.
5. कंवल भारती, डा. अम्बेडकर को नकारे जाने की साजिश, रामपुर, उत्तर प्रदेश, बौधिसत्व प्रकाशन, 2001, पृ. 9–10, एवं 12.
6. सोहनलाल शास्त्री, बाबा साहेब डॉ. अम्बेडकर के सम्पर्क में पच्चीस वर्ष, नई दिल्ली, सम्यक प्रकाशन, 2013, पृ. 8–9.
7. Talk with late N.D. Gujarati at his residence in Chopasni Housing Board, Jodhpur.
8. विस्तृत जानकारी के लिये विशेषकर देखिए, भगवान दास, बाबा साहेब भीमराव अम्बेडकर और भंगी जातियां, वहीं, 1998, पृ. 1.
9. वहीं, पृ. 1.
10. विस्तृत जानकारी के लिए विशेष तौर से एसआर दारापुरी द्वारा लिखित 'प्रस्तावना' अवश्य देखें, वहीं, 1998, पृ. i-ii.
11. डी.डी. कल्याण, 'बाबा साहेब डॉ. अम्बेडकर की वाल्मीकि जातियों अर्थात सफाई का काम करने वाली जातियों के प्रति देन' नई दिल्ली, मूल निवासी पब्लिकेशन ट्रस्ट, 2002, पृ. 1.

Part I

Untouchable Caste in India

1

The Bhangi: The Lowest of the Low Untouchable Castes

The Bhangi: Names and Titles

A caste of the removers of night soil and the cleaners of latrines belongs to a well defined group in the Indian social order. All such workers in India are, today, included under the general nomenclature 'Bhangi'. For this occupational group there are various names and titles in use in different parts of the country but the better known term is 'Bhangi'. Thus they are known in south India as 'hela'[1], meaning 'cry', and that they were called so because they had to cry out to demonstrate their identity while moving on the roads. According to another theory it is derived from the word 'hilna', meaning 'be domesticated'; another source of derivation is from 'hela', meaning basket load or 'hel' or 'hil', meaning filth mud.

The title for them in Gujarati is Halalkhor[2] – one who eats what is lawful, one whose earnings are legitimate. This euphemistic title is said to have been introduced by Emperor Akbar. 'Khakrob'[3] is from Persian words 'khaki', meaning earth, and 'rob', meaning sweeping. In Punjab, the Bhangis are known as Chuhra[4] and this name has been derived from their work of collecting and sweeping up scraps (*churaharna*). Similarly in Bombay (now Mumbai) they are known as Ghare[5] and Bhangi. The Bengali name 'Hari'[6] is supposed to have come from 'haddi' – bone. Hari was the bone gatherer and was familiar to the early settlers of Calcutta (now Kolkata) under the quaint designation of harry – wench. In Rajasthan they are called 'Mehtar'[7] and this name has been derived from Persian 'mehtar' – prince, said to have been applied to them in derision. The Bhangis might have adopted gratifying appellations as prefixes in their caste name. Thus, the Bhangis of Uttar Pradesh call themselves 'Valmiki'[8] who are followers of Valmiki Rishi, the first Sanskrit poet and the famous author of the *Ramayana*. Though this caste is known by different names, the sweeper community in most states appears to have had the same stock of traditions and legends. The title 'Bhangi' is now generally employed and has, therefore, been taken as the designation of the caste. Details regarding names have been given in Table 1.1.

Table 1.1

Various Names of the Bhangi Caste in Different States

"	[9]Bengal	Hari, Hadi
	Uttar Pradesh	Valmiki, Dhanuk
	Madhya Pradesh	Mehtar, Bhangi
	Assam	Mehtar, Bhangi
	Orissa (Odisha)	Mehtar, Bhangi, Valmiki, Madiga,
"	[10]Bihar	Mehtar
	Tamil Nadu	Thoti
	Andhra Pradesh	Madiga
	Punjab	Mira, Lalbegis, Chuhra, Balashahi, Valmiki
"	[11]Maharashtra	Ghare, Bhangi
	Gujarat	Halalkhor, Hela, Barwashia
"	[12]Delhi	Bhangi, Valmiki
"	[13]Karnataka	Madiga
"	[14]Kerala	Madiga
"	[15]Rajasthan	Bhangi, Mehtar, Chuhra, Valmiki

In the country, the Scavenging castes, are known by different names in different regions. Thus, according to Sachchidananda, they are known as 'Bhangi, Balmiki, Chuhra, Mehtar, Mazhabi, Lalbegi, Halalkhor, etc. in North India, Hari, Hela, Dom, Senei etc. in eastern India; Mukhiyar, Thoti, Chachati, Pakay, Relli etc. in south India and Mehtar, Bhangi, Halalkhor, Ghasi, Olangna, Zadmalli, Barvashia, Metariya, Jamphoda, Mela, etc. in western and central India. In 1911 census, some of them started returning as Adi Dharmi, Adi Dravida, Adi Karnataka and Adi Andhra'.[16]

From Vedic period to present day, sweepers/Scavengers of India were/are called by different names in different period. Altogether 18 different names of caste were given by S.P. Sumanakshar. According to him, they are 'Chandal, Mehtar, Bhangi, Chuhra, Hela, Lal Begi, Lal posh, Shekha, Halal khor, Bhakhiyar, Malkala, Khakrob, Berwah, Mazbi, Valmiki, Harijan, Naval-Dharmi and Adi-Dharmi'.[17]

Early Literature and Origin of Bhangi

Indians mainly live in villages. Even today more than 70 per cent of the country's population is rural. In ancient days the percentage was much higher. Being bereft of an enclosed place for defecation inside the house, people generally defecated in open fields, their women using secluded places either surrounded by trees or partly covered with crops or hidden by a raised grassy mound. The same situation is still prevalent. The people living in the town needed specified places for defecation and, hence, there was a need for disposal of night soil. In this way scavenging was not unknown even in ancient days in India. The scavenging work was done by a particular section of society constituting a caste or a sub caste.[18]

The sacred scriptures throw some light on the existence of a system for the disposal of night soil. Bindeshwar Pathak writes in his, 'Road to Freedom' (1991):

> According to the contents of sacred scriptures and other literatures, scavening specially the disposal of night soil by a particular caste or castes of Indian society, has been in existence since the beginning of civilization[19]. One of the 15 duties for slaves enumerated in the Naradiya Samhita, was to dispose of human excreta.[20] In Vajasneyi Samhita the Chandals *and Paulkasa have been referred to as slaves for the disposal of* night-soil.[21]

He further writes that during the Maurya period, Patliputra (now known as Patna in Bihar State, India) was one of the five ancient towns where the city mayor as Nagrak was the head of the organization entrusted with the task of looking after the civic affairs of the town. The Scavengers and sweepers cleaned the city and disposed of night-soil.[22]

There is a reference in the Kautalya's *Arthashastra* that during the Maurya period, the sanitary condition of towns was very much improved. Chanakya, known as Mantri (Principal adviser) to the Emperor, has mentioned that every house should have a kitchen and a bathroom. He had suggested that one who defecated in the open space must be fined. However, those who defecated due to illness or any disability, must be forgiven.[23]

Pathak has pointed out that after the advent of the Muslims in India that 'Sweeping and Scavenging' seems to have taken the form of a formal profession. According to him:

> The Muslims had brought with them some women who used the Burqua (veils) to cover their faces and they did not like to defecate in the open. The bucket privies were, therefore, designed and constructed for their defecation in Purdah. Those made captives were forced to clean latrines like bucket privies and throw the night-soil at distant places. After those captives were released, they were not accepted by their caste men and, hence, they formed a separate caste of Bhangi who were re-named as Mehtar by Emperor Akbar.[24]

Similarly Malkani (1960) and other eminent scholars have sought to establish that the Bhangis (Scavengers) of today 'are those people who were warriors made captives after they fell to the enemy'.[25]

During the British period, we witnessed the growth of Bhangis. This is evident from Srivastava's book, *Manual Scavenging in India*. Srivastava has pointed out:

> During the British period with setting up of army cantonments and Municipalities, a large number of people were perhaps required to do these services on the regular basis.[26]

Thus, according to Srivastava:

> the names of scavenging castes suggest that they are a functional community recruited from many different racial and social groups.[27]

The following extract from, 'Road to Freedom' sheds adequate light on this fact:

> Therefore, not only Kshatriyas, but also those who were engaged in cleaning night-soil since ancient time, such as Chandalas, Paulkasa and also those who were made captives in wars either in India or in Jerusalem or other parts of the world, are Bhangis and Mehtars of today. According to the 1931 Census, the total number of the Bhangis was estimated at 19,57,460, 10,38,678 males and 9,18,782 females in India.[28]

The foregoing account reveals that historical developments led to the emergence of a special class of Scavengers in India, known as Bhangis or Mehtars. This class became a hereditary occupational group with a fixed role and status in the Indian society. The unalterable role and status and the hereditary system made this class immobile and it developed into a caste or a sub-caste occupying the lowest stratum of society. With the allocation of hereditary occupation of scavenging and an immobile position, the caste or sub-caste of Bhangis became an integral part of the Indian social structure. This development was not possible without social sanctions.

The Scavengers (Bhangis) were placed at the lowest rung of the caste ladder. The nature of the job or work traditionally associated with them, or imposed upon them, pushed them to the lowest stratum of the social hierarchy of exterior castes. The task of cleaning night-soil was the most inferior job because this involved the touching of human excreta by the Bhangis. Consequently, they did not get social justice nor the human treatment. Being economically poor and socially backward, they could not revolt against the unjust sanctions nor could they rid themselves of the scavenging work.

The Possible Origin of the Bhangis and their Ethnic Relationships: A New Hypothesis

How did these persons come to be known as Bhangis? Were they declared to be outcastes first and then forced to do the filthy work or were they from the very beginning doing this work and were subsequently declared to be the lowest one. If the answer is that they were not doing this filthy work from the very beginning, but later on were compelled to do so, there arises a further question namely, what can be the reasons for it. For this we suggest the following possible reasons.

Mythological Tenet

As the question of the origin of the Bhangis has never been raised before, naturally, there exists no theory as to how the Bhangi group started performing this filthy work. There are of course the views of Hindu Dharma Shastras. The most relevant and frequently quoted story of the origin of the Bhangi caste in Dharma Shastras and the Smrities, can be referred to as 'Chandala'. According to Manu:

> Chandala is declared to be born from a Brahmani mother and a Sudra father, whose occupation was conveyance of corpses and task of acting as Public Executioner.[29] Other reports give him a less respectable pedigree, for he is said also to be the offspring of Musalia father (Sudra who pounds the Brahman called Musalia) by a

woman fisherman, whose occupation is to clean the street every morning and evening, remove the night soil, and receive the corpses.[30] And again he is said to be the son of Dom, one of the most despised of the groups having Nisad as his father and Sudra as his mother.[31] According to Osnash Smiriti, he is declared to be the offspring of Chandala father and Vaishya mother.[32]

One cannot draw any definite conclusion from these statements of Dharma Shastras. According to N. Prasad:

> It is abundantly evident that these sacred books contain no uniform or consistent account of the origin of the castes, but on the contrary, present the greatest varieties of speculation on this subject.[33]

Historical Tenet

The next question that arises is whether the caste indicated by the term Chandala is the same as that indicated by the term 'Bhangi' which socially means Scavengers, the lowest in the caste hierarchy. In other words, are they only different names for the same class of people? It is a fact that Dharma Shastras do not answer this question. For this we must go to the Chinese travellers who visited India and placed on a record what they observed in the form of modes and manners of the Indian people. Of these Chinese travellers, Fa-Hien came in 400 AD during the reign of Chandra Gupta II and has left an authentic record of the people of this country. Unfortunately he has noted very little about the untouchables of India. Still whatever little he says about the life of the untouchables is of value. Referring to the social life, Beal, quoting Fa-Hien, writes:

> The people are very well off, without poll tax or official restrictions. Only those who till the royal lands return a portion of profit of the land. If they desire to go, they go, if they like to stop they stop. The kings govern without corporal punishment; criminals are fined, according to the circumstances, lightly or heavily. Even in cases of repeated rebellion they only cut off the right hand The king's personal attendants, who guard him on the right and left have fixed salaries. Throughout the country the people kill no living thing nor drink wine, nor do they eat garlic or onion with the exception of Chandalas only. The Chandalas are named 'evil men' and dwell apart from others, if they enter a town or market, they sound a piece of word in order to separate themselves, then men knowing they are, avoid coming in contact with them. In this country they do not keep swine nor fowls and do not deal in cattle, they have no shambles or wine shops in their market places. In selling they use cowrie shells. The Chandalas only hunt and sell flesh.[34]

On reading this brief description of Chandalas we can say with some confidence that the term Bhangi was not in existence at the time of Fa-Hien. It gives us some idea of untouchability prevailing at the time of Fa-Hien. Here the observations of Dr Ambedkar are worth mentioning.

> Certain parts of this description of the treatment given to Chandalas do seem to lend support to the conclusions, that is, a case of untouchability.[35] But there is no indication in this passage whether they (Chandalas), even if they formed untouchable caste, were at all the Bhangis. In all probability, it was the name given to those people who were living on the outside of the villages.

The next Chinese traveller who came to India was Yuan Chwang. He came to India in 629 AD. He stayed in India for 16 years and has left most accurate record of his journeys up and down the country and of the manners and customs of the people. About the general characters of the cities and buildings of India, Walter, quoting Yuan Chwang, writes:

> As to their inhabited towns and cities the quadrangular walls of the cities (or according to one next, of the various regions) are broad and high, while the thorough – fares are narrow tortuous passage. The shops are on the highways and booths or (inns) line the roads. Butchers, fishermen, public performers, executioners and scavengers have their habitations marked by a distinguishing sign. They are forced to live outside the city and they sneak along on the left when going about in the hamlets.[36]

This description is too short and too brief for drawing a definite conclusion thereon. There is however, one point which deserves our attention in Fa-Hien's description. We find the reference to Chandalas only in Fa-Hien's description while the description given by Yuan Chwang applies to different communities other than the Chandalas. This is a point of great importance. It is, therefore, just possible that when Yuan Chwang came to India, untouchable groups and untouchability had emerged. The following extract from Dr Ambedkar may be quoted in support of this conclusion:

> We can conclude that while untouchability did not exist in 200 AD, it had emerged by 600 AD.[37]

We may now turn to the question as to who the Bhangis are and how the Bhangi caste originated in India. These are the main issues which we would like to investigate. Unfortunately no such study has so far been attempted. The result is that though people are aware of the existence of the Bhangis among the Hindus yet they do not know the causes of their origin. A definite idea of this unique feature is, however, essential not merely for a real understanding of the Bhangis, but also as the best means of emphasizing the need of investigating about the origin of this caste.

True, the origin of the Bhangi caste appears to be a complex problem. Races and invasions, institutions and governments of different periods in the history of India have left their imprint on the caste. Hence, there is a need for a historical perspective for understanding the origin of the Bhangis in India.

The first thing to be noted is that this caste group is predominantly 'non-Aryan' or 'Dravidian in character'.[38] The reason for this is explained by Crook in the following terms:

> Non-Aryan or Dravidian races were at an early time reduced to servitude and compelled to perform the vilest functions of the Aryan Common Wealth.[39] It is therefore, obvious that they did the work of the scavengers which is the filthiest of the filthy occupation.

But today the caste is a very large one and it would be difficult to account for it merely on this ground. As now constituted, the caste is made up of a 'heterogeneous' or of 'different elements'[40] of the people. There are few salient points on which reliance is placed. With these presumptions, we enter the other tenets of the hypothesis.

Anthropological Tenet

With some confidence, it can be said that the original caste group (which was of aboriginal origin) may be the ancestors of the present Bhangis and other untouchables of India. For this there are two tests we can apply to find the truth. One is anthropometric test and the other is ethological.

Considered in the light of the anthropometric characteristics of Indian people, Ghurye has something very striking to say in his volume on *Caste and Class in India* from which the following extract is reproduced:

> Taking the Brahmin of the United Provinces as the typical representative of the ancient Aryans we shall start comparisons with him. If we turn to the table of differential indices we find that he shows smaller differential index as compared with the Chuhra and the Khatri of the Punjab than with any caste from the United Provinces except the Khatri. The differential index between the Khatri and the Chuhra is only slightly less than that between that the Brahmin of the United Provinces and the chuhra. This means that the Brahmin of the united provinces has closer physical affinities with the Chuhra and the Khatri of Punjab than with any caste from his own province except the very high caste of the Khatri. The Brahmin is as much akin to the Chuhra as the later is to the Khatri of the Punjab.[41]

With this evidence, it cannot be doubted that there was a time when both the Brahmins and Chuhra (Bhangi) were one and the same people.

When Aryans came here as conquerors, they retained themselves the religious and military functions of the social order. So as the time went on, they held the functions of priests and nobles and became the great landed proprietors and ranch men.

The conquered people were kept in subjection. They performed the most lowly task of life and that lowest task was scavenging only. This is what Stanley Rice has said:

> Thus the Dravidians applied to the Paraiyanş the same test which the Aryans are assumed to have applied to the conquered inhabitants. They reduced them to the position of serfs and assigned to them those duties which it was thought beneath their own dignity to perform.[42] 'Therefore he further adds': There is strong probability that the outcastes were the survivor of the conquered peoples, who, as castes tendered to coincide with occupation, became the drum- beating, leather working and farm labouring classes to which as serfs they had been relegated from early times.[43]

Again there are some variations in the features of the members of the caste. This may be illustrated from the Bhangi caste of northern India. Some idea of this may be obtained from the following summary given by Crook:

> Some Bhangis have dark complexion, stunned figures and peculiar dark flashing eyes which is so characteristics of Dom.
>
> Others again are of a much taller form and fairer complexion.[44]

The reasons for this racial mixture are explained again by Crook in the following terms:

> Partly by the fact that their admittance as servants into high class families facilitates illicit connection with superior class and partly that tribe habitually recruits itself by admission of outcaste from superior tribes.[45]

Ethnological Tenet

There is yet another section of ethnological scholars who believe that certain classes were unable to maintain their identity and prestige with changing order and that consequently they have sunk to the lowest level. Perhaps these contentions are borne out by many *Got* (*Gotras*) names: for instance, Chouhan, Solanki, Gehlot, Parihar, Rathore, Pandit, and Kalla. These are the names of Rajput and Brahmin *Gotras* and are also found in the Bhangis. But they suggest dependency. Let us see what authorities have to say on this subject. This is what Dr Ambedkar has to say on the subject in his book, *The Untouchables*:

> As I have said if totem, kul and Gotra have significance it means that those who have the same totem must have been kindred. If they were kindred they could not be persons of different race.[46] Prof. Atal says that 'these Jatis (Gots or Gotras) suggest the past affiliation of these groups (Untouchables) with Rajputs'.[47]

Descent of Kshatriyas and Bhangis from the same sources has been justified on the basis of similarities by D.S. Chaturvedi. Quoting Chaturvedi, Bindeshwar Pathak[48] writes ... Kshatriyas and Bhangis have descended from the same source. For, he says, one notices a marked similarity between them. He has cited the following similarities:

BHANGI :	Vas, Vasvar, Bir Gujar, Bhadwaria, Bisen.
MEHTAR :	Bundelia, Chandala, Chauhan, Nado, Yaduvanshi, Kachhwaha, Kinwar, Thakur.
RAJPUT :	(99) Bundela (48) Bargujar Panna (222) Panna Dajoha or Yaduvanshi Gujar Panna (248) Rout.

The people belonging to the Chandala caste requested the census officer in 1911 to accord them the status of the Brahmins as they had the Brahmin origin. In that respect their customs, rituals and other sacramental roles are identical with those of Brahmins. There is no doubt that the Chandalas were made to dispose of sullage. These Chandalas took the initiative to enroll themselves as Brahmin only after they became affluent. Obviously, the castes engaged in the disposal of human excreta were not at all divergent of a single caste.[49]

If the above mentioned analogies are correct then it would be quite logical (from ethnological point of view) to say that the Bhangis at one time did belong to a high social status.

Conversion and Ex-Communication Tenets

Besides all this, however, there are other links connecting the Bhangis of northern India with higher castes. Direct evidence on this issue could be had if higher castes converted as Bhangis had been studied. Unfortunately, the study of converted Bhangis has not yet been undertaken either by the students of sociology or of anthropology. When such data is collected it would enable us to give a decisive opinion on the possibility that the Bhangis were high caste men. For the present, we are satisfied in this regard from the information we have collected from the high caste converted Bhangis from different districts of Rajasthan.

In this connection reference may be made to the tradition among the Hindu society, according to which breach of established social norms and usages was a social crime. Anyone who violated these approved social laws was guilty and was forcibly declared an outcaste. This means that the position of the ex-communicated had been lowered and they were treated as untouchables and were also prohibited from following their traditional occupation. Now they were with no means of livelihood. Without it they would starve. It would be natural in these circumstances for these outcastes to agree to give to others their services as sweepers. In Hindu society this often happened from the early times. This process is still going on. As a consequence there always existed in early times a floating population consisting of persons of different castes. Risley's thesis that:

> ... Almost every caste professes to have traditional occupation, though many of its members have abandoned it, but that the adoption of new occupation or of changes in the original occupation may have given rise to sub-division of the castes which ultimately developed into separate and distinct castes.[50] can be accepted in case of the Bhangi's origin.

This can be clearly supported from the following observations of B.N. Srivastava:[51]

> The names of scavenging castes suggest that they are a functional community recruited from many different racial and social groups. It is very likely that people belonging to the lowest strata were compelled to take on this profession especially in the urban areas due to economic necessity. The great variations in the physical features of the different sections of this community, but also the varied recruitment from higher castes of 'broken men' outcastes destitute etc. shows that the members of various castes have joined this profession at different points of time obviously due to economic compulsions as this occupation was regarded as unpleasant by the economically better off sections. This only proves that the members of different castes and communities have taken up to this vocation mainly due to economic constraints.

Invasion Tenet

From the ancient Indian history, we also know, that subjugation of a tribe after a tribe has been a recurring phenomenon in India. The subjugation occurred over wide areas. Indian history fully illustrates this fact and we may observe rising and falling of tribes and castes under repeated foreign and local waves of conquest. But then what were the social consequences? History has recorded very useful information. As N. Prasad points out:

... the force of class struggle always determined the status of a class or its classified form, caste.[52] This can be clearly supported from the following observations of H.P. Shastri:[53]

> The people of Bengal who, after the downfall of the Hindu rule, did not accept either Brahmanism or Islam but stuck to their old mode of worship, became the untouchables of today. History is not without such examples.

In the case of the Bhangis, the same principle was at work. Malkani, who has made a general study of the Bhangi caste, says:[54]

> The Bhangi is essentially a recent product of urban life, first created as an occupation by Muslims and later on in British rule, made into hereditary caste.

Traditions Regarding Origin of the Term 'Bhangi'

In the absence of any authentic, written record about the origin of the Bhangis, one has to depend necessarily on the oral traditions. In the following pages, an attempt has been made to use information collected and references available in the history, and the meaning and origin of their community names.

As Descendants of Valmiki Rishi[55]

According to narrative handed down from generation to generation and at present current in the older generation of the Bhangis, they are decedents of Valmiki Rishi – the first Sanskrit poet and famous author of the Hindu epic Ramayana. Their supposed connection with Valmiki rests on occupational and not on racial occupation and not on racial identity. Valmiki's story, as it prevails among the Bhangi, represents him as a low caste and as such as having taken to the living of a robber. Owing to this abhorrent activity of Valmiki, he was designated as a sweeper. The relics of this mythological narrative are still prevalent among the Bhangis.

In *The Tribes and Castes of Central Provinces of India*, there is a detailed reference as to the origin of Bhangis. It runs as follows:[56]

> The religion of the sweepers ... centres round the worship of two Saints Lal Beg or Bale Shah and Balnek or Balmik, who is really the huntsman Valmiki, the reputed author of the Ramayana. Balmiki was originally a lowcaste hunter called Ratnakar, and when he could not get game, he was accustomed to rob and kill travellers. But one day he met Brahma and wished to kill him, but he could not raise his club against Brahma, and the God spoke and convinced him of his sins, directing him to repeat the name of Rama until he should be purified of them. But the hunter's heart was so evil that he could not pronounce the divine name and instead he repeated 'Mara Mara' (Struck, Struck) but in the end by repetition this came to the same thing. As a small spark of fire burneth up a heap of cotton, so the word Rama cleaneth a man of all his sins. So the words 'Rama', 'Rama' were taught unto Ratnakar who ever repeated them for sixty thousand years at the self-same spot with a heart sincere. All his skin was eaten up by the white ants. Only the skeleton remained. Mud had been heaped over the body and grass had grown up, yet within the mound of mud saint was still repeating the name of Rama.

After sixty thousand years Brahma returned. No man could he see, yet he heard the voice of Rama, Rama, rising from the mould of mud. Then Brahma bethought that the saint was beneath. He sought Indra to pour down rain and to wash away the mud. Indra complied with his request and rain washed away the mud. The saint came forth. Naught save bones remained. Brahma called loud to the saint. When the saint beheld him, he prostrated himself and spoke. 'Thou hast taught me the words "Rama Rama" which have cleaned away all my sins'. Then spoke Brahma 'hitherto thou wast Ratnakar. From today thy name shall be Valmiki (from Valmik, an ant hill). Now do thou compose a *Ramayana* in seven parts, containing the deeds and exploits of Rama'. Valmiki had been or afterwards became a sweeper and was known as 'Cooker of Dog's food (Swapach), a name applied to sweepers, who have adopted him as their eponymous ancestor and patron Saint'.

The following is the text in English of Bhangis origin from Marwar Census 1891.[57]

One day God Brahma (Creator of the world) was passing through a street. There, God Brahma saw a dump of refuse. To get it removed, God Brahma immediately rubbed his skin and from its greasy material (the layer form on the skin by sand, perspiration and other skin discharge) produced a man and named him 'Matrak'. Matrak removed the refuse from Mahi earth. Since then he was known as 'Mahithar' and later on it turned into Mehtar. They were called the Bhangis because the children of the Matrak ate the flesh of the dead animals and entered into the temple of the Goddess Matangi without bathing. Upon this, the Goddess was shocked and cursed them that they will always sweep and remove the night soil. Therefore they are known as Bhangis.

In the first volume of his book entitled *Tribes and Castes of N.W.P* and *Oudh*[58] Crook has dealt with all castes found in the Hindu society. There are 18 legends dealing with the origin of the Bhangis. Out of 18, one important runs as follows:

... The Holy Prophet (Hazrat Paighambar), Saint (Mehtar) llias, or the prophet Elias, attended the court of the Almighty God, where many prophets were sitting. Mehtar llias coughed and finding no room to spit in, he spat upwards and his spittle fell upon the prophets. They all felt disgusted and complained to Almighty God, who directed that he should serve throughout the world as a sweeper. Mehtar Ilias begged that some prophet should be created in the world to intercede for him, and it was ordered that such a one should be born. According to the order of the God of Mercy he came into the world and took to sweeping and passed many days in the hope of forgiveness. One day the great Saint Bare Pir Sahib, Pir-I-Dastagir or Sayyid Abdul Qadir jilani took his coat (Chola) off and gave it to Mehtar llias to wear. Mehtar llias put it into an earthen pitcher (Matka) and intended to wear it at some auspicious time. One day the great Saint asked him why he did not wear the coat. He answered 'My work is to sweep and it would become dirty. I will wear it on some lucky day'. The great Saint said 'wear it today and come to me'. He agreed and went to open the pitcher, but it was shut so fast that he could not open it. He came to the Saint and said that the pitcher would not open. The Saint said 'Take my name and say to the pitcher that the Pir Sahib calls you'. Mehtar llias went and did as he was bidden, and putting the pitcher on his head brought it to the Saint. The Saint said Nikalao, Lal Beg – 'come out quickly my boy' (Lal is 'my dear boy', Beg means

> 'quickly'. Immediately out of the pitcher came a fair man wearing red clothes, and the Saint said to Lal Beg. 'This was the order of Almighty God that you should be the prophet of the sweepers and interecede for them at the day of Judgment'. Mehtar Ilias took him home, and placing him under a nim tree filled his pipe for him (a custom of the sweepers to the present day towards their religious teachers) and worshipped him. Lal Beg became at once invisible, and Mehtar llias went to the great Saint and told him the story. The great Saint said that Lal Beg had disappeared because he did not approve of his religion. 'However, worship him, and he will interecede for you'. He then ordered Mehtar Illias to do penance, and said, 'In the first age the ghatmat (vessels worshipped to represent Lal Beg) will be golden, in the second, they will be of silver, in the third, copper, in the fourth earthen'. This is why the sweepers now worship vessels of earth, and believe in Lal Beg as their prophet.

These traditions, both ancient and modem, do not however, account for the origin of the Bhangis. They merely show how some persons were degraded into sweeper working group.

Etymological Meaning and Definition of Bhangi

The word 'bhangi' is originally derived from Sanskrit root 'bhang' – hemp and bhangi meaning 'hemp addict'.[59] Crook in support of this derivation advances the Buria custom of calling their leader Bhangi or hemp addict as title of honour.[60] Sir H.M. Elliot[61] also derives the term 'Bhangi' from the same word in the sense of their drinking habits. Editors[62] Gove and Webster further confirm Crook's and Elliot's findings and indicate that Bhangi is one 'addicted to bhang'. The Bhangis are to be regarded as a group of hemp drinkers.

A much wider connotation of the term 'Bhangi' has been put forward by an eminent economist and sociologist late professor D.R. Gadgil. According to him 'Mehtar Bhangis are castes traditionally confined to the business of removing night soil. They are on this account considered among the most degraded in Hindu society. Moving out of the caste occupation is therefore, extremely difficult for them.[63] Professor Sahay supports these views in his article 'Eradication of Untouchability and the Caste System'. According to him,[64] 'Bhangi' 'means' those who are associated with filthy work like carrying of night-soil, cleaning of drains and the like.

Harold R. Issacs,[65] while defining the term Bhangi writes, 'Night soil ... has traditionally been the task of the untouchables at the bottom of even the untouchable's scale. This kind of scavenger is known as Bhangi and Bhangis are a people apart from even among people apart'. Again, editors James Brodly, Craigie and Onions[66] say that Bhangi means 'a person engaged in sweeping a room, chimney etc. and in India it would apply particularly for a person of lowest caste'. Lynch also used the term 'Bhangi' in this limited sense.[67]

Bhangi according to Chauhan,[68] are 'Those who have broken away from society and it is, therefore, derogatory in meaning'. Ghurye[69] quoting Enthoven writes 'Bhangi is one who performs the useful functions of removing night soil. It is a term probably applied to the caste simply as a token of contempt for those who are broken or out caste'. Occupationally today the Bhangi corresponds to the remover of night soil.

Position of the Bhangis in Caste System

Because of their low caste status, the Bhangis are in some sense less a part of the community of Jodhpur than are most of the other higher castes. But the community also incorporates them in a particular way because it could not survive without them.

Caste and Social Status

The status of the Bhangi caste has openly been described as untouchables. In Jodhpur they are often dubbed with vernacular term 'Bhangi' which means just that. Elsewhere too, their status has been actually that of the untouchable. It is true that social gradation among the untouchables follows a pattern which is basically similar to that prevalent among the upper castes. Blunt, has drawn attention to such a factor operating in the past 'eleven caste will not touch a Bhangi'. He further adds that '... being touched by such an untouchable required a good Hindu to bathe himself and wash his clothes'.[70] Dumont's[71] study also indicates that out of a total 25 untouchables there are 12 castes which do not touch the Bhangi. Hutton places the Bhangi caste in the lowest grade of Hindu social system. According to him:[72]

> Occupation again is also in part at any rate, the reasons for low standing of ... Khateek, who is a butcher or the Chamar who tans hides, and works in leather. Below all these are the scavenging castes, the various grades of the Bhangis or sweepers.

The position of the Bhangis differs vitally from that found in various parts of India. Bhangis accept food at the hands of any other castes but do not accept it from Dhobis and Dholis. Gupta[73] supports this statement in his discussion of the leather workers and untouchable group of the village of Awan. He writes 'The Bhangis accept scraps of food from the plates of the eaters ranked above the Balai, save the Dhobi, the Dholi and the Mogya'.

This is further proved by the following extract from Marwar Census Report, 1884.[74] We (Bhangis) consider ourselves polluted by the touch of Dhobi and Dholi. In that case we have to take off our clothes, sprinkle Gangajal (water of Ganga) over ourselves and bathe. Everywhere Dhobi and Dholi rank higher than Bhangis but they are regarded as untouchables and their status is superior to Bhangis. This superiority has been shown very clearly also by Gangrade,[75] in a study of Dhobis in a village near Delhi. Even Bhangis refuse food touched by them and it is only in recent years that the Bhangis have started to eat from their hands. The Bhangis of Delhi who work in Dhobis' houses are also paid for their services in cash and are given food at the time of marriage.[76] Similarly, Butchers (Khateek) are higher caste (as mentioned earlier) yet Bhangis of Kishan Garhi (UP) do not accept food from them.

This is proved by the following extract from McKim Marriott's[77] publication entitled *Castes Ranking and Community Structure in Five Regions of India and Pakistan*:

> Butchers locally claim to be Rajput. In support of this claim, they give themselves famous Rajput clan names and cite their external ties of marriage and descent with other groups of equally illustrious Rajput nomenclature elsewhere. At the same time members of the sweeper (Bhangi) caste in Kishan Garhi regard Butchers as too low in rank to receive sweeping services and too low to be able to give inferior bread as payment to sweepers or to any other caste.

'When Bhangis walk along a street or road', wrote L.S.S.O. Molley,[78]

> ... they (Bhangis) have to give warning of their presence by calling out 'Payse or Paraysa (Keep at distance) and sweeper was required to wear a crow's feather on his turban to show his unclean caste.

When high caste persons refer to a Bhangi as untouchable they mean only that they cannot take food or water from him and that his touch will pollute food, water and utensils used for food and water. The Bhangis are regarded as defiled especially because of their repugnant traditional occupation of removing night-soil and tanning and because of their eating carrion beef and meat of other dead animals.

Since the name 'Bhangi' has acquired abusive connotation as on the phrases – 'Dirty as Bhangi', son of Bhangis, the Bhangis prefer to designate themselves by other names. Some Bhangis call themselves Valmiki taking the name of their most famous Saint Valmiki. Other Bhangis of whom there are many from different districts, style themselves 'Harijan'. The word 'Harijan' means the 'Children of God' and was first coined by Mahatma Gandhi. A few call themselves Arya. But the Bhangis prefer to be called by name of Harijan.

Old Bhangis extended some kinship terminology and behaviour to higher caste persons. Some address higher caste persons as 'Mai-Baap' (Mother-Father). Older Bhangis feel that *jajmans* (patrons) should receive the same respect as mother or father. Older member of higher castes often address their Bhangis as their children. Now very few persons use those terms and their use in general is resented by the Bhangis. The Bhangi caste's status relation with Brahmin and castes below Brahmin are clearly structured. Food, water and vessels are kept strictly separate and the Bhangi is never permitted to enter the house of higher caste. If a man of higher caste works at a Bhangi's house for construction or repair of the house etc. he will have his own vessel for water or will go somewhere else for water.

There is a potential bond among the Bhangis and all other low caste people, no matter what their relative status is. They are all low in caste in relation to members of higher castes. All are somehow or the other economically dependent upon the members of the higher castes.

Ceremonial Status

The Bhangis occupy an isolated position in the ceremonial life of Jodhpur. Although they follow the customs and rituals of the members of the higher castes, they worship Gods, Goddesses separately in their own houses or Bastis. Similarly, they do not join with members of the higher castes in any ritual. As traditional workers for all higher castes, the Bhangis receive food and other domestic things at important festivals, such as Holi, Diwali, Sheetla Ashtami. Rakhi, etc. but they do not celebrate these festivals on equal terms with the members of the other higher castes.

Economical Status

Bhangis are economically tied to the city especially to members of higher castes as traditional workers and labourers. The Bhangi's traditional work is sweeping and removing refuse in the city. For this purpose, the city has been divided among different Bhangi families. Each family has been divided among different Bhangi families. Each family has been serving a certain number of houses (*jajman* families) from generation to generation. The *jajman* compensates his Bhangi for his work through periodic payment in cash or/and kind made throughout the year, mainly on monthly basis. Bhangis may also receive gifts such as free clothing, food, raw materials, etc., on festivals like Holi, Diwali and other important occasions like marriage, birth and death.

It is an unwritten law that if a Bhangi wants to move out of the city or is ill, he would have to find a substitute in his place. In this matter the high castes have no choice as to who would work for them. If they want to sell the work of a street in which they are working, they could do so to another family of their own caste. This sale is only effective on the condition that in that particular area no other Bhangi has any claim and also that people who bought it are satisfied. The price would be fixed according to the income of the area. We can have a clear picture of this practice from an autobiography of a Bhangi.[79]

> *The Purchaser:* How many landlords have you and what is the size of each of their families?
>
> *The Seller:* I have six Muslim households. One land lord is the Subedar Major in the King Emperor's service and other five are landowners, their land has been covering ten villages outside the town.
>
> *Purchaser:* How much cash per year do you receive from each house? How much grain, oil and sugar do you receive and what is the average number of marriage?

On this depends the sale, but no one ever thinks of asking how much work there is to do, because it is understood that once the purchaser takes over the responsibilities he would do whatever there is to be done. Besides, if there is any extra work, the *jajman* always compensate his Bhangi. But the sale of this nature takes place very rarely as it means the losing of one's birth-right and family reputation. Also, this is the only means of livelihood open to Bhangis and the richer the *jajmans* they serve, the higher the prestige and honour they get, not only among neighbours but also in the district itself and that means a lot to them, because this is the only basis on which depends their status in the community.

Outside employment is a recent phenomenon among the Bhangis of this region. Some of the Bhangis[80] joined the Army and fought in the Second World

War in Burma, Afghanistan and other places. Others have been noted as servants of British residents. The trend of outside employment has been further accelerated in recent years as non-traditional occupation has become possible, in and outside Jodhpur. Jodhpur is one of the most rapidly growing city in Rajasthan. Its economy is highly diversified, employment being provided by the university and other educational units, the Government Medical College Hospital and other medical centres, several small-scale industries and State Government offices, location of the Rajasthan High Court has added to the population and resumption of non- traditional occupation by the Bhangis has helped to improve steadily the economic position for them within Jodhpur.

Outside employment has gradually increased. Until 1976 there were few Bhangis of Jodhpur residing and working outside the region. With the exception of a few families which have sufficient economic sources, some of the Bhangi families have still been doing the work of removing night-soil. Although there is temporary mobility of the Bhangis from this city to other places over the last two generations, only a countable number of Bhangis from Jodhpur are known to have settled permanently in other place.

Political Status

Until the middle of the 20th century, the Gujarati Gotra Bhangi[81] the Scavengers (Kamin) of His Highness of Jodhpur State, were judges and arbitrators for Bhangis and for three other untouchable castes namely Kuchbandia, Satia and Sansi of the whole Jodhpur state. This was told to us when we approached one of the oldest living eminent persons of Gujarati Gotra Bhangi. The chief of Gujarati Gotra Bhangi met at the Panchayat to discuss matters of interest to the Bhangis themselves and to the other untouchables and to arbitrate disputes of every nature that might arise within or between the three untouchable castes of Jodhpur state. The members of the Panchayat who know the castes and caste members intimately and pride themselves on their own integrity, could find out the facts, arrive at a decision and enforce it too. They were empowered by His Highness of Jodhpur State to impose penalties like fine, punishment, ex-communication from the caste and also imprisonment for six months. The decisions of Panchayat chief were not subject to appeal before any higher authority. Through fear, the Bhangis and other lower caste people were peaceful and followed the political leadership of their Gujarati Gotra Bhangi.

Notes

1. Crook, W., *The Tribes and Castes of N.W.P. and Oudh*, Vol. 1 Calcutta: Office of the Superintendent of Government Printing India, 1896, p. 260.
2. Ibid. p. 260.
3. Marwar Census Report, Report on the Census of 1891, Vol. II, Jodhpur, Jodhpur Press, 1894, p. 179.
4. Russell, R.V., *The Tribes and Castes of Central Provinces of India*, Vol. IV London: MacMillan, 1916, p. 215.

5. Gunarthi, R.C., *Rajasthani Jatio ki Khoj*, Ajmer: Vedic Yantralaya 1950, p. 278.
6. Russell, Ibid. p. 215.
7. Marwar Census Report 1894, Ibid. p. 179.
8. N.R. Malkani, Report of the Committee on Customary Rights to Scavenging. Delhi, Ministry of Home affairs, Government of India, 1966, p. 131.
9. Based upon the list given in the Order in Council, issued under the Government of India Act of 1935 and the same was reproduced by Dr B.R. Ambedkar in *The Untouchables*, Balrampur, Jetavan Mahavihar Shravasti, 1969, pp. 17, 18, 20, 23 and 24.
10. Malkani, Ibid, pp. 61, 130 and 131** Ambedkar, Ibid., p. 19.
11. Gunarthi, Ibid. pp. 278–279.
12. Ram Ratan, Ibid, p. 179.
13. Ishwaran, K., *Tradition and Economy in Village India*, Bombay, (now Mumbai) Allied Publishers, 1966, p. 70.
14. Dass, Bhagwan 'Valmiki, Jyanti Aur Bhangi Jati', Jullundur, *Bheem Patrika* Publication, 1973, p. 15.
15. Ethnographic Atlas of Rajasthan, 1969 with reference to Scheduled Castes and Scheduled Tribes, Delhi: The Manager of Publications, 1969, pp. 24–30.
16. Sachchidanand, *People at the Bottom: A Portrait of the Scavengers.* New Delhi: Concept Publishing Company 2001, p. 15.
17. Sumanakshar, S.P. Prachin, *Adimjati Valmiki- Dharm Sanskriti and Itihas* (Hindi), Delhi: Bharatiya Dalit Sahitya Academy, 2008, p. 3.
18. Pathak, Bindeshwar, *Road to Freedom: A Sociological Study on the Abolition of Scavenging in India*, Delhi: Motilal Banarasi Dass Publishers, 1991 p. 37.
19. Ibid., p. 37.
20. Ibid., p. 37.
21. Ibid., p. 37.
22. Ibid., p. 37.
23. Ibid., p. 37–38.
24. Ibid., p. 38.
25. Ibid., p. 38.
26. Srivastava, B.N., *Manual Scavenging in India: A Disgrace to the Country.* New Delhi: Concept Publishing Company, 1997, p. 17.
27. Ibid., p. 17.
28. Pathak, Bindeshwar, Ibid. p. 38–39.
29. Crook, ibid. p. 261.
30. Gunarthi, ibid, p. 275.
31. Ibid., p. 274.
32. Ibid., p. 274.
33. Prasad, N., *The Myth of Caste System*, Patna: Samjana Prakashan, 1957. pp. 18–19.
34. Beal, quoted by Ambedkar, ibid., p. 190.
35. Ibid., p. 190.
36. Walters, quoted by Ambedkar, ibid., p. 198.
37. Ambedkar, ibid., p. 199.

38. Crook, ibid., p. 261.
39. Ibid., p. 261.
40. Ibid., p. 261.
41. Ghurye, G.S., *Caste and Class in India*, Bombay (now Mumbai): Popular Book Depot, 1957. pp. 120–121.
42. Rice, Stanley quoted by Ambedkar, ibid., p. 56.
43. Ibid., p. 55.
44. Crook, ibid., p. 261.
45. Ibid., p. 261.
46. Ambedkar, ibid., p. 82.
47. Atal, Yogesh. *The Changing Frontier of Caste*, New Delhi: National Publishing House, 1968, p. 261.
48. Pathak, Bindeshwar, 1991, ibid., p. 38.
49. Ibid., p. 38.
50. Risley quoted by Prasad, op. cit. p. 24.
51. Srivastava, B.N., 1997 ibid., p. 17.
52. Op. cit., p. 46.
53. Shastri, quoted by Prasad, op. cit., p. 46.
54. Malkani, ibid., p. 137.
55. Story as narrated by the Bhangis.
56. Russell, op. cit., pp. 225–226.
57. Marwar Census Report 1894, ibid., p. 179.
58. Crook, ibid., pp. 262–267.
59. Crook, ibid., p. 260.
60. Ibid., p. 260.
61. Ibid., p. 260.
62. Gove, P.B. and Webster, W. (ed.) *International Dictionary of English Language*, Vol. I, USA: G&C Merriam, 1966, p. 210. See also Dube, G.S., A.K. Harijan Bustee, Varanasi: Navchetna Prakashan, 1970, p. 7 and 9.
63. Gadgil, D.R., Poona: *A Socio-Economic Survey*, Part II, Publication No. 25, Poona, Gokhale Institute of Politics and Economics, 1952, P. 94.
64. Sahay, K.N., 'Eradication of Untouchability and Caste System', Ranchi: *Journal of Social Research*, Vol. XVIII No.2, 1975, p. 4.
65. Issacs, ibid., p. 53.
66. James, A.M. Brodly, M.H. Craigie, W.A., and Onion, C.I, (ed.) The Oxford English Dictionary, Vol. X Sa!e X. U.K. The Clarendon Press, 1961, p. 306.
67. Lynch, Owen M., *The Politics of Untouchability: Social Mobility and Social Change, in a City of India*, New Delhi: National Publishing House, 1974 p. 131 'a job which only a sweeper caste will do in India. Since it involves contact with human faeces.'
68. Chauhan, B.R., *A Rajasthan Village*, Delhi: Vir Publishing House, 1967, p. 18. These characteristics have been drawn from writings of some other writers. More particularly reference is made to the following in addition to Chauhan and Ghurya. Gunarthi, ibid. – p. 21, Dube, ibid., p. 5. Verma, R.C., Manak Sabdha Kosh Vol. IV, Prayag Sahitya Sammelan, 1965, p. 164. Mehant, Nagarmal, Mehtar Mimansa, Bikaner: Harijan Sewak Sangh/Vikram Samvat 2004, p. 8.

69. Ghurye, G.S., *Caste, Class and Occupation*, Bombay, (now Mumbai) Book Depot, 1961, p. 32.
70. Blunt, ibid., p. 99 and 102.
71. Dumont Louis, *Homo Hierarchicus: The Caste System and Its Implication*, Delhi. Vikas Publishing House, 1970, p 136.
72. Hutton, ibid., p. 34.
73. Gupta, ibid., p. 39.
74. Marwar Census Report, 1894, ibid., p. 180.
75. Gangrade, K.D. 'Panchayat Election of 1959 and 1963: Ranchi, *Man in India*, Vol. XlVI, No. 11 p. 138.
76. Mitra Channa, Subhadra, The Cultural Relation of Occupation. A Dhobi Case. Ranchi. *Man in India*, Vol. IV, No. IV, p. 319.
77. Marriott, McKim, *Caste Ranking and Community Structure in Five Regions of India and Pakistan*, Poona : Gokhale Institute of Politics and Economics, 1965, p. 27.
78. Molley, L.S.S.O., *Indian Caste Custom*, Delhi. Vikas Publishing House, 1974, p. 150.
79. Hazari, ibid, p. 6.
80. Talk with Tudji & Bhera. Inhabitants of Hanumanji ki Bhakri, who fought in IInd world war.
81. Talk with Mangi Ram Gujarati.

2

The Bhangi: Some Socio-Demographic Characteristics

Bhangis in British India: Census of 1901 and 1931

Though the census operation started in British India in 1871[1], it was only in 1881 that a systematic broad-based all-India census on uniform basis was conducted. It was decided to have enumerations decennially thereafter, resulting in subsequent census reports of 1891 and 1901. These reports though a considerable improvement, continued to be limited in scope. None of these censuses made special efforts to collect separate all-India statistics of untouchables, not even a rough estimate of their number in India could be obtained. D. Ibbetson's[2] attempt in 1881 was the first of its kind to collect some data about a few selected castes and tribals in selected areas, followed by Richard Burn during the census operations for 1901, who classified castes on the basis of social precedence and native public opinion.

Later on, in addition to the census operations, for the first time the Government made an estimation of the total numbers of untouchables along with their literacy rate in Seventh Quinquennials review of progress of education in India 1912–17.[3] Since then the number of untouchables has grown in the official records, because until then the very existence of untouchables was ignored.[4]

Thus, the data of the governmental agencies[5] were rough and sketchy. Census operators hardly realized the very existence of the untouchables.

Since 1871 Census, like other untouchables, the Bhangis, too due to stigma of untouchability, were marginalized and consequently they were neither acknowledged nor properly documented.

Later on, in addition to the census operations, for the first time, the Government made an estimation of the total number of the Bhangis/Scavengers in India in 1901. Thus, according to H.H. Risley[6], the estimated number of Bhangis in 1901, were 9,86,004 (Bhangi 6,56,586; Chuhra 13,29,418).

Similarly, none of the census reports of 1911, 1921 and 1931 made special efforts to collect separate all India data of Bhangis. But a rough estimate of their number in India was made. Hutton's[7] attempt in 1931 was the second of its kind to make estimation of the total number of Scavengers in India. Thus, an estimation of total number of Scavengers were: 19,57,460 (10,38,678 male and 9,18,782 female) in India.

Bhangis in Independent India: Census of 1961 Onward

When India achieved Independence in 1947, surprisingly enough, the Government did not take the initiative to census the persons engaged in scavenging. Consequently, they got neither social justice nor human treatment. Being economically poor and socially nowhere, they could not revolt against the unjust sanctions nor could they rid themselves of scavenging work.

Bhangis have very wide geographical distribution. They are distributed all over the country. According to 1961[8] Census (Figures of 1971, 1981 and 1991 census are not available) the total number of workers engaged by themselves as scavengers and sweepers was just over 8 lakh. According to 1961 Census, the Bhangis constitute 0.1 per cent of India's total population. The state-wise break-up is given in Table 2.1.

Table 2.1

State-Wise Bhangi Caste Break-up, 1961 Census

S. No.	State/Union Territory	Population of Sweepers/Scavengers
1.	Andhra Pradesh	43,883
2.	Assam	7,018
3.	Bihar	37,430
4.	Gujarat	35, 111
5.	Jammu & Kashmir	5,230
6.	Kerala	15,730
7.	Madhya Pradesh	58,770
8.	Madras	38,518
9.	Maharashtra	72,535
10.	Mysore	30,174
11.	Orissa	6,573
12.	Punjab	1,04,445
13.	Rajasthan	50,832
14.	Uttar Pradesh	2,19,604
15.	West Bengal	48,943
16.	Andaman & Nicobar	197
17.	Dadra & Nagar Haveli	13
18.	Delhi	24,480
19.	Goa, Daman & Diu	246
20.	Himachal Pradesh	1,076

Cont'd...

...Cont'd

21.	Laccadive Islands	14
22.	Manipur	217
23.	Nagaland	237
24.	NEFA	194
25.	Pondicherry	796
26.	Tripura	297
	Total	8,02,336

Source: fHarijan Seva, New Delhi, Vol. 21. No. 1, January 1972, p. 36–37.

Estimated Number of Scavengers in 1981

In the light of above stated fact, the number of Scavengers who were engaged in removal of night soil was 3,86,725 which can be projected as 6.18 lakh for 1981.

State-wise Estimated Number of Scavengers in 1989

The task force constituted by the Planning Commission, Government of India, had estimated the number of Scavengers in respect of Scheduled Castes for the year 1989[9] at 40 lakh, out of which 3,33,779 were in urban areas and 67,229 in rural areas. In urban areas 2,06,612 were males and 1,27,167 females. In the rural areas, 53,335 were estimated to be male and 13,865 female. This rural and urban distribution of scavenging caste shows that 83 per cent Scavengers are located in urban areas and 17 per cent in rural areas. State-wise estimated number of scavengers in 1989 is given in Table 2.2.

Table 2.2

State-Wise Estimated Number of Scavengers in 1989

States/UTs	*Area*	*Male*	*Female*
	Rural	3,812	2,086
	Urban	6,296	5,537
	Total	10,108	7,623
Assam	Rural	—	—
	Urban		
	Total		
Bihar	Rural	2,187	15
	Urban	12,922	7,274
	Total	15,109	7,289
Gujarat	Rural	4,372	959
	Urban	13,339	11,854
	Total	17,711	12,812
Haryana	Rural	—	—
	Urban	—	—
	Total	—	—
Himachal Pradesh	Rural	1,742	625
	Urban	2,593	1,168

Cont'd...

...Cont'd

	Total	4,335	1,793
Jammu & Kashmir	Rural	149	12
	Urban	115	52
	Total	284	64
Karnataka	Rural	1,846	492
	Urban	9, 168	5,682
	Total	11, 034	6, 174
Kerala	Rural	108	181
	Urban	874	1, 164
	Total	982	1,335
Madhya Pradesh	Rural	4,909	1,088
	Urban	11,660	12,235
	Total	23, 569	13,325
Maharashtra	Rural	2,009	1,299
	Urban	17,096	14,633
	Total	19, 186	15,932
Meghalaya	Rural		
	Urban		
	Total		
Manipur	Rural		
	Urban		
	Total		
Mizoram	Rural		
	Urban		
	Total		
Nagaland	Rural		
	Urban		
	Total		
Orissa	Rural	4,568	7,905
	Urban	10,665	10,475
	Total	15,233	19,380
Punjab	Rural	2,276	878
	Urban	10,310	3, 376
	Total	8,034	4,802
Rajasthan	Rural	12, 137	7,277
	Urban	12,841	9,837
	Total	24,978	1,711
Sikkim	Rural		
	Urban		
	Total		
Tamil Nadu	Rural	9,680	2, 587
	Urban	20,057	14,300
	Total	29,737	15,887
Tripura	Rural	99	60
	Urban	241	205

Cont'd...

...Cont'd

	Total	340	265
Uttar Pradesh	Rural	4,378	-
	Urban	43,735	18,226
	Total	45, 191	13,848
West Bengal	Rural	1,255	615
	Urban	5,290	2,703
	Total	6,545	3,318
Arunachal Pradesh	Rural		
	Urban		
	Total		
Andaman & Nicobar	Rural		
	Urban		
	Total		
Chandigarh	Rural		
	Urban		
	Total		
Delhi	Rural	2,219	1,225
	Urban	22,264	6,314
	Total	24,483	9, 539
Goa, Daman & Diu	Rural		
	Urban		
	Total		
Dadra and Nagar Haveli	Rural		
	Urban		
	Total		
Pondicherry	Rural	12	2
	Urban	102	136
	Total	138	136
North East Frontier Agency	Rural		
	Urban		
	Total		
Laccadive, Minicoy, and Amindivi Islands	Rural		
	Urban		
	Total		
All India	Rural	53,355	13,865
	Urban	2,06, 612	27, 157
	Total	2,59,96	1,41, 932

Source: Akash Gulalia, *Scavengers in Twenty First Century, Realities of Rehabilitation*, New Delhi: Saloni Publishing House, 2003, p. 142- 144, Annexure 1.

State-wise Estimated Number of Scavengers in 1998

Like earlier estimation of the Planning Commission of India (1989), the NSLRS (National Scheme for Liberation and Rehabilitation of Scavengers and their Dependents, 1992) of India, 1998[10], had estimated the total number of persons engaged in the occupation of scavenging as 5,77,228 lakh in the country. State-wise estimated number of Scavengers in 1998 is given in Table 2.3.

Table 2.3

State-Wise Estimated Number of Scavengers (NSLRS) in 1998

S.No.	Name of State/UT	No.of Scavengers
1.	Andhra Pradesh	14,701
2.	Assam	16,673
3.	Bihar	40,249
4.	Gujarat	64,195
5.	Haryana	25,279
6.	Himachal Pradesh	5, 100
7.	Jammu & Kashmir	4, 150
8.	Karnataka	14,555
9.	Kerala	1,339
10.	Madhya Pradesh	80,072
11.	Maharashtra	42,563
12.	Orissa	20,178
13.	Punjab	31,290
14.	Rajasthan	57,736
15.	Tamil Nadu	35,561
16.	Uttar Pradesh	72,483
17.	West Bengal	30,000
18.	Delhi	17,420
19.	Nagaland	1,800
20.	Meghalaya	607
21.	Pondicherry	476
22.	Sikkim	400
	Total	5,77,228

Source: Akash Gulalia, *Scavengers in Twenty First Century*, New Delhi: Saloni Publishing House, 2003, p. 146. Annexure 3.

The Present-Day Scenario of Scavengers in India, 2011

The position of the Scavengers has not improved much. The majority of Scavengers are still engaged in the lowest type of unskilled work like sweeping. They have been treated as untouchables. The profession of the Bhangis is lowest in caste hierarchy. Blunt[11] has drawn attention to such a factor operating in the past, 'eleven castes will not touch a Bhangi'. He further adds that being touched by such an untouchable required a good Hindu to bathe himself and wash his clothes. Dumount's[12] study also indicates that out of a total 25 untouchable castes there are 12 which do not touch the Bhangis. Hutton[13] placed the Bhangi castes in the lowest grade of Hindu social system.

In India, majority of Scavengers are living in towns and cities. Although their working conditions have slightly improved yet manual removal of night soil is still persisting. Head-loading is still in practice in cities and towns of India. Above all, the social stigma against them has not been done away with so far and traditional social hierarchy is still in existence. The Bhangis have grievances against government authorities – social, political and the bureaucratic set-up and have complained that their approach towards Scavengers is unjust and discriminatory.

NGO: Safai Karamchari Andolan Informed[14] the Supreme Court: 4.97 lakh Dry-Toilets Serviced by Animals, while 7.94 lakh Serviced Manually

Almost 22 years earlier, the Parliament had passed the Employment of Manual Scavengers and Construction of Dry-Latrines (Prohibition) Bill, 1993, to abolish scavenging and ban the construction of dry latrines, but the figures/data culled out from 2011 Census report by NGO 'Safai Karamchari Andolan' dealt[15] a severe blow to the sanitation claims of successive governments.

How many persons are still engaged in manual scavenging in India? How many dry latrines are cleaned by animals? If the people of India today have the answers to these questions, it can be attributed to the work of NGO Safai Karamchari Andolan (SKA) for social reform.

Activist Bezwada Wilson started 'SKA' in 1986 from Karnataka to take up the cause of Bhangis. Its work includes abolition of scavenging and ban on the construction of dry latrines and helping the Bhangis to ensure their human dignity enshrined in Article 21 of the Constitution. This initiative has been a ray of hope for lakhs of men, women and children in India.

A PIL was filed by this organization in the Apex Court in 2009[16] making it mandatory for the Government to ban construction of dry-latrines in the country. The Employment of Manual Scavengers and Construction of Dry Latrines (Prohibition) Law 1993 to protect scavengers is not enough. They had needed a law for a total ban on the construction of dry latrines by 2012–2013 to protect lower caste. Safai Karamchari Andolan aims to bring about Government accountability in the process of abolition of scavenging. It relies a big network of partner organization whose volunteers work for its programme. Bezwada Wilson believes SKA has helped make it an issue of national debate. All grassroot socio-political workers support this. We, however, need to build public and judicial pressure.

Throwing some light on the miserable conditions of Scavengers in India, on Tuesday, 4 September 2012, Senior Advocate[17] P.S. Narasimha and K. Parmeshwar appearing for the NGO, informed a bench of Justice Swatanter Kumar and S.J. Mukhopadhaya, 'Of a total 24.6 crore households in India, over 26 lakh toilets were termed insanitary as they discharged excreta directly into open drain (13.14 lakh toilets) or were cleaned manually or serviced by animals (12.91)'.

NGO Safai Karamchari Andolan[18], *The Times of India* has pointed out, informed the Apex Court that 4.97 lakh dry toilets were serviced by animals while another 7.94 lakh were serviced manually.

Notes

1. Yagati, Chinna Rao, *Dalits Struggle for Identity*, New Delhi: Kanishka Publishers, 2003, p. 107.
2. Ibid., p. 107.
3. Ibid., p. 110.
4. Ibid., p. 110.
5. Ibid., p. 110.
6. H.H. Risley, Census of India, 1901, Vol. 1, Part-1, Report, Summary Tables, Table XIV. Statistics of main Castes, p. 619, Calcutta (now Kolkata), Office of the Superintendent Printing India, 1903.
7. Pathak, Bindeshwar, *Road to Freedom: A Sociological Study on the Abolition of Scavenging in India*, Delhi: Motilal Banarsidass Publishers, 1991, p. 39.
8. हरिजन सेवा, हरिजन सेवक संघ की मुख्य पत्रिका, नई दिल्ली, वर्ष 21, अंक 1, जनवरी 1972, पृ. 36–37। यह भी देखें: Gulalia, Akash, *Scavengers in Twenty First Century: Realities of Rehabilitation*, New Delhi: Saloni Publishing House, 2003, p. 35.
9. Gulalia, Akash, 2003, ibid., p. 35, also see, p. 142–144, Annexure 1.
10. Gulalia, Akash, 2003, ibid., p. 36, also see, p. 146 Annexure 3.
11. Shyam Lal, *The Bhangi, a Sweeper Caste: Its Socio-Economic Portraits*, Bombay, Popular Prakashan, 1992, p. 24.
12. Ibid., p. 24.
13. Ibid., p. 24.
14. 'Animals Clean 5 Lakh Toilets, Top Court told', in *The Times of India*, Jaipur, Tuesday, 4 September 2012.
15. Ibid.
16. 'Manual Scavengers not Identified in Urban SECC', in *The Times of India*, Jaipur, Saturday, 3 December 2011.
17. 'Animals Clean 5 Lakh Toilets, Top Court told,' in *The Times of India*, Jaipur, Tuesday, 4 September 2012.
18. Ibid.

3

The Bhangi: Poor and Marginalized

The facts analysed earlier presented a brief account of the social status and pathetic condition of Scavengers in Indian society where it has not only been an occupation, but also a social institution marked by social taboos, religious ostracism and social degradation. The social disabilities pushed Scavengers down to the lowest level to get only sub-human treatment. The practices associated with untouchability in general, and with Scavengers, in particular, amounted to a denial of social justice. In an age of rising consciousness for human rights, social sanctions against Bhangis cannot have a defence. Moreover, the norms of a democratic society and a Welfare State demanded end to such inhuman and unjust discriminations.

Hence, in the post-Independence era, social reformers, welfare agencies and the State and Central Governments paid special attention to this problem and made sincere efforts to abolish untouchability and to liberate Scavengers from the job of cleaning night-soil; for it was realized that the end of the job of disposing of human excreta and involvement of the people of this section in different jobs will help in improving their social and economic conditions. Various agencies, national as well as international, have been working in the field of sanitation. Although their efforts are aimed at providing good sanitation and not at the liberation of Scavengers, yet the consequences of providing sanitary toilets in place of service latrines help in liberating the Scavengers. The following account presents in brief the efforts made by, various organizations and agencies.

Since Independence, the country has made tremendous progress in almost all areas. It is a matter of concern that despite such achievements, the country has not made desired progress in certain areas like social development and social justice. It is, indeed, alarming that even after a period of 65 years, a large number of people amongst the untouchables are still involved in the hereditary occupation of human scavenging. The occupation is despicable and degrading for those involved in it. The Scavengers are cut off from the mainstream of the society and are no doubt the most oppressed and disadvantageous section of the society.

While Indian democracy completes yet another cycle of elections in 2014, an editorial in *The Tribune*[1] (New Delhi, Haryana edition, Tuesday, 13 September 2012) about 'Manual Scavenging' across the country has shaken us all. However, this plight is not new. Imagine the plight of those who actually do it. Manual scavenging euphemism for picking up human excreta by hand was supposed to have been banned in 1993 by law. That never happened. The technology to do this with machines exists, but the will does not. Perhaps the age of caste system has something to do with that.

Similarly, another shocking report – 'Animals Clean 5 Lakh Toilets, Top Court Told' – in *The Times of India*, Jaipur[2], (Tuesday, 4 September 2012) talks about the cleaning of nearly 13 lakh insanitary dry toilets across the country, where human beings and animals, play almost equal role. NGG[3] Safai Karamchari Andolan 'culled out the data from the 2011 Census report to inform the Apex Court that 4.97 lakh dry toilets were serviced by animals, while another 7.94 lakh were serviced manually'.

In the last 65 years, as a member of Scavenging community, as a student of University, as a college teacher, as a researcher, as a university professor and Head and as Vice-Chancellor of three universities, I have witnessed various forms of discrimination against Dalits in general and sweepers (Bhangis) in particular. We, sociologists, tell people that modernization will bring about a social change. Yet with every passing year, the frequency, form and styles of discrimination have only increased.

Notwithstanding the social and political struggle for abolition of scavenging by Bhangis in the 20th century, it was the state that negated the social and political movement. No matter which party/ideology formed the Government, the dominant social groups have took lukewarm attitude towards abolishing scavenging. This was done in three ways since 1947.

First, the dominant social groups adopted a patronizing stance towards the Bhangis. Aided with liberal and radical instruments, they wanted to remove social evils. This started in the year following Independence and continued in the later years because the dominant castes were confident that even if the traditional scavenging was abolished their control of economic, social and political resources would keep them miles ahead of the rest. The result was that India failed in implementing social reform and social development in different regions of the country. In the name of new Legislation (1993) on abolition of scavenging, new commissions were created at Centre and in the States. India, Pakistan and Bangladesh are perhaps the only countries in the world to have created caste-based occupations that correspond with specified social groups, thus creating social segmentation in these countries.

Second, the two-faced profile of the high caste dominated and elitist bureaucracy deliberately excluded Bhangis from harnessing the benefits of social, political and economic policies of the state. To illustrate this point, let's discuss the amount sanctioned for abolition of scavenging in the country.

As stated earlier, in 1993, the Central Government created a National Commission for Safai Karamcharis[4] and released ₹ 464 crore to launch a national scheme to identify, train and rehabilitate manual Scavengers throughout the country, as it was with the social and economic conditions of the scavengers, so also with the ideals of social Liberty, Justice and Welfare of the downtrodden. And the scavengers thus liberated will also find jobs. But the scheme did not attain a considerable significance socially and economically.

As regards training, identification and rehabilitation of manual Scavengers throughout the country, the position was far from satisfactory and no tangible results could be achieved. Thus, implementation of NSLR of Scavengers was dismal. In 1997, it was reported by the National Human Rights Commission, New Delhi, that the progress 'has not been altogether satisfactory[5], and had *benefitted* only' a handful of Safai Karamcharis and their dependents.[6] It was also noticed that' one of the reasons for unsatisfactory progress of the scheme appears to be inadequate attention paid to it by the State Governments and concerned agencies'.[7]

In spite of legislations passed by the Parliament and various government schemes, manual scavenging continues to be practised in our country, with an estimated 8 lakhs of people, majority of them being women and children, who continue in this stigmatized practice. There was no indication of expenditure by many states. One can only draw two conclusions: 'No money has been spent or no report has been sent about utilisation of the funds'[8] stated R.V. Pillai, CERD Member and Former Secretary General of the National Human Rights Commission.

It was also found that the Finance Ministry has earmarked ₹ 98 crore for rehabilitation of manual Scavengers, of which the Social Justice and Empowerment Ministry plans to spend ₹ 36 crore on survey, it has not even begun.[9] 'It is also significant to quote Bezwada Wilsen[10] that the SECC 2011 could have been used to do this ... but this opportunity has been missed'.

In another case, the Ministry of Social Justice and Empowerment[11], Government of India, initiated the Self-employment Scheme for Rehabilitation of Manual Scavengers (SRMS) in 2007. An amount of ₹ 735.60 crore was allocated for the rehabilitation of 3,42,468 individuals. This scheme was for the period from January 2007 to March 2009, but was extended till March 2010. Under this scheme, only 1,18,474 individuals showed interest to avail the benefits out of which 78,941 individuals were benefitted and 39,533 individuals could not, due to various reasons. According to the Ministry, a total of ₹ 231 crore were released under this scheme between the financial years 2006 and financial year 2009–2010. Under this scheme 13,275 individuals were benefitted. Rashtriya Garima Abhiyan Jan Sahas conducted a survey on the implementation status of SRMS in three states of India in the year 2010–2011. Some of the findings of this study are given below:

i. The beneficiaries of scheme includes 76 per cent such people who were not involved in manual scavenging.
ii. The scheme was not launched in 25 per cent of districts and it was said that manual scavenging practice did not exist in those districts. But during the study it was found that manual scavenging practice was going on in those districts.

iii. 98 per cent of people engaged in the profession are women. But it was found that benefits of SRMS were given to 51 per cent of men in those three states.

iv. 85 per cent people said that they had faced various types of problems to get benefits of the scheme like time wasting, bribe, misbehaviour etc.

It was also found that the Finance Ministry[12] has earmarked ₹ 98 crore for rehabilitation of manual Scavengers, of which the Social Justice and Empowerment Ministry plans to spend ₹ 36 crore on survey, it has not even begun. It is also significant to quote here Bezwada Wilson[13], National Convenor, Safai Karamchari Andolan, that, 'The SECC 2011 could have been used to do this (as it any way has to) ... but this opportunity has been missed.'

Third, the institutional safeguard mechanism, particularly those constituted for welfare of the Bhangis have weakened. Mahatma Gandhi and makers of our Constitution believed that the dream of an independent and progressive nation could not be fulfilled without removing scavenging, which is a blot on the country and adhering to the principles of Social Justice. Legislation on abolition of scavenging, Safai Karamchari Ayog in Delhi and in various State capitals have been established. In addition to these, there are national panels on abolition of scavenging in various regions. But none of these institutions is allowed to work independently. Someone or other tries to protect the interest of the dominant castes/groups overtly or covertly.

These problems have existed separately or simultaneously in time and space.

Legislation on Abolition of Scavenging Passed by Parliament in 1993

Perhaps the first organized effort for the employment of Manual Scavengers and Construction of Dry Latrines (Prohibition) Bill, 1993, was passed by the Parliament to abolish scavenging and ban the construction of dry latrines. These efforts, of course, have been historic decision. However, no time limit was put by which the system of manual scavenging would be totally abolished in the country. Thus, the very purpose of the Bill was defeated. There were other reasons also.

The first reason was that the employment of Manual Scavengers and construction of Dry Latrines Act itself provided so many loopholes[14] that it remained meaningless. A State Government can choose which areas to notify the Act in, and cannot notify unless 'adequate' facilities for the use of water seal latrines in that area exist. This immediately negates the possibility of enforcing the Act in the vast expanse that is rural India as well as a major part of the urban and semi-urban areas where there is no water supply or sewerage.

Second, lacuna in the Act is now sought to be corrected by the Government through a proposed Bill – it will include people cleaning sewers and septic tanks, who were not covered under the 1993 law.[15] This was essential as a lot of manual scavenging has now shifted from latrines to septic tanks, especially in areas that have piped water supply but not sewerage. None of these, however, is going to wipe out the demeaning practice till every home has water and disposal system, which is a long way off in a country where more than half of the city population does not have piped water or sewerage system. Manual scavenging is not a pleasant work and dry latrines are not convenient. But both exist for want of alternatives.

Third, a lot that can be done even under the circumstances is also not being done. Manual scavenging continues at government facilities and those run by civic bodies or Panchayats. Workers[16] are not provided even elementary equipment like gloves and boots.

Lastly, in a State like Punjab, where many villages also have piped water, septic tanks are common, but these are all cleaned manually, mostly late at night to escape attention. The technology to do this with machines exists, but the will[17] does not. Perhaps the age of caste system[18] has something to do with that.

The National Commission for Safai Karamcharis Act, 1993[19]

The National Commission for Safai Karamcharis was constituted under Section 3 of the National Commission for Safai Karamcharis Act, 1993. The power and the functions of the Commission as laid down in Section 8 of the said Act are as follows:

The Commission shall perform all or any of the following functions, namely:

i. Recommend to the Central Government specific programme of action towards elimination of inequalities in status, facilities and opportunities for Safai Karamcharis under a time-bound action plan.
ii. Study and evaluate the implementation of the programmes and schemes relating to the social and economic rehabilitation of Safai Karamcharis and make recommendations to the Central Government and the State Governments for a better coordination and implementation of such programmes and schemes.
iii. Investigate specific grievances and take in moto notice of matters relating to non-implementation of:
    a. programmes or schemes in respect of any group of Safai Karamcharis.
    b. decisions, guidelines or instructions, aimed at mitigating the hardships of Safai Karamcharis.
    c. measures for the social and economic upliftment of Safai Karamcharis.
    d. the provision of any law in its application to the Safai Karamcharis.
    e. taking up such matters with the authorities concerned or with the Central or the State Government.
iv. Making periodical reports to the Central and State Governments on any matter concerning Safai Karamcharis, taking into account any difficulties or disabilities being encountered by Safai Karamcharis.
v. Any other matter which may be referred to it by the Central Government.
vi. In the discharge of its functions under sub-section (1), the Commission shall have power to call for information with respect to any matter specified in that sub-section from any Government or local or other authority.

The functions and responsibilities of the Commission are fairly widespread and encompass the entire area of activities of the Central Government, State Government, local authorities and other authorities in so far as they relate to or otherwise affect Safai Karamcharis engaged in or employed for manually carrying human excreta or any sanitation work.

Tenure

The Act was passed on 4 September 1993, but this Commission was constituted on 12 August 1994. According to sub-section (4) of section 1 of the Act it shall cease to have effect after the 31 March 1997. Therefore, the Commission would have a short life span of two and a half years.

Jurisdiction

The Commission is not in a position to protect and serve a large section of the Safai Karamcharis for want of appropriate jurisdiction.

Power

The Commission has been vested with power to call for information with respect to any matter falling within its jurisdiction from any government or local authority, but does not have powers of a Civil court as vested with other National Commission.

Financial Powers

The Central Government shall, after due appropriation made by the Parliament by law in this behalf, pay to the Commission by way of grants such sums of money as the Central Government may think fit for being utilized for the purpose of this act.

Status of Chairperson

The Chairperson of the National Commission for SC/STs, the National Commission for Minorities and the National Commission for Backward Classes have been accorded status of Union Cabinet Minister. However, the Chairperson of this national-level Commission is assigned with functions and responsibilities that are equally important, and has been given status of a Union Deputy Minister.

A comparative study of the powers, functions, status and tenure of all the four National Commissions under the Ministry of Welfare would reveal the discrimination meted out to National Commission for Safai Karamcharis.

Administrative Set-up

The National Commission for Safai Karamcharis was constituted on 12 August 1994, in pursuance of provision made in Section 3 of the National Commission for Safai Karamcharis Act, 1993. The Commission as per Act shall consist of:

i. A Chairperson
ii. A Vice-Chairperson

iii. Five members to be nominated from amongst the persons of eminence connected with the socio-economic development and welfare of Safai Karamcharis, by the Central Government of whom at least one of the members shall be a woman.

As per the provision of the National Commission for Safai Karamcharis Act, Chairperson, Vice-Chairperson and every member shall hold office for such period not exceeding three years as may be specified by the Central Government in this behalf or up to 31 March 1997, whichever is earlier.

The Central Government vide Notification dated 12 August 1994, constituted the Commission consisting of the following persons:

i.	Shri Mangilal Arya	Chairperson
ii.	Shri J.P.D. Salappa	Vice-Chairperson
iii.	Shri Vasudeorao Changra	Member
iv.	Shri Mangal Ram Premi	Member
v.	Padamshree Ishwar Bhai Patel	Member
vi.	Smt. Maya Devi	Member
vii.	Dr. Hanuman Prasad	Member

For financial year 1994–95 (for seven months), a budget provision of ₹ 50 lakh was made. For 1995–96, ₹ 55 lakh was provided, which was raised to ₹ 59.80 in 1995–96. For 1996–97, against a budget proposal of ₹ 160 lakh submitted to the Commission, only ₹ 70 lakh was provided. The Commission had proposed ₹ 80 lakh in R.E. 1996–97 and ₹ 146 lakh in 1997–98. The budget position at a glance is as under:

Table 3.1

Budget Figure in BE and RE

Financial year	*BE*	*RE (₹ in lakhs)*
1994–95	50	50
1995–96	55	59.80
1996–97	70	80
1997–98	146	

The Budget figures in RE 1996–97 and BE 1997–98 are projected by the Commission for the approval of the Government.

The Commission has a sanctioned a strength of 46 persons, including one Chairperson, one Vice-Chairperson and five members. Other sanctioned posts include Secretary (One), Under Secretary (One) Deputy Director (One), Principal Private Secretary (One), Assistant Director (One), Section officer (One), Private Secretaries (Seven), Personal Assistants (Seven), Assistant (two), Senior Hindi Translator (One), Research Assistant (two), Steno Grade 'D' (two), L.D.C. (Four) and Staff Car Drivers (eight). There is no sanctioned post of Group 'D'. The Commission has already recommended creation of additional 69 posts to the Government.

The Chairperson holds the rank of Deputy Minister of Central Government, Vice-Chairperson and Members are in the rank and pay scale of Secretary to the

Government of India. The Secretary to the Commission is in the rank and pay scale of Joint Secretary to the Government of India and post is covered under Central Staffing Scheme and the incumbent is drawn from Group 'A' services of the Central Government. Other Secretariat posts have been filled on transfer or deputation basis.

Some of the main developments that took place due to lukewarm attitude of Government were summarized in *Jan Satta*, New Delhi Daily newspaper, as given below.[20]

> It is a sorry tale. It is rather ridiculous that after passing the bill in Parliament in August 1993, the government took nearly one year in appointing Chairman and Members of Commission. Further after the lapse of three months, the Commission was constituted. Not only this, the Commission is temporary, as the tenure of the Commission would expire on 31 March 1997. Thus, one-third period of the Commission was lapsed in its formation'.

Describing the miserable infrastructure facilities, the paper stated that since its inception the Commission requested to the then Prime Minister again and again and also tried its best to procure 69 employees for its proper functioning but it failed in the attempts. So far as the budget is concerned, the Government sanctioned in all ₹ 50 lakh for the first year, 1994–95, and for the year 1995–96, the Government sanctioned only ₹ 55 lakh. Similarly, as a part of infrastructure facilities the Government provided two cars out of eight.

It should also be noted here that in order to perform their duties with sincerity and also to do something for the betterment of the community, the Commission requested the Government for a suitable office building and residential accommodation for members. In this regard, in the month of January 1995, necessary directions were issued from the Prime Minister's Secretariat for the allotment of residential accommodation for members. After an interval of nine months or so, a meeting was held on 11 October 1995, the Government assured to Commission that by 15 October 1995, accommodation will be allotted. But this time also Government failed to do so. This was the attitude of the Government. The Commission cannot function in vacuum nor can it build up its machinery or infrastructure.

High and increasing expectations of AISMC on the one hand and the lukewarm attitude of Government to provide basic requirements on the other, as discussed above, caused the tension and dissatisfaction in the AISMC. Such attitude of the Congress Government discouraged Chairman Mangilal Arya and his fellow members. They continued their attempts but were conscious enough not to antagonize the party in power for these reasons. First, they knew that AISMC did not have the capacity and resources to obtain political power on its own strength. For that they have to work through a party. Secondly, Congress being a dominant party, was the only party capable of satisfying their demands. Lastly, Buta Singh and Mangilal Arya, who dominated the Sabha were Congressmen since very beginning. The Sabha's leader, therefore, made attempts to win over the sympathy of the Congressmen for the organization.

In such circumstances, the Congress-minded Buta Singh, who was also an ardent champion of Bhangis' cause, found himself in an embarrassing situation. He, therefore, took a middle course and worked for compromise between the Party and his caste brothers.

Then complaints were raised in the meeting of Welfare Ministers, held at Delhi on 3 February 1996 to discuss and analyse the socio-economic conditions of SC, ST Minorities and OBC. Mangilal Arya, Chairman, National Commission for Safai Karamcharis, strongly criticized the government for its step-motherly attitude towards the Commission. Though we have worked with the Congress, it has failed to understand our feelings. We are being neglected. No one welcomes us. Therefore, he said in the meeting 'It is my humble request to all the ministers and senior officers to visit the Bhangi Bastis at least once and observe, how they are living'. In such circumstances, Arya expressed some of the anti-Congress feeling, finding it difficult to work properly.

The then Prime Minister P.V. Narasimha Rao, on the other hand, was emotionally ready to accept the feelings of Arya. Ideologically, he felt that in the present circumstances the problems of Scavengers have become a critical issue for the country. Despite this regrettable fact, the State Governments have taken little interest in the all-round development of the sweepers. The then Prime Minister requested to Welfare Ministers and senior Government officers that they should concentrate their full energy for all-round development of the sweeper class, etc. 'I want to involve you in my emotions as I had to face a lot of difficulties in Constitution of this Commission in particularly', the then Prime Minister had said.

People's Commission on Abolition of Scavenging[21]

In spite of many Commissions and Committees, including the National Commission for Safai Karamcharis set up in 1994, the degrading practice of manual scavenging still continues. Hence Sulabh has set up People's Commission on abolishing scavenging which will take a holistic view of the problem and suggest ways to abolish it. The terms of reference of the proposed Commission are:

i. To ascertain the nature and extent of the problem of manual scavenging in its historical and contemporary perspectives.
ii. To determine the extent to which manual scavenging has been reduced in the country.
iii. To develop a socio-economic profile of Scavengers in rural and urban areas.
iv. To examine the working and living conditions of Scavengers.
v. To find out participation of Scavengers in education and other development programmes.
vi. To study and evaluate the effectiveness of various schemes on the abolition of manual scavenging.
vii. To make recommendations for the Scavengers with a view to finally abolish this practice totally.

Role of NGO

As stated earlier, scavenging has been legally banned through various legislations and provisions given in the Constitution of India. This inhuman practice exists in degrading forms through out the country. The Government of India fixed a time limit to end this inhuman practice since it was outlawed. However, the deadline has been continuously extended eight times by the Central Government.

Beside Sulabh International as the most effective and dynamic voluntary organization contributing to the liberation of Scavengers, a few voluntary agencies are doing pioneering work in this context in the country. The important among them are the Rashtriya Garima Abhiyan, Safai Karamchari Andolan and Nav Sarjan Trust. A brief mention of these agencies is also desirable to understand the movement for the liberation of Scavengers.

Rashtriya Garima Abhiyan, 2001[22]: National Campaign for Dignity and Eradication of Manual Scavenging

Rashtriya Garima Abhiyan came into existence in 2001 after legislation on abolition of scavenging was passed by the Parliament in 1993. Theoretically, the crisis was resolved, but the Government of India did not fix a time limit to end this inhuman practice. To fix a time limit to end this inhuman practice a new organization named 'Rashtriya Garima Abhiyan' was formed in 2001. The founder Chairman of this organization was Ashif Shaikh. The entire community stood in support of this move, morally and politically. Ashif Shaikh and Lali Bai Valmiki tried to turn it into a national movement and within a few years of its inception, they spread it throughout the country with utmost zeal and devotion.

In 2009, it was resolved in Bhopal under the Presidentship of Ashif Shaikh that the practice of carrying human excreta should be eradicated in all its form from the Hindu society. To struggle for the freedom and liberation for those involved in the practice of carrying human excreta a new campaign named 'Maila Mukti Yatra, 2009' was launched from 6 November 2009 to 1 December 2009. The *yatra* started on 6 November 2009 from Mhow, the birth place of great fighter against caste system, Dr B.R. Ambedkar, and culminated at Bhopal on 1 December 2009. Communication was established with more than 1,400 women during the *yatra* who were engaged in the practice and 502 women members decided to leave the practice.

These efforts, of course, met with success. But Rashtriya Garima Abhiyan in MP thought of launching a national campaign on this design. After a few years, national people's march for total eradication of manual scavenging was decided with following objectives:

i. To liberate other Dalit women engaged in the practice in 200 districts of 18 States of India through those who have already come out of it.

ii. To associate and sensitize other sections of society and involve them in this liberation movement.

iii. To provide a common platform to women liberated from this practice to fight for their rights and rehabilitation.

iv. To build a common and larger consensus and movement for eliminating this practice.

v. To increase goodwill to address this issue.

Later, the organizers declared publicly about the Maila Mukti Yatra's plan to take out a nation-wide march of its rank and file that would commence on 30 November 2012 from the country's north, south, east and west and culminate in a public rally in Delhi on 31 January 2013.

During the 63 day Maila Mukti Yatra, they covered in all 200 districts of 18 states – Maharashtra, Rajasthan, Uttar Pradesh, Bihar, Jharkhand, Madhya Pradesh, West Bengal, Orissa, Chhattisgarh, Andhra Pradesh, Tamil Nadu, Karnataka, Gujarat, Haryana, Punjab, Himachal Pradesh, Uttarakhand and Delhi.

When Maila Mukti Yatra 2012–13 launched the 63-day campaign, a large number of women freed from this evil participated in this *yatra*. They went to colonies and Bastis of women engaged in this evil and motivated them to get free from this practice instantly. They explained that though they may be deprived of a few stale *chapatis*, few old clothes, some money, though they may be pressurized or boycotted yet they should not continue doing this work. 'We won't do this and live with dignity' was the motto. 'We won't take human excreta on our head and will live a life of dignity'.

With the sincere efforts made to discard the evil practice, most of the women decided to leave this practice.

After launching of Maila Mukti Yatra from 30 November 2012 to 31 January 2013, it was engaged in various activities during the *yatra* such as awareness generation campaign, meeting with government departments and other *stake-holders*, out-reach campaign in other districts, community mobilization, State and national consultation and convention, Press conference and documentation. Rashtriya Garima Abhiyan has been working for total eradication of manual scavenging in 18 states of India. This produced a great impact on the masses. A large number of people heard the speeches of speakers, inspired by their thought and stopped the practice of manual scavenging. Rashtriya Garima Abhiyan facilitated the processes of social, political and economic rehabilitation throughout the country for liberated families. It also sensitized and generated awareness throughout the country within the stratified Bhangi Communities to build Dalit unity to address all forms of untouchability, discrimination and social exclusion practices.

The Rashtriya Garima Abhiyan also struggled for restoring the human rights to the scavengers of society. It was realized that for the uplift of Scavengers, improvement in the level of literacy was necessary. It was also planned to work with other stakeholders like NGOs, People's Movements, community-based organizations, media etc.

Maila Mukti Yatra made a country-wide tour, travelling several miles and 55-day night stay between November 2012 and January 2013. These efforts of RGA were exclusively for Scavengers.

The Prohibition of Employment as Manual Scavengers and their Rehabilitation Bill 2012 tabled in Parliament (Lok Sabha)

It has been stated earlier that the Employment of Manual Scavengers and Construction of Dry-Latrines (Prohibition) Act, 1993, is in operation and considerable number of scavengers have already been liberated through it. It was expected after making a law to abolish it in 1993 that the practice of manual scavenging in India will be abolished soon. Regarding this, it is important to point out that in more than two decades, since its inception in 1993, many political parties have come into power but none of them tried to put an end to this practice.

Consequently, the programme of abolition of manual scavenging through EMSCDL Act has not attained full success. That Act totally failed. The extent of adoption or passing of this act by the State Assemblies even after 20 years varies from State to State. Such an analysis also facilitates the discovery of hurdles standing in the way of implementing the programme which is of great help in implementing the EMSCDL Act 1993. It is also evident from the above analysis that liberation of Scavengers through the EMSCDL Act is important not only from the social point of view, but also for economic planning and development of the country. The nature of the problem attracts the attention of not only sociologists, but also of economic planners, leaders and persons and agencies engaged in the welfare activities.

Consequently, the present issue attracted not only attention of NGO and changes in the present Act, but repeated adjournments sought by the Union Government for getting the prohibition of employment of manual scavengers and their Rehabilitation Bill, 2012, had irked a bench headed by Justice H.D. Dattu so much that it had observed on last Friday that if the Bill was not getting through the legislative process, the Government must bring an ordinance to put an end to manual scavenging.[23] Hence, intervention of Apex Court on this issue is of vital significance.

Speaking on behalf of Government of India Attorney General G.E. Vahanvati[24] assured the bench of Justice S. Dattu and Ranjan Gogai that centre was fully committed to an early passage of the Bill which gave comprehensive definition of insanitary latrines and manual scavengers.

The Attorney General[25] further said to court:

> 'The government will make an earnest request to Parliamentary Standing Committee on social justice and empowerment to expedite its deliberations and present its report to the Lok Sabha at the commencement of the forthcoming Budget Session (21 February 2013) and there after make every effort to ensure that the law is enacted as expeditiously as possible'.

In the light of the above discussions, it is evident that it took 19 years for the states to ratify the existing Employment of Manual Scavenging and Construction of Dry Latrines (Prohibition) Act 1993. Wiser by the experience, the Centre has decided to take a route through entry 97 of the Central list for the proposed law to bind the States to follow the law. The States will have no choice but to accept. The centre is no longer dependent on volition of States. 'We are talking of human dignity enshrined in Article 21 of Constitution. We are aware of it and whatever is needed will be done'.[26]

In the light of the above discussions, the objectives of Rehabilitation Bill, 2012, according to Maila Mukti Yatra, may be summarized in the following ways:

i. On the basis of experience of studies, to define the term 'Manual Scavengers' afresh and to include manually cleaning, carrying, disposing or *other wise* handling in any manner, human excreta in an insanitary latrine or in an open drain or pit, etc.

ii. To announce some important provisions regarding to identification, monitoring, vigilance, rehabilitation and penalties.

Notes

1. For details, see particularly 'Cans Just Flush it away, End of Scavenging needs Infrastructure', in *The Tribune*, New Delhi, Haryana edition, Thursday, 13 September 2012.
2. See particularly, 'Animals Clean 5 lakh Toilets, Top Court told' in *The Times of India*, Jaipur, Tuesday, 4 September 2012. Also See, '8 lakh toilets cleaned manually, S.C. told', in The Times of India, Jaipur, Tuesday, 4 September 2012.
3. Ibid.
4. See, 21 Page small booklet entitled 'Maila Mukti Yatra: Rashtriya Garima Abhiyan', Dewas M.P., Dated 17-11-2012, p. 7.
5. Ibid., p. 8.
6. Ibid., p. 8.
7. Ibid., p. 8.
8. Ibid., p. 9.
9. See, 'Manual Scavengers not identified in urban , in *The Times of India*, Jaipur, Saturday, 3 December 2011.
10. Ibid.
11. See, 21 Page small booklet entitled, 'Maila Mukti Yatra: Rashtriya Garima Abhiyan' Dewas, M.P., Dated 17-11-2012, p. 14. Also see, मैला मुक्ति भारत यात्रा जयपुर पहुंची, दैनिक भास्कर, जयपुर, गुरूवार, 17 जनवरी 2013.
12. See, 'Manual Scavengers not identified in Urban SECC' in *The Times of India*, Jaipur, Saturday, 3 December 2011.
13. Ibid.
14. See, 'Can't Just flush it way ...' in *The Tribune*, New Delhi, Haryana edition, Thursday, 13 September 2012.
15. Ibid.
16. Ibid.
17. Ibid.
18. Ibid.
19. See particularly, 'The National Commission for Safai Karamcharis' in Shyam Lal, *The Changing Bhangis of India: A study of Caste Association,* Jaipur: Sublime Publications, 1999, p. 157-178.

20. Ibid., p. 157–158.
21. Sachchidananda, *People at Bottom: A Portrait of the Scavengers*. Concept Publishing Company, New Delhi, 2001, p. 96–97.
22. A full account is provided in 21 page booklet, entitled 'Maila Mukti Yatra: Rashtriya Garima Abhiyan', Dewas, M.P., dated 17–11–2012.
23. See, Particularly, 'Anti Manual Scavenging Law Soon: Govt. to SC' in *The Times of India*, Jaipur, Wednesday, 9 January 2013.
24. Ibid.
25. Ibid.
26. Ibid.

Part II

Dr Ambedkar and the Bhangis

4

Ambedkar's Contribution to Untouchables and Human Rights

Social stratification has been a fact of Indian society for around 3000 years. Different classes of people are placed on a vertical plane characterized by hereditary hierarchy of socially superior and inferior ranks. These classes are broadly categorized as Brahmins at the top in hierarchy followed by Kshatriyas, Vaisyas and Shudras at the bottom. This is known as Chaturvarna Vyavastha. This system draws its sanction from the Shastras. With the juxtaposition of *varna* with *jati*, the caste system emerges. There is a fifth category outside and below the four *varnas* viz. untouchables or outcastes. Their status is the lowest in the Hindu social arrangement. The untouchables were called 'Dalits' or 'Depressed Classes' by Dr Ambedkar, Harijan by Gandhi and designated as Scheduled Castes by the Indian Constitution.

The untouchables are the most discriminated, deprived and exploited section of Hindu society. They have been denied basic human rights and education. They have been forced to live in segregated localities. The whole community has been compelled to lead a secluded life, unexposed to the development around. For centuries, they have been forced to exist at sub-human level by the exigencies of Hindu social order. The extent of violations of human rights cannot be truly imagined of people whose shadows were polluting and inviting punishment. Dr Ambedkar was a born untouchable. The indignities and deprivation that his community faced, moved him to take up the gauntlet to fight for its rights. His life had been a long stretched struggle to fight for their socio-economic and political rights. He articulated and pressed hard for their legitimate claims before the British and caste Hindus. He demanded and ultimately, secured for them some special privileges as means to a greater realization of their human rights.

Caste: The Greatest and Longest Hurdle of Human Rights of the Untouchables

As stated earlier, different castes, on the basis of their occupations were assigned the ranks one above another on a vertical scale. The status of members in caste groups is ascribed and hereditary. The superiority of some vis-á-vis others as well as inferiority of some vis-á-vis others is maintained and justified as the natural order of things by the institution of caste. According to Khurram:[1]

> 'Thus, Caste system came to be characterised by social hierarchy, inequality, fixing of occupations and continuance thereof by heredity, ascribed status, endogamy, social segregation, commensal restrictions, authorisation of power to upper castes on a permanent basis and continuous denial and humiliation of lower castes. There, of course, exists a sort of religious sanction behind it'.

He further stated:[2]

> 'The worst victims of the hierarchised and closed social order have been the untouchables. They have suffered untouchability the most heinous crime against human dignity ever experienced on earth. This phenomenon, in certain respects, is unique to India. It connotes the practice of non-touching of the outcastes by the caste Hindus, implying the notion of ritual impurity. It means separation, segregation and isolation of a people within a society. It has resulted in the greatest and the longest violation of human rights of a community ever experienced by humanity. The word untouchable is itself, the most obnoxious. It is an epitome of suffering and deprivation of a people. The condition of untouchables was even worse than the slaves of Europe and Central Asia. ... The untouchables, however could never revolt because they were deprived from participation in common activity of society'.

Untouchability has been legally abolished and it is severely punishable offence, today. But the notion of ritual impurity is still surviving in the minds of the people. Its practice is continuing, sometimes, with complete disregard to the law and frequently, in various concealed and subtle forms.

The Terms Human Rights and Human Dignity

Human beings need rights because of their being human. K.C. Daiya[3] held that 'The term "human rights" could be generally defined as those rights which are inherent in our nature without which we can not live, as human being.'

Human Rights, according to traditional international law[4], are inherent in all individuals because of their being human and irrespective of caste, creed, religion, sex, language, ideology, etc. These rights originate with the very birth of the individual and are essential for the development of human personality and for human happiness and progress. Due to their inextricable link with human beings, these rights are known as human rights'.

Political philosopher, Laski[5], held the rights to be essential conditions of human life. Thus, rights are required by humans to realize their freedom, their personality, their humanity. They need the rights to live with dignity. Dignity is an essential component of human self-consciousness. Therefore, it is the cornerstone of human rights.

Our Supreme Court[6] has interpreted Fundamental Rights to life as constituting right to live with human dignity.

The preamble of the United Nations Charter[7], while providing equal rights, emphasizes on maintaining the dignity and worth of human beings. The universal Declaration of Human Rights states that human beings are 'born free and have equal dignity and rights and are therefore entitled to all rights and freedom, set forth in the Declaration' without distinction of any kind, such as race, colour, sex, language or religion.

In short, it can be said that dignity can be ensured when every member of society has a feeling that he or she is a respectable member and no one can humiliate, exploit or insult him on the basis of caste, creed, sex, status, etc.

Ambedkar and Human Rights of Untouchables

Bhim Rao Ambedkar is popularly known as the messiah of the poor, the downtrodden and the untouchables. Born in a Mahar (untouchable) family he suffered all kinds of humiliation in his early life. He decided to dedicate his life to the cause of untouchables. It became his life's mission. As he wished to annihilate caste in order to achieve equality of social status for his community, he vehemently protested against social, political and economic segregation practised against the untouchables. Thus, he emerged as the greatest champion of the human rights of the poor, oppressed and untouchables.

Ambedkar had undergone the entire gamut of experience of social injustice and victimization because of untouchability. He was the victim of this cruel practice and had suffered the ignominy of having thrown files by peon at his face while he was Military Secretary of Maharaja of Baroda; had been beaten up for staying incognito as a paying guest in a Parse Inn etc. As a young boy, he was denied a gulp of water from evening till late night, mere touching of his note books or razor would be considered unclean by his teachers or barber a mere contact with his hair while the razor could be used without fear of pollution for shaving buffaloes. He roused consciousness in the Dalits where does 'to fight for eradication of untouchability, to claim equality of treatment, status and opportunity and of equal rights – civil, political, social and economic – and of dignity of person. He preached the grand universal law that liberty is never received as a gift but it has to be fought for. That is the clarion call given by Ambedkar who is the crusader for human rights of the untouchables in India.

The Constitutional Design: Abolition of Untouchability and Promotion of Equality

Ambedkar had entered the Constituent Assembly with the only hope of safeguarding the rights of the downtrodden. He explained:[8]

> I came into the Constituent Assembly with no greater aspiration than to safeguard the interests of the Scheduled Castes, I had not the remotest idea that I would be called upon to undertake a more responsible function. I was therefore, surprised when the Assembly elected me to be its Chairman.

Ambedkar, as the champion of the downtrodden, was convinced beyond doubt as to the need for a Bill of Rights in the Indian Constitution.

The Constitution of India[9] proclaims in the Preamble the objective of achieving for all its citizens, justice, social, economic and political and equality of status and opportunity.

Part III of the Constitution deals with fundamental rights to which every citizen is entitled. Article 14 declares that the 'state shall not deny to any person equality before law or the equal protection of laws'. Under Article 15, discrimination by the State only on the grounds of religion, race, caste, sex, place of birth was prohibited. Keeping in view the problem of untouchability, clause (2) of Article 15 further states that no person only on the grounds of religion, race, caste, sex or place of birth shall be subjected to any disability, liability, restriction or condition with regard to (a) access to shops, public restaurant, hotels, places of public entertainment, or (b) the use of wells, tanks, bathing ghats, roads and places of public resort maintained wholly or partly out of State funds or dedicated to the use of general public. Clause 3 of Article 15 provides for special legislation for women and children. Clause 4 provides for reservation of Backward Classes.

While clauses 1 and 2 of Article 15 prohibit discrimination on grounds of religion, race, caste, sex or place of birth, etc. clause 3 and 4 are exceptions to clause 1 and 2, thus permitting some discriminatory treatment of favour to women, children and socially and educationally backward classes, including the Scheduled Castes and Tribes.

Article 16 of the Constitution is to secure equality of opportunity. Article 16 (1) guarantees equality of opportunity for all citizens in the matter of appointment to any office or of any employment under the State. Clause 2 laid down that no citizen shall on grounds only of religion, race, caste, sex, descent, place of birth, residence or any of them, be ineligible for, or discriminated against, in respect of any employment or office under the State. Clauses 3, 4, 4a and 5 of Article 16 are the exceptions to this general rule of equality of opportunity.

Clause (3) empowers the Parliament to make a law prescribing residence within a state, a qualification for appointment or any government post. Clause (4) enables the State to make provision for the reservation of posts in government jobs in favour of any Backward Class of citizens which, in the opinion of the State, are not adequately represented in service of the State. The newly added clause (4a) (added by 77th amendment, 1995) empowers the State to make any provision for reservation in matters of promotion for SCs and STs which, in the opinion of the State, are not absolutely represented in the services under the State. Clause (5) saves a law from the operation of clauses (1) and (2) which provide for the incumbent of any office a religious qualification for appointment.

By Article 17 'untouchability is abolished and its practise in any form is forbidden'. The enforcement of any disability, arising out of 'untouchability' has been made an offence punishable in accordance with the law.

Under Article 29 (2), the practise of discrimination (on any of the grounds) in offering admission into any educational institutions maintained by the State or receiving aid out of the State funds is proscribed. Article 23 forbids forced labour, commonly part of the dominant caste rule or feudal regime. Article 25 guarantees freedom to profess, practice and propagate religion, and is specially made subject to other fundamental rights provisions and is explicitly qualified by the provision that: '(a) Nothing in this article shall affect the operation of any existing law or prevent the state from making any law, and (b) Providing for social welfare to reform or the throwing open of Hindus religious institutions of a public character to all classes and sections of Hindus'.

All these fundamental rights are judicially enforceable. Under Article 32, every citizen has a right to move the Supreme Court for the enforcement of rights. The High Courts under Article 226 have power to issue directions, orders or writs in the nature of 'Prohibition'. Under these powers, the courts can direct the individual or State to desist from the practice of untouchability.

These are the main provisions concerning equality and non-discrimination in the Constitution. The above Constitutional provisions provide two-fold approach to achieve the aim of promoting human rights of untouchables: the negative approach and the positive one. Under the former many Legislative Acts are enacted to make the Constitutional provisions on the removal of untouchability work more effectively, whereas the latter approach enjoins a scheme of protective measures, such as Legislative reservations, job reservation and educational facilities to the untouchables.

Article 17 of the Constitution is on the lines of the provisions of Article 2 of the Universal Declaration of Human Rights. It is a very important and significant provision from the point of view of equality before law. It guarantees social justice and dignity of man, the twin privileges which were denied to a vast section of the Indian society for centuries together. Article 17 is similar to the 13th Amendment of the Constitution of the United States of America which abolished slavery.

Removing Night Soil by the Bhangi: A Slur on Our Culture and Disgrace to Our Society

While we take pride in our past glory, we forget that we have also got some dark spots on our heritage and culture – untouchability, scavenging, etc. and prevalence of caste system in our society. We should look into our own past record and see the abominable way we have treated our Scheduled Castes and Scheduled Tribes brothers and sisters and hang our heads in shame. We still have temples which refuse entry to Bhangis. We have Shankaracharyas who quote sacred texts to justify discrimination against the lower castes in general and Bhangis in particular.

India is the only country in the world where only a particular section of the society is traditionally responsible for keeping the habitation clean by removing human excreta through primitive methods. This is a disgrace to the country. After 66 years of Independence, even today one can see people carrying night soil on their heads in the buckets or removing human excreta by physical touch.[10] The country which won freedom from the slavery of British people 66 years ago, but could not liberate more than half million people who are called, Mehtars, Valmikis, etc. from human bondage and are still engaged in their traditional occupation of sweeping and scavenging. Is it not a shame on us when we force a person to clean excreta of others?'[11]

Thus, scavenging is a human rights question, because it violates Article 1 (all humans are born free and equal inhuman dignity and human rights), Article 4 (none will be held in slavery), Article 5 (nobody shall be subjected to cruel inhuman or degrading treatment) and Article 23 which says, 'Every one, without discrimination, has the right to equal pay and equal work'.[12]

Scavenging also violates the Preamble of universal declaration of Human Rights[13] (signed on 10 December 1948) which, among other things, says 'The charter affirms faith in the dignity and worth of human person and in the equal rights of men and women. Scavengers, who are made untouchable in their own country, need protection under the charter not less than the victims of apartheid in South Africa, ethnic conflicts in the Balkans, of the victims of prejudices anywhere else in the world. Scavengers, however, do not get media attention because they have been suffering the indignity of physically cleaning and carrying human excreta for centuries without protest and with total resignation.

Observations of Commissions and Committees on the Pitiable Plight of Bhangis

Many of the national leaders have expressed their anguish on the problems of Bhangis. For want of space the opinion of all of them can not be reproduced here. However some of the most important ones are quoted here.

National Concern on Scavenging

The national concern on scavenging has been expressed in a number of the reports of the Government-appointed Commissions and Committees right from the days of Independence. The concern was more forcefully voiced in the Report of a Committee of the National Labour Commission on the working and service conditions of sweepers and Scavengers (1968-69). The Report says:[14]

> 'The question of working conditions of sweepers and scavengers is not merely a matter of employer/employee relationship, but an issue that has figured prominently in the social and political discussions of the country for almost a generation. The question of untouchability, caste differentiations, the stigma and repugnance attached to this occupation, the age-long suppression, privations and afflictions suffered by these communities of sweepers and scavengers involve the social conscience of the whole nation. The upliftment of this class of people requires breaking of traditional attitudes and a long process of education not only of the higher castes but of sweepers and scavengers themselves, to pull them up from the state of despair to which they have a fatalistic approach.

'That a section of humanity should be condemned to such degrading condition is slur on our culture and disgrace to our society'.[15]

The pitiable plight of Scavengers is best summed up in the following two observations: One made by the Backward Classes Commission in 1956 and the other by the Father of the Nation in 1927.

> 'The condition of Bhang is extremely miserable and the betterment of this unfortunate section is one of the crying needs. When compared with the average income of the common people, the earnings of the Bhangis attached to local bodies and municipalities may not be very low. Yet the condition of these people is extremely

miserable. Drinking and gambling habits, lack of education and lower standard of living are responsible for many of their ills'.[16]

'Socially they (Bhangis) are lepers and economically they are worse than slaves. Religiously, they are denied entrance to places we miscall 'House of God'.[17]

Mahatma Gandhi

The obvious reasons are that peculiar situation exists in our country. Nowhere in the world this occupation is confined to a particular caste as in India and that the job of scavengers is considered as the meanest. In the words of Mahatma Gandhi:[18]

> 'We have reduced them to the level of beast, they earn a few coppers but only at the expense of their human dignity. The weights of oppression have crushed them. It is enough to break one's heart to see them eating their food covering under the shadow of the latrine wall'.

Gandhiji was really moved by the appalling living conditions and social degradation that Bhangis suffer in the Hindu society and had started, even during those days, the Bhangi Mukti Campaign. His approach to this problem was not only humanitarian but also social and revolutionary. His concern about the Bhangis can be described in his own words. He says:[19]

> I do not want to attain Moksha. I do not want to be reborn. But if I have to be reborn, I should be born an untouchable, so that I may share their sorrows, sufferings and the affronts levelled at them. In order that I may endeavour to free myself and them from that miserable condition. I therefore pray that I should be born again. I should do so not as a Brahmin, Kshatriya, Vaishya or Shudra but as an Atishudra – a Bhangi.

> This was the spirit which inspired many social reformers to raise their voice against the inhuman conduct of many towards them.

It was in pre-Independence days, when Babasaheb Ambedkar was the Labour Minister, that he appointed the first Committee the 'Pande Committee' to go into the problems of the sweepers employed by the local authorities. A Report was prepared and submitted to the government – but without any positive action. Then came the 'Barve Committee in Bombay' (1949) with very valuable suggestions and recommendations followed by the report of the Renuka Roy Committee appointed by the Planning Commission and then the famous Malkani Committee sponsored by the Government of India, Ministry of Home Affairs. This committee, under the Chairmanship of Professor N.R. Malkani, after very intensive study and tour of the country, submitted a detailed report in 1960. While submitting its recommendations, Professor Malkani has described the unbearable and inhuman working conditions of the Scavengers. It says:[20]

> 'Even today after 13 years of freedom, it is common sight to see a scavenger moving with a heavy load of night soil on his head earned in a bamboo basket or a leaking drum, the matter trickling over his face and body. The passer by avoids his sight as he considers it inauspicious to meet with such a scene but gets reconciled to it as if it is inevitable. He perhaps does not trouble himself to arouse his conscience which

> is bound to tell him that such sights could be avoided and scavengers made not to carry any head loads of night soil. If per chance, a scavenger comes in the close proximity, he is showered upon with all sorts of filthy remarks and so often with abuses. No sooner, a scavenger with a head load or night soil cart comes into sight, men start pulling out their handkerchiefs, the ladies the "pallas" of their sarees and cover their noses. Even the Office-in-charge of public health who is supposed to remain daily in close touch with the scavenging work and look after their welfare, for which they are paid, have been noticed drawing out their handkerchiefs and trying to remain as far away as they could, from the spots of filth, the spots where the scavengers are required to work for hours together day in and day out for his whole life'.

Another Plague Spot

Earlier N.R. Malkani drew public attention to the disgraceful conditions of the Bhangi bastis of Allahabad. Later on he again sent to *Hindustan Times*, his impression of Delhi Bhangi Basti which were published. These impressions show that the Delhi bastis are not much better than the Allahabad ones. There is the same tale of indescribable filth and consequent degradation. The Scavengers, on whose careful labour largely depends the health of the inhabitants of Delhi, are housed in cells which are windowless and lightless holes. I cannot do better than reproduce Malkani's closing sentences:[21]

> 'It had been raining very hard and several bastis had become quagmires inside and pools outside. One could not walk, but only skip over stones placed to order or be lifted up by sportive scavengers. We were a party – including some Delhi notables. One entered and returned reeling, as he walked over unnamable filth. Another returned, and would not go again, for the bowels of his compassion had been moved and he felt like vomiting for ease. A third wondered how "these people living in filth had become filth-like". One brave soul, living in Easy Street, blurted out "Oh! my house is leaking, where is the house in Delhi that is not leaking? Why worry? His opinion is on all fours with the opinion of many Bhangis, who think, poor souls, that born in filth they must live and die in filth. Why worry?" ... Living in a world of smells and sight, day and night, the Bhangi himself becomes a smell and sight, a human waste-heap. Life in these bastis is ugly, almost hideous. It is too terrible for over statement.'

Extracts from Jawaharlal Nehru's Speech[22] in a Public Meeting of Sweepers held at Ramlila Maidan on 2 January 1964

> 'When you asked me to address your meeting I felt some hesitation, though I liked the invitation. I had heavy work to do which I could not easily leave behind. But I could hardly refuse to attend this special gathering of Safai Mazdoors. So here I am before you this evening. Now it is embarrassing for me to find words for speaking to you. In fact in this matter I feel somewhat ashamed. I visited several times, several years back, the places where you live. Seeing your huts I felt unhappy and ashamed, I therefore hesitated to appear before you now and then and yet be reconciled to your miserable conditions. This is our Government and we have our own Constitution which provides that our worker comrades and those who are

considered as 'low' should receive special care and protection. It is our duty to abolish this evil of high and low by birth and specially to improve the condition of those who do sanitation work'.

Everybody is conscious of this fact (inhuman system of carrying and handling human excreta manually), and we have discussed this many times and there is no doubt that this is a disgrace and it should be eradicated as early as possible'.

Indira Gandhi[23]

'The continued practice of scavenging is the most undesirable form of social derogation. Under the 20-Point Programme (1986), we are determined to eradicate it. To do so we will require the active cooperation of all citizens and particularly of local bodies and Governments which are responsible for approving construction activity or have their own housing programmes. This will also require rehabilitation of Scavengers which will mean training and resettlement in new occupations'.

Rajiv Gandhi[24]

Legislation on Abolition of Scavenging, 1993

Two decades ago, the Government had decided to bring in a central legislation for abolition of manual scavenging from the country and introduced a Bill in this regard in the Parliament. As a result of all this, the Parliament passed the Employment of Manual Scavengers and Construction of Dry Latrines (Prohibition) Bill, 1993, to abolish scavenging and ban the construction of dry latrines. This was no doubt, a historical decision but no time limit had been given, by which the system of manual scavenging would be totally abolished and thus, very purpose of the Bill was defeated. For more details see particularly Chapter III.

Notes

1. Khurram, 'Dr Ambedkar's Approach Towards Human Rights', in Mohammad Shabbir (ed.) *Ambedkar On Law, Constitution and Social Justice,* Jaipur: Rawat Publications, 2005, p. 323.
2. Ibid., p. 323–324.
3. K.C. Daiya, B.R. Ambedkar: The Crusader for Human Rights of Untouchables, in Shyam Lal and K.S. Saxena (ed.) *Ambedkar and Nation Building*, Jaipur: Rawat Publications, 1998, p. 252.
4. Ibid., p. 252.
5. Khurram, 2005, ibid., p. 319.
6. Khurram, 2005, ibid., p. 319.
7. K.C. Daiya, 1998, ibid., p. 252.
8. K.C. Daiya, 1998, ibid., p. 257
9. K.C. Daiya, 1998, ibid., p. 257
10. B.N. Srivastava, 'State Action for the Liberation of Scavengers' in National Seminar on Action Sociology and Liberation of Scavengers, New Delhi, 8–10 February

1992. Sponsored by Indian Associartion of Action Sociologists and Sulabh International, p. 24.

11. Ibid., p. 24.
12. Sachchidanand, *People at the Bottom: A Portrait of Scavengers*, New Delhi: Concept Publishing Company, 2001, p. 95.
13. Ibid., p. 95.
14. S.P. Srivastava, 'Issue in Scavenging: An Overview of the Problem, Programmes and Policies', in National Seminar on Action-Sociology and Liberation of Scavengers, New Delhi, 8–10 February 1992, ibid., p. 15.
15. Ibid., p. 16.
16. Ibid., p. 13.
17. Shyam Lal, 'Upliftment of Bhangis: A National Challenge' in National Seminar on Action Sociology and Liberation of Scavengers, New Delhi, 8–10 February 1992, ibid., p 75.
18. Ibid., p. 76.
19. Ibid., p. 76.
20. Ibid., p. 77.
21. M.R. Malkani, 'Clean People and An Unclean Country', Delhi, Harijan Sevak Sangh, 1969, p. 157–158.
22. Ibid., 1969, p. 153.
23. S.P. Srivastav 'Issues in Scavenging: An Overview of Problem, Programmes and Policies', in National Seminar on Action Sociology and Liberation of Scavengers, New Delhi, 8–10 February 1992, ibid., p. 16.
24. Ibid., p. 16.

5

Ambedkar: Mobilization and Bhangi Solidarity Movement

The Bhangis are placed at the lowest rung of the caste hierarchy. The nature of the job or work traditionally associated with them or imposed upon them, pushed them to the lowest rank. The task of cleaning night soil is the inferior most job because this involves the touching of human excreta. Consequently, they did not get social justice nor human treatment. Being socially lowest of the low, and economically poorest of the poor, they could not revolt against the unjust nor could they rid themselves of scavenging work.

Since the Independence of the country social scientists, more particularly sociologists, social anthropologists and political scientists have shown their increasing interest in the study of Dr Ambedkar's contribution in nation building. Although there is a considerable body of empirical literature on Constitutional stewardship of social justice, egalitarian social order, the vision of national development of natural and mineral resources and social, political, economic and educational aspects of traditionally lower untouchable castes yet formation of a separate Commission for Safai Karamcharis to document the difficulties of Safai Karamcharis, their working conditions and social status, etc. were some of the Babasaheb's noteworthy achievements in his capacity as Labour Minister. But significance of his role is still to be adequately assessed and documented. In this chapter, efforts of Babasaheb Ambedkar for liberation of Scavengers has been brought to the fore.

Growth of Ambedkar's Influence amongst the Bhangis

News came in the third week of June 1942 that the Viceroy Linlithgow was about to expand his executive council of Ministry and will appoint five new ministers. Among the probable names were Sir C.P. Ramaswami Iyer, Sir Mohammad Usman, Dr B.R. Ambedkar, Sir J.P. Srivastava, Sir Jogendra Singh, M.N. Roy, Jamnadas Mehta and Sir Shanmukhan Chetty. On 2 July, names were announced and except the last three all were included in the executive council making the strength of Indians 14 as against five Europeans.[1]

Babasaheb was apppointed the Council's Labour Member, a department usually allotted to Scheduled Caste leaders. Most people of the untouchable castes used to work as sweepers, garbage collectors, factory labourers and railway workers. For most of the time, they were daily wage earners. Babasaheb's followers belonged overwhelmingly to this section.

A few parties tried to organize the working class under their banner. Communist party activists were among the first to work among the working classes. Their slogan was 'Mazdoor aur Kisan Sangathit ho Jao' (Workers and Peasants Unite). This slogan was taken from the communist Soviet Union. Mao Zedong formulated a similar slogan in China. The Communists in India also built a working class organization, the All India Trade Union Congress or AITUC.[2]

The Congress also organized labourers – their organization was called INTUC, the Indian National Trade Union Congress, and was meant to prevent the workers from coming solely under the communist party banner. Many Congress supporters were industrialists and capitalists. But Babasaheb wanted the working class to form an independent organizational front with a progressive leadership and he told them to fight a collective battle and wrest political power.[3]

First Commission for Safai Karamcharis during British Rule

Among the untouchables, the lowest and most humiliated section is that of the sweepers – those who sweep the roads, clean drains and carry away from traditional dry toilets, many castes in India are also involved in this kind of work. Known as Safai Karamcharis (sanitation workers), they find work through municipal committee, corporation, cantonment boards, the railways, hospitals and in residential colonies. When a person has been collecting garbage in a particular area for many years he/she gets a kind of exclusive property right over the work. For instance, if a person were to quit the job of garbage collecting because of low wages or poor working conditions, no other person would replace him by mutual agreement. Some courts recognized this tradition as a right or property on the basis of which a worker could even get a loan or bail from court.[4]

To better understand the Safai Karamcharis' problems, Babasaheb formed a separate commission to which P.T. Borle and R.R. Bhole were appointed members. They travelled to various provinces across India, to document the difficulties of the Safai Karamcharis, their working conditions and social status and submit a report to the Labour Department for discussion.[5]

Achievements of the commission in a short span of time were incredible. It should be noted that in 1945 R.R. Bhole[6] was sent by Ambedkar to International Mazdoor Congress held at Philadelphia as a representative of Safai Karamcharis. Bhole presented and explained the difficulties of the Safai Karamcharis, their working conditions and social status. All these developments took place only after Ambedkar took up the leadership of Labour Ministry and Bhangi cause. Ambedkar's efforts were an asset to the Bhangis in many ways. Later, Bhole became the High Court Judge. After his retirement he was elected as a Member of Lok Sabha.

Ambedkar's Anguish, Love and Affection for the Bhangis

Dalits from different regions used to meet Ambedkar at his residence at New Delhi. They had detailed discussions with him – the sole Dalit leader – about their grievances. Ambedkar was highly pained by the socio-political atrocities, economic exploitation and social injustice by upper caste Hindus and others. In reply to their grievances, Ambedkar wrote letters to Collectors, Commissioners and sometimes even to the Viceroy too. Ambedkar was grieved to see that such people were harassed, tortured and treated as animals by higher strata of the society. For instance Devi Dayal, a librarian, who looked after the library work at Ambedkar's Bungalow at New Delhi from 1943–51, published a book 'डॉ बाबा साहेब भीमराव अम्बेडकर की दिनचर्या' from Lucknow, Uttar Pradesh, in 1989. He was also a keen listener of the conversations between Ambedkar and dignitaries and others. According to him:[7]

> '14 सितम्बर : आज चार मेहतर अपनी दु:खभरी कहानी सुनाने आए। एक मेहतर के शरीर की खाल चटकी हुई थी और उनसे थोड़ा-थोड़ा खून झलक रहा था। मुख पर ऐसे चिन्हों को देखकर बाबा साहेब ने कहा 'यह क्या हो गया है?' मेहतर ने जवाब दिया 'हुजूर! अफ़सरों के हुकूम से मैंने कल गंदी नाली में डुबकी लगाई। मल की गंदगी की गर्मी से मेरी खाल कट गई। इनसे बड़ी पीड़ा होती है।'

On hearing this, Ambedkar was not pleased with the pitiable conditions; it only increased his anguish. Ambedkar[8] expressed his anger to them in these words:

> 'मैं इन मेहतरों से इतनी घृणा करता हूं कि जिसकी तुम कल्पना भी नहीं कर सकते। मैंने वर्षों तक सुधार का काम किया। मैं सबको समझा सका कि उन्हें मनुष्य की भांति रहना चाहिये। किन्तु मैं इस कोम को नहीं समझ सका। वे इतना नारकीय जीवन व्यतीत करते हैं किन्तु उससे बचने का कोई उपाय न तो स्वयं करते हैं और न दूसरों की सुनते हैं, वे इतने पतित हो गये हैं कि न तो उन्हें अपने मनुष्य होने पर और न अपने काम का मूल्य समझ में आता है। वे दो पैसों के लिए महीना भर गंदगी उठाते हैं और यहां आकर तनख्वाह बढ़वाने के लिए रोते हैं। यदि वे दो महीने तक अपना काम छोड़ देने का संकल्प करें तो सम्पूर्ण समाज विनाश को प्राप्त हो जाये और लोग 100/- रूपए माहवार देने के लिए तैयार हो जायें। किन्तु ये मूर्ख तो अपना मूल्य कभी नहीं समझेंगे।'

Besides his anguish, Ambedkar also showed his love and affection from the very beginning. Affection was also one of the Ambedkar's constructive programmes and was one of the main programmes of reform, which Ambedkar had initiated much earlier. There were eight Dalit families residing in Ambedkar Bungalow. All families took care of Ambedkar by rendering their services to him. Ambedkar also cared and helped his staff in crisis. For instance, Devi Dayal[9] had drawn our attention:

> 'एक बार उनके जमादार ''भगली'' को जो कोठी में सफाई का काम करता था, कुछ तकलीफ हो गई। बाबा साहेब ने उसे अपनी कार से अस्पताल भेजा और अपना काम रोके रखा। धोबी के बारे में यह बात बहुधा हुआ करती थी।'

As mentioned earlier, there was a strong feeling amongst untouchables not to accept food and water touched by a Bhangi. Ambedkar was against it and the charismatic influence of Ambedkar pleaded for removal of restriction regarding inter-dinning. For instance, according to Devi Dayal:[10]

> 'उनका सबसे प्यारा मेहतर उनको खाना खिलाने का भी काम करता था और तेल मालिश भी करता था।'

Karamcharis have certain specific problems. On the one hand, people assume that they are quite powerful - were they to stop work' for even a few days, any government would be forced to accept their demands from fear of the prospect of the unsanitary conditions that would result into consequent spread of disease. On the other hand, most Safai Karamcharis are living in conditions of extreme poverty, ignorance and helplessness. There are many masters above them who exploit and use them. This makes it very difficult for them to organize and sustain a struggle.[11]

The Bhangis and their Participation in Scheduled Castes Federation

Every political party gives preference (at the organization level) to certain dominant SC people connected with that particular party and often it is the Bhangis who end up being neglected altogether. The overall perception is that the Congress has fared badly. What is blatantly obvious is the plight of the Bhangis.

While all parties have upheld reservation for the SCs/STs, they have not been able to evolve a consensus on the rights of the Bhangis. Parties claiming to be secular and saviours of the Bhangis have paid no attention to welfare schemes. This is especially true of Bhangis who remain the lowest of the low untouchables. The national concern on the pitiable plight of Bhangis was expressed in a number of reports of the Government-appointed Commissions and Committees right from the days of Independence.

Much of the responsibility for this shameful neglect must be placed at the door step of the Congress which has been in power at the Centre longer than any other political formation. The BJP and its affiliates have played an altogether different role at ominous time.

The Bhangis are, thus, caught in pincer movement. On the one hand the parties, particularly the Congress, have failed to deliver the Constitutional rights of the Bhangis to them and on the other hand, the BJP has also neglected them. As a result of political parties' negative attitude, the Bhangis were never nominated or given the ticket to fight the election.

Envisaging the need for a powerful organization to reach the masses, 'Independent Labour Party[12] came into existence at Bombay in 1936. In 1942, it was re-christened as 'Scheduled Castes Federation'. From time to time, it organized conferences which were attended by Dalits, weaker sections of society and other persons belonging to different castes. It should be noted here that Ambedkar gave an opportunity to the Bhangis. Thus, under Ambedkar's guidance, Balmukund and Teluram Baidwan became President of Scheduled Caste Federation and General Secretary of Scheduled Castes Federation of Shimla unit, respectively.[13] This news was widely publicized and Ambedkar earned the appreciation and goodwill of the Bhangi masses.

Here I would like to discuss in a nutshell the Scheduled Castes Federation Movement (SCFM) in Shimla. The branch of Scheduled Castes Federation was active in Shimla prior to 1942, where Teluram Baidwan born in Punjab had migrated to Shimla long back and worked as a cleaner and caretaker at a beauty parlour run by an English woman. With the encouragement of Ambedkar, Baidwan launched socio-political activities of Scheduled Castes Federation, which involved a large number of untouchables. The federation was becoming a powerful organization in the region. He used to spend most of his time in reading and working for untouchables rights and justice. Baidwan impressed upon the sweepers and others the need of SCF in order to fight for citizenship rights. Many people from other castes, such as Koli and Chamar, used to come to him with their problems to seek his guidance. However, the members of the Congress Party and other Hindu groups used to call him 'Badman' instead of Baidwan.

In his campaign, Puran Chand, another sweeper activist, was assisting him. Baidwan and his colleagues organized several agitations and meetings of the Scheduled Caste Federation during his school days. Bhagwan Das was highly impressed by Baidwan and his socio-political activities. Thus, under Baidwan's guidance, Bhagwan Das involved himself in SCFM.

After Ambedkar, parties had not yet made enough efforts to provide them opportunities.[14] Bhagwan Das in his book 'बाबा साहेब भीमराव अम्बेडकर: एक परिचय-एक संदेश' made a statement attacking the leaders of the Republican Party.[15]

> 'यदि रिपब्लिकन पार्टी सफाई मजदूर और खेत मजदूर को संगठित करने का काम हाथ में ले लेती तो न सिर्फ उसकी शक्ति बढ़ती बल्कि वह एक क्रांतिकारी काम भी कर पाती।'

The most significant event that occurred after Ambedkar's death was the re-christening and in 1957 it became the Republican Party.[16]

During the British rule, the untouchables in general and Bhangis in particular were not recruited to public services because they were untouchables. With the appointment of Ambedkar as Labour Member in 1942, aspirations arose among the untouchables because of the accessibility to Ambedkar. Besides other untouchables, it was the educated Bhangis who exploited these opportunities but in a small way. A noteworthy issue which had attracted widespread attention among the Bhangis and in which Babasaheb Ambedkar played an important part was 'recruitment to public service'.

As Labour Member, Ambedkar's office was partly in Delhi and partly in Shimla. Another department, the civil pioneer force, deployed in constructing and repairing roads and bridges, was also brought under his supervision. Brigadier C.P. Clark was its Commander.

Ambedkar first came to Shimla as Labour Member in 1943. He stayed at Khan Bahadur Mustfaq Ahmed Gurmani's residence. It is significant to note that local association called 'Scheduled Castes Federation' (SCF) was founded by Ambedkar with the objective to propagating his teachings. The socio-political philosophy of Ambedkar was considered to be a path of truth, conduct and wisdom. It was regarded as the beacon of new knowledge and moonlight in dark. It is also significant that SCF was centred around the teachings of Ambedkar. In order to understand the part played by SCF in uniting the untouchables, it is necessary to know the aims and objectives of the SCF. According to its constitution[17], 'the object of the All India Scheduled Castes Federation is the attainment by the Scheduled Castes of status as distinct and separate element in the national life of India and to obtain for them their political, economic and social rights to which they are entitled by reason of their needs, their numbers and their importance'. Through SCF, headed by local Bhangi called Tuluram Baidwan, message of Ambedkar spread all over Shimla and reached the masses at village level. He was a very devoted activist and influential in the Himachal Hill terrain. Whenever he went to meet Ambedkar, 'he talked at length about the problems of Dalits'.[18]

Baidwan used to work as cleaner and caretaker at a beauty parlour run by an English woman. He used to spend most of his time reading and working for untouchables' rights and justice. Many people from other castes, such as Koli and Chamar, used to come to him with their problems to seek his guidance. It should, however, be noted that 'the members of the Congress Party and other Hindu groups used sarcastic remarks and called him "Bad Man"' instead of Baidwan.[19]

Baidwan was President of SCF, Shimla. He worked in close association with Ambedkar and continued to play an important part in SCF. Besides Baidwan the foremost Bhangi workers of SCF were:[20] Mothan Singh, Chanan Ram Kalyanpuri, Budhram Kapoor, Giya Lal, Puranchand, Master Udho, etc. who also managed the Safai Karamchari Union.

During Baidwan's leadership, Koli, another untouchable caste, who also worked as Safaiwala in the northern part of Himachal, hated the Bhangis and Chamars. They strongly opposed the SCF and remained out of the Federation. Bhagwan Das in his book wrote why Koli dissuaded the SCF from making an active political career. First, leaders of Koli were under the influence of Arya Samaj. Secondly and lastly, Kolis claimed for themselves the title name 'छोटे राजपूत'.[21] Hence they maintained a socio-political distance with other untouchable castes. The objectives of SCF were to propagate Ambedkar's teachings, to fight for Dalit cause and create socio-political awakening and unity among untouchables. It is also true that SCF had made progress in social and educational field.

As we have noted earlier, it is a fact that a sizeable section of the Bhangis had allied itself with SCF and they continued to play an important part in establishing the branches of SCF in Punjab and other states. For instance, the leadership of SCF in this phase was in the hands of Balmukand[22], who was General Secretary of SCF and continued for a long period.

Another notable person was Khalid Siddique. We get an idea of how Khalid Siddique was converted to Bhangi caste, with the growth of Arya Samaj influence from the account of Bhagwan Das's book.[23]

Khalid Siddique was originally a Muslim by birth in Punjab. He came under the influence of Arya Samaj and consequently converted himself into the Hindu fold. Then he took membership of Bhangi Samaj. As a result, he was known as Virendra Satyawadi. Later, he became the President of PEPs. He made a bid to win the Bhangis to his side by dissociating them from the Congress. After India achieved her Independence, he was once elected as a member of the Parliament. Besides Bal Mukand, Baidwan and Virendra Satyawadi, the foremost Bhangi activists of SCF were:[24] Harwant Singh (Ferozepur, Punjab), Ram Rakha Subha (दो आब), Chuni Lal Thappar, Rahav Ram, Fakeer Chand Nahar, Bhagmal 'Pagal', Mohan Singh Gill, Puran Chand, Jiya Lal, Braj Lal and others.

Samata Sainik Dal and Mobilization of Bhangis

Samata Sainik Dal (SSD) also gained the support of the Bhangis at the local level, especially in the regions where the SSD was influential. For instance, SCF and SSD movement in Allahabad grew steadily and some of the notable Bhangis of Allahabad joined both. The Bhangis not only joined the SCF and SSD, but also supported the Ambedkar programmes.

The growth of the Congress influence[25] had an adverse effect on SCF movement. Later Kalyan Chand was elected as the member of the Rajya Sabha. Similarly, Badri Prasad (popularly known as Badri Prasad Balmikanand) led several delegates of SCF and SSD. Badra Prasad as chief supporter of SCF and SSD in Allahabad, continued to do so.

The untouchables, under the leadership of Ambedkar, united under the banner of SCF and aimed to fight for Dalits' cause. The strength of SCF increased because Bhangis and Chamars – the dominant communities, were its stronghold. It should be noted that whenever Ambedkar toured Punjab, both Bhangis and Chamars made joint efforts to organize public meetings of Dalits. They tried to give good impression to the public. For instance,[26] on 27 October 1951, Ambedkar came to Jalandhar to address the public meetings. Seth Kishan Das, who was the president of SCF, organized a public meeting and Master Bhagmal who was also Prachar Mantri of SCF conducted the proceedings of the meeting. But in 1937, there was a split in SCF[27] between the Bhangis and Chamars due to distribution of tickets. Seth Kishan Das was born in Jalandhar in a family of Chamars. Seth Kishan Das, who was the chairman of SCF, was also a big leather businessman in Calcutta. It was alleged that Seth Kishan Das was not willing to give the tickets to Chura (Bhangi) as they demanded or desired. Thus, there arose serious differences amongst the members of SCF due to distribution of tickets.

Rift in SCF[28]

In 1937, the internal cleavage in SCF emerged between Seth Kishan Das and his group on the one hand and Bhagmal and his group on the other. The rift to a great extent was also an expression of Chamar dominance. Seth Kishan Das, being an important SCF leader pursued an informal policy of eliminating the Bhangis from SCF. The Bhangis opposed Seth Kishan Das's policy and used SCF to propagate Ambedkar's ideas.

In those days, *The Times of India* and *The Statesman* were two main English newspapers, both had English men as editors and were published from Bombay and Calcutta respectively. *Hindustan Times* was owned by the Gandhians . *The Times of India* and *The Statesman* printed Dr Ambedkar's articles and speeches. Thus, English press also played an important part in publicizing the views, ideas and philosophy of Ambedkar, across the country. But *Hindustan Times* pleaded mainly about Gandhi and the Congress.[29] Bhagwan Das was at that time a regular reader of the two main English newspapers. As a result of all this, he was so impressed that he became a staunch supporter of Dr Ambedkar during the period.

Recruitment of Educated Bhangis in Public Services and Strategies to Protect their Interest

Being the lowest of the low, Bhagwan Das, a Bhangi, was very keen to see Dr Ambedkar too. After a few months, Dr Ambedkar first came to Shimla as a Labour Member in 1943. Here he stayed at Khan Bahadur Mushtaq Ahmed Gurmani's residence. Members of the Scheduled Castes Federation and other activists wanted to meet him.

As stated earlier, Bhagwan Das wanted to see Ambedkar, though he was neither a politician nor an officer. One day he reached there and met Ambedkar's personal assistant, who was a young Maharashtrian. The personal assistant assured Bhagwan Das that he would arrange the meeting. Bhagwan Das waited from morning to evening in order to see Ambedkar. After waiting for seven hours, the personal assistant took him inside the office. Ambedkar asked his name and then enquired about his father. Bhagwan Das then told Ambedkar that his father had expired on 14 May that year and their house had been burnt down just a month later.[30] He further told that he had completed his matriculation and was working in the accounts department of CPWD. Ambedkar then asked Bhagwan Das, 'What do you want?[31] Bhagwan Das replied, 'I was not prepared for this question, as I was already a government employee, but I knew that if I could find employment in a Central Government office, my pay would be double the amount I was getting. I thought a little and answered, I want to work in your department. I sent a letter a few days ago and I have not yet received any reply. He (Ambedkar) asked for my address and I gave it to him, thanked him and took his leave'.[32]

After 15 days of this meeting, Bhagwan Das received an appointment letter from Labour Division for the post of a B-grade clerk. He deposited ₹ 51 with CPWD and they accepted his resignation. In the Labour Department, his salary was certainly higher.

Besides Bhagwan Das another Bhangi clerk was Pritam Lal, who mainly did the typing during its early days in Labour Department, Shimla. But he had problem with English. Because of this, his work suffered. He suspected that his services may be terminated at any time. Before it happened so, Pritam Lal asked his uncle Mohan Singh for help. As a Safai Karamchari's union leader, Mohan Singh knew many Congressmen. It may be noted in this connection that in the year 1943–44, an attempt was made by Pritamlal to meet Dr Ambedkar at his bungalow on Prithviraj Road, Delhi, to seek his help and guidance. Dr Ambedkar listened to his problem.

The response from Dr Ambedkar was encouraging. He rang up the head of Shimla office and told him:[33]

> 'My boys are not here to be discharged or dismissed. Try to find some other work for him'.

Pritam Lal came back to Shimla. No orders were issued for his discharge and he was sent to another department, where a Hindu superintendent taught him English with love and patience. After this Pritam Lal learnt English, did well and was promoted.

This was the zeal with which Dr Ambedkar recruited educated Bhangis to the offices of public services and worked out various strategies to protect their interest.

Movement within Bhangis

Ambedkar's Visit to Matang Samaj, 1937

In an attempt to address general meeting of Independent Labour Party and to preside over a district conference of the depressed classes at Masur and other places, Ambedkar toured all over Maharashtra in 1937.

On 30 December 1937, Ambedkar left for Pandharpur to preside over the Sholapur District Conference of the Depressed Classes. On his way, he was enthusiastically received at Kurduwadi Station. Then he and his party were taken in a special bus to Pandharpur. On their way, Ambedkar made a brief halt and made a short speech before Matang Samaj at Karkam village. Addressing the Matang Samaj, Ambedkar was able to perceive the deprivation felt among the Matang Samaj and he 'advised them to be on their guard against the Congress which, he said, comprised their exploiters, oppressors and blood suckers, who professed welfare of poor under the garb of white dress and cap.'[34]

Matang Conference, 1938[35]

Similarly, from Pandharpur, Ambedkar went to Sholapur to address the Matang Conference. On his arrival he was presented with a welcome civil address by the Sholapur Municipality on the morning of 4 January 1938 at the Bhagat Chitra Mandir. The address was read and presented by Rao Bahadur, Dr V.V. Muley, who had helped the cause of the untouchables at Sholapur in the capacity of the President of the Municipality. In reply Ambedkar made a very important speech, expressing his views on the working of 'Parliamentary Democracy'. 'In the political situation', he declared, 'that has grown up in this country, there has grown only one political party, the Congress.'[36]

Thus, Ambedkar used the opportunity of addressing the Bhangi Samaj and Bhangi Conference as a weapon of agitation against social discrimination and deprivation in promoting the cause of the Bhangis welfare. The underlying motive in both the meetings was the desire for involvement of Scavengers in its movement.

Equality of Citizenship

One of the most significant events of the Ambedkar Movement was to promote inter-mixing between untouchable castes communities and between Bhangis and other untouchables. All untouchable castes considered the Bhangi as most degraded untouchable and, therefore, had no commensal relations with them. Ambedkar, realized the contradiction, in that while Dalits were fighting against pollution as practiced by the castes above them, they were themselves treating the Bhangis as the most untouchable. Ambedkar advocated castelessness and started a programme of inter-dining. The credit of having started a movement of self correction among the untouchables goes to Ambedkar B.K. Gayakward, the closest colleague of Ambedkar, narrated in D.D. Kalyani's book[37] 'Whenever Ambedkar visited Nasik, some caste Hindus and Brahmins met him and invited him to have food with them'. However, it may be noted that Ambedkar used to visit his friend's, Rambhau Palajimaro's[38] home and stayed there. Here Ambedkar took food. Ambedkar fought for equality of citizenship movement for removal of restriction regarding inter-dining. It should be noted that Rambhau Palajimaro was born in a family of Bhangi. Some of his Dalit followers played an important role in publicizing Ambedkar's inter-dining and inter-marrying campaign in Nasik. D.D. Kalyani[39] wrote: 'उन्हीं (अम्बेडकर) की शिक्षा को क्रियात्मक रूप देने के लक्ष्य से नासिक में महारों और भंगी जाति में परस्पर अनेक शादियां हुई।'

The Congress and the Bhangis[40]

Even before Ambedkar started the process of organizing the Bhangis on national level, they were under the influence of Gandhi, Pandit Jawaharlal Nehru, Indian National Congress, etc. They not only kept the Bhangis away from Ambedkar, but also created ill feeling among them and led anti-Ambedkar Movement.

Some literate persons of the Bhangis of Delhi and Bombay wanted to have the advantage of Ambedkar's leadership and guidance for the upliftment of the caste and for overcoming their socio-economic discrimination. Their effort was to spread Ambedkar's message among the caste fellows. The fear that Gandhi and the Congress supporters might harass and torture them, if they did so, always haunted them. As a result of all this, a large number of Bhangis never joined organizations started by Ambedkar.

Several workers and leaders of Gandhi Congress carried on the propaganda against Ambedkar and did much to maintain the distance between Ambedkar and the Bhangis. They wanted that the Bhangis who were associated with Ambedkar should be detached from him and affiliated to Gandhi. The poor and the unlettered Bhangis considered the Congress as their messiah and therefore accepted it. To a great extent, the Congress succeeded in its mission all over

India.[41] Yet, the Bhangis were under the influence of Ambedkar. They appreciated agitation and movement launched by Ambedkar against social discrimination. A few Bhangi workers bought the books of Ambedkar and read them. The Bhangis were also highly impressed by Ambedkar's speeches.

Formation of Municipalities Kamgar Sangh, 1936

Ambedkar was dedicated to the upliftment of the untouchables, the downtrodden and the weaker sections of the society. But at the same time he also took special interest in improving the pitiable plight of the Bhangis in Bombay Municipality. He encouraged them to form an organization (Union) and, thus, Bombay Municipal Kamgar Sangh[42] came into existence in 1936, which was headed by Ambedkar himself. The Bhangis were treated with contempt. Ambedkar organized Bhangis to fight for their rights.

Organizational activities among the Bhangis in different parts of the country, got linked up with the programme of action initiated by Ambedkar on the one hand and the Scheduled Castes Federation (SCF) on the other. We can identify two regional centres of activity, each one functioning under a leader or a team of leaders. The two regional centres were at Bombay and Delhi.

In fact, Ambedkar's heart bleed for the suffering of the people, particularly for untouchables - the Bhangis - and he realized the importance of having national, regional and local organizations. Thus, the idea of forming an organization as a weapon was exploited by Ambedkar in promoting the cause of the Bhangis. On 4 June 1943–44,[43] he organized a combined mass gathering of Delhi and Bombay Bhangis at 22, Prithviraj Road, New Delhi, encouraging them for formation of Municipalities Kamgar Union for the removal of discrimination against them in all spheres. This was the first set of significant events. Ambedkar asked the workers for formation of their own organization union so that they would not be exploited and discriminated in the municipalities and states. His appeal did evoke positive response from workers. Thus, the Municipal Kamgar Union came into existence at Delhi in 1944. Ramesh Jadhav assumed the leadership as President of the newly founded organization, Municipal Kamgar Union, to fight injustice done to the Bhangis in the field of education and employment in municipalities. This was the first (set of) event which sparked off a mass movement. Ramesh Jadhav was a resident of Nasik, Maharashtra, and was contractor in the PWD. However, in order to understand the part played by Ambedkar in transforming the caste, it is necessary to note his views.

Ambedkar and Upliftment of the Bhangis

From an account of work carried out by Dr Ambedkar for the upliftment of the Bhangis given by one of the biographers, B.R. Skampla[44] (2003), it will be seen that the miserable conditions of the Bhangis in Delhi was also not better than that of the Bhangis in Bombay. In the sphere of recruitment to Delhi Municipality, the Bhangis were not given jobs directly. They could enter municipalities only through contractors/*thekedars*. The role of *thekedars* had adverse effects on the Bhangis as they exploited the Bhangis in a big way. So much so that the Bhangis who were appointed through *thekedars* were paid less amount.

If a Bhangi employee did not turn up for a week, his services were not only terminated but he was even sent to Jail for 15 days.[45] The dependence of the Bhangis on their *thekedars* being great, they could not afford to displease the authorities. This was to a very considerable extent not only responsible for their backwardness but also restricted their efforts for emancipation. This situation partly explains why the movement among the Bhangis could not start in Delhi and Bombay where exploitation and discrimination against them in the municipalities was severe.

During the British India certain Municipal Acts had already been enacted with the aim of harassment and punishing the Bhangis. The clause of these Acts had an adverse effect on the Bhangis. In 1890, the Bombay Government enacted Bombay Municipal Servant Act, 1890. This led to a series of Municipal Acts of some important municipalities, such as Uttar Pradesh Municipalities Act 1920, Madras Municipalities Act 1920, Rajasthan Municipalities Act 1923 and Municipal Act Bengal 1923. There were serious clauses whereby the Bhangis could harassed and even sent to jail for a few months. For instance, according to the Article 71 of Municipal Act Bengal 1923, if a Bhangi without prior permission of the Commissioner, remained absent from the duty, then he/she would be either sent to Jail for one month or fined ₹ 50 or both. It was also true that Madras Municipalities Act 1920 had included hard clauses to punish Bhangis for minor mistakes. Thus, according to Article 318 of Madras Municipalities Act, 1920, a Bhangi could be sent to jail for two months in case he remained absent from duty.[46]

Another notable case was from UP. We get an idea of how a Bhangi was punished and sent behind the bar, from the account of D.D. Kalyani's book. Kalyani states:[47]

> 'बसवा नामक एक सफाई मजदूर (भंगी) 6 अगस्त 1934 को काम पर नहीं गया, क्योंकि उसने नियमों के अनुसार त्याग पत्र दे दिया था। बसवा ने त्याग पत्र मंजूर होने का इंतजार किए बगैर काम छोड़ दिया। सैशन जज ने उसे एक महीना कारावास का दण्ड दिया। हाई कोर्ट में जब अपील की गई तो सजा तो बहाल रखी, किन्तु अवधि कम कर दी गई।'

The Labour Ministry introduced a number of measures which benefitted the lower caste sections (all untouchables, including Bhangis) in coal mines, mills, factories, workshops, printing press industries, hospitals, port trust, municipalities, military cantonments, railways, etc. Later on various Municipalities Acts which were primarily used against the Bhangis for harassing, humiliating and socio-economic exploitation were declared illegal.[48] The poor Bhangis not only felt happy but expressed gratitude to Ambedkar.

Today even in nagar nigams, cantonment boards by-laws and laws are there through which Bhangis could be punished severally. But due to fear of strike by Bhangis, very few authorities used them. After Independence the by-laws, etc. were not applicable.[49]

Scavengers Free India

Since caste was associated with traditional occupation, i.e. sweeping and scavenging, Ambedkar advocated that Bhangis give up their occupation of scavenging. He wanted 'Scavengers Free India' and encouraged them to take other jobs, and indulge in trade and commerce. He believed that progress in employment and education was the basis for upward social mobility.[50] He took this step in generating new views and thoughts and instilling its value in the lives of caste fellows. He firmly believed that giving up of the traditional occupation was the only basis of progress without which the basic inequalities and suffering could not be fought. Thus, he laid supreme emphasis on social strength with a view to gaining self-respect and esteem.

From an account of views and thoughts of Ambedkar given by one of his supporters and followers, Bhagwan Das, it will be seen that Ambedkar was deeply concerned with regard to the upliftment of the Bhangis.

A few Bhangis were influenced by Ambedkar, notably Bhagwan Das. Contemptuous curiosity prompted him to meet Ambedkar in 1943 at Shimla, and was so impressed that he became his staunch follower. In one of his book, 'सफाई कर्मचारी दिवस, 31 जुलाई', he asked Ambedkar Mission Society, followers of Ambedkar and other Ambedkar organizations to make 'Scavengers Free India'.[51] Ambedkar Mission society is dedicated to the spreading of Ambedkar message. Every year it organizes conferences, seminars and meetings which is attended by Ambedkarites, well-wishers and other scholars belonging to different castes. Thus, he urged[52] the local association to support the following objectives which were part of the Ambedkar campaign in early 1930.

First, it is necessary that parents be asked not to allow their children to do the same dirty work, which lowers their social status and forbid them to enter temples, educational institutes, government services, etc. but to do other jobs.

Second, they are poorest of the poor across the country. Therefore, it is significant to raise a special fund to provide them financial assistance for those who want to do business, trade, etc.

Third, those parents who allowed their children for sweeping and scavenging must be socially boycotted and also financially be fined so that they may be discouraged.

The conditions that prevailed at that time were such that across the country, the caste fellows had undesirable social practices, norms, customs and habits, such as eating dead animals and their left over and it was considered bad, because this practice also stood in the way of improving their low social status. Hence, Ambedkar appealed them to stop all this.[53]

Introducing Uniform Rules in Municipalities

It should also be noted here that Ambedkar as the Labour Minister considered old rules unnecessary. He reformed the recruitment rules and introduced a simple uniform rule which included direct appointment of sweepers in municipalities.

Delayed payment to Bhangis in municipalities was another area, where they were tortured and harassed. Hence, Ambedkar improved the system of payment and issued new directions to the authorities to pay them well in time.

Deeds of the Congress

In order to understand the part played by Delhi Municipality Kamgar Sangh in removing Ambedkar's name from the letter head, it is necessary to discuss this case here.

As it was stated earlier that Ambedkar was the founder of Delhi Municipality Kamgar Sangh and was associated with the upliftment programmes with regard to the Bhangis. He took an active interest in fighting against the social discrimination.

Soon after the death of Ambedkar in 1956, a year later, attempts were made in 1957 by certain Congress influential Bhangi leaders in Kamgar Sangh to remove the name of Ambedkar from the letter head.[54] They successfully removed the name of Ambedkar – the founder. It was the worst incident during the Congress rule at Centre. The Congress influential leaders asked their people to follow the Congress ideology, stop the praising of Ambedkar's activities in public meetings, gatherings and *sammelans.* Thus, the Bhangi association became centres of the teachings of Gandhi.

The lack of enthusiasm for Ambedkar by the Bhangis of north India can be explained in terms of certain inter-related factors.

First, Gandhi and his followers offered a more satisfactory lifestyle and Indian view, within the framework of Hinduism. It was this which largely attracted the Bhangis to कांग्रेसीकरण, Gandhi's influence was wide spread and Bhagwan Das, an enlightened intellectual, recognized that it was Gandhi who had fenced up a community from going out to seek refuge under Ambedkar.

Second, the Bhangis were more attracted by lip service of Gandhi Congress and reform programmes initiated by it, though they were least interested in improving their social status. This made the Bhangis to remain with the Congress.

Third, it was mainly due to Gandhi's influence that a large number of Bhangis became staunch supporters of Congress, and only a small number of Bhangis remained staunch followers of Ambedkar.

The Conversion Question

The question of conversion from Hinduism to any other religion did not come up for the first time in 1935, in fact it was a recurring phenomenon as mentioned earlier. Consequently 12 untouchables[55] had embraced Islam. With great efforts, great energy and great hope Ambedkar had launched the campaign for temple entry, but the caste Hindus showed no sign of common sense and reasoning. They were impenitent and relentless as before. Gandhi and his men did nothing more than evince a flutter of emotion.

It was on the eve of the Yeola conference that it was convened by leaders of depressed classes to review the political and social situation in the light of their 10-year-old struggle and initiating the reforms.

The conference met at Yeola on 13 October 1935 and was attended by about 10,000 untouchables of all shades of opinion.[56]

In a tremendously feeling speech, Ambedkar recounted the plight of the depressed classes in all spheres, economic, social, educational and political and pointed out the immense sacrifices made by them to secure the barest human rights as member of the same community under the aegis of Hinduism. He said that it gave him a very painful realization that time and money spent on and efforts made to achieve those objectives had proved utterly fruitless.[57]

He then exhorted them to severe their connection with Hinduism and seek solace and self respect in another religion, but warned them to be very careful in choosing the new faith and to see that equality of treatment, status and opportunities was guaranteed to them unreservedly.[58]

Referring to his own personal decision in the matter, Ambedkar said:

> 'Unfortunately for him he was born a Hindu untouchable. It was beyond his power to prevent that, but he declared that it was within his power to refuse to live under ignoble and humiliating conditions. I solemnly assure you that I will not die a Hindu'.[59]

Independent Labour Party and the Congress

As noted earlier, Ambedkar played a significant role in politicization of castes. In 1936,[60] Ambedkar established a new party called 'Independent Labour Party' (ILP) which was confined to Bombay only. ILP included almost all minor and major untouchable castes of Bombay – the Mahar, Mang, Chamar and others.

A new Act popularly known as 1935 India Act came into existence in the same year (1935). Soon after, elections held in 1937[61] showed that ILP had distributed 17 tickets amongst Mahar, Mang, Chamar and other castes. ILP won 12 seats out of 17 seats, demonstrating the strength of the party in Bombay.

In 1937, there was a keen contest between Congress and ILP, during which Congress shouted the slogans like[62] 'असेम्बलियों में कौन जायेगा, भंगी, तेली और चमार'. However, the ILP fought the elections in Bombay. Ambedkar was the main target of the Congress and they backed Balu, who was from Chamar caste and also a known cricketer in 1937. But despite the support from the Congress, Balu could not resist the tide of Ambedkar Movement and Scheduled Castes and others supported Ambedkar. As a result, Ambedkar was elected to Bombay Legislative Assembly.

Imperative of Education

A milestone of the 20th century, which attracted attention of Ambedkar and in which Ambedkar played an important role was opening of educational institutions. In 1945, Ambedkar formed 'People's Education Society'[63] (PES) in Bombay for neglected section of society and the downtrodden. The PES not only provided educational facilities and employment opportunities but also encouraged the poor, the downtrodden in general and the scheduled castes in particular for higher education. In collaboration with PES, Ambedkar opened 'Siddharth College of Arts and Science'.[64] Thus, the untouchables, the scheduled castes, the poor and others achieved success in getting higher education. But a significant consequence of opening of a college was the widespread social opportunity with regard to higher education which was denied to them earlier and which came as a result of the efforts made by Ambedkar. In 1950, another college namely 'Milind College' was established. On 1 September 1951, Dr Rajendra Prasad[65] the first President of the Republic of India, laid the foundation of Milind College at Aurangabad (Maharashtra). Ambedkar[66] said in his speech, 'I know the importance of education as I belong to the lowest of the Low ...'

On 14 October 1956, a remarkable phenomenon was initiated by Dr Ambedkar's public adoption of Buddhism at a *diksha* (conversion) ceremony held at Nagpur. According to Adele Fiske,[67] an estimated 3.5 million of India's former untouchables embraced Buddhism. Ambedkar's speech on this occasion discussed that they are very poor and their position in Hinduism is miserable as they are untouchables and they could not enter in a temple and had suffered social ostracism. The speech also pointed out:[68]

> हिन्दू धर्म ने अछूतों के सम्मान से जीना और प्रगति की इच्छा छीन ली है। आज जब ब्राह्मण औरत बच्चे को जन्म देती है तो उसका मुंह हाई कोर्ट की ओर होता है, वह सोचती है कि मेरा बेटा बड़ा होकर हाईकोर्ट का जज बनेगा। परन्तु जब हमारी औरतें बच्चों को जन्म देती है तो वह सोचती है कि नगरपालिका में सफाई कर्मचारी की नौकरी खाली होगी तो मेरा बेटा वहां लगेगा।

Therefore, Ambedkar emphasized that most of the Dalits, particularly Scavengers, are narrow-minded and were indifferent to others, coupled with an appeal for Scavengers to educate their children and facilities for higher education.

If Scavengers become educated they would end untouchability and achieve a recognized status in the community. In fact, Ambedkar argued that the man is the maker of his own destiny. Many educated Dalits have achieved a higher status equal to that of upper caste persons through education.

Dalits and their Participation in Foreign Universities for Higher Studies

Ambedkar as a Labour Minister introduced several positive programmes for reforms. All Dalit castes/communities were economically poor and rarely had any opportunity for higher education. Ambedkar, therefore, pleaded and introduced foreign scholarship and sent them (untouchables) abroad for further studies. Such decisions were publicized and praised and this was enthusiastically followed by untouchables from all over India.

Some of the untouchable students[69] may be listed for sake of illustration, Yashwant Roy, Kolta, NG Uke, Nafere, Koyla and many other students were sent to universities of UK and USA for further studies. In all, 16 Dalit students were sent abroad for higher studies.

Having mentioned the name of students with respect to higher studies abroad, I shall now discuss some of the well known personalities for sake of illustrations.

Yashwant Roy,[70] born in Bhangi caste, was from Punjab State. He was sent to a university of UK and subsequently he was popularly known as 'Professor Yashwant Roy'. Later, he was nominated as member in Punjab State Assembly. He was one of the ministers in Punjab cabinet. Besides Yashwant Roy, there was Kolta[71] who was too sent abroad and became Director of Education of Haryana Government. After his retirement, he established a college in Chandigarh called 'Ambedkar College' which was closed within a few years. Kolta was born in Punjab in a family of Chamars.

Besides intellectual elite, Ambedkar wanted a number of Dalit (Bhangi) doctors, engineers, jurists, military officers, etc. One of the well known jurists was George[72] Corniliyus (hence forth called George). George was born in Kashmir in the family of the Bhangi. His father and grandfather had been doing the traditional work in Kashmir, but later embraced Christianity. Subsequently, George got good English education. He appeared in ICS exams and became ICS officer. After Partition in 1947, he left India and went to Pakistan. Besides his professional achievement, George was a keen student of Law. With such rich experience and background, George became Judge of Pakistan High Court. This was a great event in his career. These achievements had made the Bhangi people aware of the importance of education in society. Ambedkar encouraged the education for Bhangis particularly. This was the main cause of socio-cultural and political mobilization.

Sending of Dalit students in the foreign universities for higher studies was responsible for emergence of intellectual elite. A successful scheme tends to have an impact on other poor section of Dalits. Judging by this standard, studies of Dalits extended its direct influence on Dalits. On their return, they realized to help other poor and helpless persons. Dalits claimed its intellectual heritage from Ambedkar's slogan 'शिक्षित बनो, संगठित हो और संघर्ष करो'. However, it arose mainly as to compete with higher caste Hindus in securing modern education and economic opportunities and political power.

Ambedkar also played an important part in introducing various kinds of training in his Ministry in 1942. Labour Ministry includes publicity and recruitment and technical and apprenticeship training. Soon the department started technical and apprenticeship training, etc.

It should be noted that there were two outstanding officers. Brigadier AWH Ree and Khan Bahadur Mushtaq Ahmed Gurmani. Brigadier AWH Ree was Director of the Technical Training Wing for a long time. Another notable officer was Khan Bahadur Mushtaq Ahmed Gurmani who was also incharge of publicity and recruitment in the Ministry of Labour. These officers were empowered to fill in vacancies in the ministry and also select the candidates for training, as Bhagwan Das has mentioned in his book 'बाबा साहेब भीमराव अम्बेडकर और भंगी जातियां'.[73] 'more educated Bhangis were recruited in Simla office as Assistant. While there was only one Mahar Assistant, namely Desh Bhrata, there was only one Deputy Secretary namely P.K. Pushpa Raj, a Tamil untouchable and that too from Periyar community. It is obvious that recruitment of Bhangis as Assistant closely related to educational mobility. Similarly, during 1942–1945, the Labour

Ministry in its Shimla office recruited the peon, guard, watchman and pharas from Chamar, Koli and other untouchables in good numbers.[74]

This initiative during its early years helped the Dalits in general and Bhangis in particular. The Bhangis were not particularly interested in the economic and education programmes of Ambedkar, but were attracted by occupational reformation programme of Ambedkar. This was significant, as an indicator of upward social mobility of Bhangi caste, for it means increasing access to the non-traditional occupation.

Achyutananda Movement

A notable leader, who was associated with the activities of social reform amongst the untouchables during 1917 in UP was Achyutananda of Manpuri. Achyutananda, born in 1879[75] in village Umri, district Mainpuri, was from childhood directly affected by the inequalities and status of untouchability. His father, Moti Ram was a man with progressive ideas. Achyutananda passed his middle school and while he was wandering, he met Swami Sachidanand who was then a well known Arya Samajist. Achyutananda was highly impressed by him and became Arya Samajist. Later, he became a school teacher. He was not satisfied in Arya Samaj and soon left it.[76] In 1917[77] he took the lead in organizing a Vishal sammelan of untouchables in Delhi against social discrimination, untouchability and deprivation. Chaudhary Jankidas, Devidas, Jagatram and others cooperated with Achyutananda in organizing 'Achchut Sammelan' in Delhi.

Thus, Achyutananda assumed the leadership to fight injustice being done to untouchables. This was the first set of events which sparked off a mass movement.

In this connection it should be noted that while Achyutananda was holding 'Achchut Sammelan' in Delhi, he met Dr Ambedkar[78] who was then the most popular Scheduled Castes leader. As an ardent admirer of Ambedkar, Achyutananda not only co-operated with Ambedkar in launching agitation for untouchables, but also had already started working for the upliftment of untouchables of UP. He also took a lead in an agitation against abolition of all kinds of disabilities and presided over many meetings. The socio-political agenda of Achyutananda was closely related to Ambedkar movement.

In 1919,[79] he submitted a memorandum to the Government demanding admission of untouchables in schools, job reservation in public services and abolition of all kinds of disabilities. This has to be seen in context of the Montagu-Chelmford Reforms of 1919.

This was the zeal with which Achyutananda spearheaded the agitation, mobilizing public opinion among the Dalits. He was mainly responsible for the publication of the first newspaper, the *Achchut*.[80] Later, it was renamed to *Adi Hindu*. He had literary interests and wrote several books on various themes.

Congress Instigates the Bhangis and their Resentment against Ambedkar

Once, when Ambedkar was touring all over UP and reached Kanpur railway station, a large gathering of Bhangi agitators assembled. The agitators were shouting slogans against Ambedkar. The agitated leaders wanted to know:

i. What Ambedkar had done for the Safai Karamcharis and expressed their anguish for doing nothing for them.
ii. They too were saying what Ambedkar did for his own Mahar caste fellows.
iii. They also expressed their appreciation for the Congress for doing something for them and the demonstration was continued.

Ambedkar soon realized that it was a strategy of some opposition parties. He immediately sent a message and invited their leaders for a talk. A few leaders came and held conversation with Ambedkar for the Bhangi's related issues. The agitators behaved with dignity and peace conditions prevailed.

Ambedkar wanted to show the truth to the agitators. Eventually, Ambedkar asked the leaders of agitation to go to his train cabin's office and note the names and castes of persons working there. They went to cabin to note their names and castes. They then went back and presented the list to Ambedkar. It was clear from the list that 18 persons were Bhangis, one each was Christian and Scheduled Caste.

Thus, Ambedkar demonstrated that 18 out of 20 persons working in his Secretariat were Bhangis. This probe was in response to one of the queries. Ambedkar himself was concerned about the Bhangis' pitiable conditions. He was the first Dalit leader to have shown an administrative ability to do something for the betterment of this neglected section of the society. As stated earlier, the most notable work was the formation of separate commission for safai karamcharis, to document the difficulties of Safai karamcharis, their working conditions and social status.

When the agitators, who were demonstrating against Ambedkar, came to know the truth, felt themselves ashamed. They bowed in the feet of Ambedkar and tendered apology. They too regretted for this shameful act. They revealed the truth thus. The demonstration was planned and instigated by Congressmen, leaders and their sympathizers. The Bhangi community was in dark. They were misguided and shocked by the strategy of the Congress.

In 2011, Agnelal and Rahul Raj, former Professor and Assistant Professor respectively, in the Department of Ancient Indian History and Archaeology, Lucknow University, Lucknow and Banaras Hindu University, Banaras, respectively narrated a significant incident in their book, 'उत्तर प्रदेश में दलित आन्दोलन':[81]

> 'कानपुर के दलित सम्मान संघर्ष की एक दूसरी झलक दूसरे रूप में दिखाई देती है। एक बार जब बाबा साहेब डॉ. अम्बेडकर अपने सैलून से कानपुर होकर यात्रा कर रहे थे, उस समय किसी राजनैतिक पार्टी के लोगों के उकसाने पर सफाई कर्मचारी समाज के लोगों ने विरोध प्रदर्शित किया। उन्होंने कहा कि बाबा साहब ने अपनी बिरादरी के लिये क्या किया है, हम सफाई मजदूरों के लिये कोई कार्य नहीं किया। हमारे लिये तो कांग्रेस ही कार्य कर रही है। इस तरह से जो कुछ उन्हें बताया गया था, वह सब कुछ कहकर उन्होंने विरोध प्रदर्शित किया।
>
> बाबा साहब भली-भांति यह समझ गये कि यह हवा कहीं से सफाई कर्मचारी, समाज में भरी गयी है। अस्तु उन्होंने पूरे विरोध प्रदर्शन के बाद में प्रदर्शनकारियों के प्रमुख दो-तीन लोगों को आमंत्रित किया और उनसे वार्ता की। अन्त में उन्होंने कहा कि 'जाओ और सैलून के कार्यालय भाग में जो लोग कार्य कर रहे हैं, उन सभी के नाम और जाति लिखकर लाओ' वे लोग गये और कार्यालय में कर्मचारियों

की पूरी सूची बनाकर ले आए। उसमें अधिकांश सफाई कर्मचारी ही थे। शायद एक अन्य अनुसूचित जाति या और दूसरा क्रिश्चियन था। कर्मचारियों की संख्या 20 से कम न थी। वे लोग यह देखकर बहुत शर्मिंदा हुए और बाबा साहेब के चरणों पर सिर रखकर कहा कि हमें कांग्रेस नेताओं ने ऐसा करने को कहा, बाबा साहब हम लोग अंधकार में थे आपने यह अंधकार दूर कर दिया।'

Emergence of Bhangi Propagator of Buddhism

When Ambedkar adopted Buddhism in Nagpur on 14 October 1956, the national scenario was changing fast. There was competition among the untouchables to spread Buddhism in different communities. Buddhism was gradually rising in many regions: Punjab, Delhi, Rajasthan and others.

During this time, in Punjab the person whose work did much to carry Ambedkar's Mission forward was L.R. Balley.[82] As stated earlier, he published many of Babasaheb's books in Urdu, English, Hindi and Punjabi. His contribution to the spread of *dhamma* remain unmatched in Punjab. Because of his influence, many Indians living in England, such as Rattan Lal Sampala, Bhagat Ram Sampala and Chanan Chahal also became propagators of Buddhism.

Similarly, many people were responsible for the propagation of Buddhism. One such was Vijay Desavar. Vijay Desavar was born in Balmiki caste[83] (sweeper) in Punjab. He 'took inspiration from Ambedkar's Buddhism' and became staunch propagator of Buddhism. He made extensive tours, propagating Ambedkar's new message, visiting several places in Punjab and meeting Dalits. He firmly believed that acceptance of Buddhism was the only basis of religious conversion, without which inequalities and sufferings could not be fought. Thus, he laid supreme emphasis on spiritual strength with a view to gaining self-respect and self-esteem.

Vijay Desavar worked hard to strengthening and spreading of Buddhism that Ambedkar had brought about in 1956. Contemptuous curiosity, prompted him to organize a Vishal congregation in Ludhiana, Punjab, which was attended by thousands of Dalits.[84] All Ambedkar propagators made a spirited speech urging the Dalits to abandon Hinduism as it was impossible to overcome all kinds of deprivation and humiliation by the upper castes. Vijay Desavar also spoke on this occasion and had advocated Buddhism as a means of emancipating the Dalits. There was a strong wave on the part of untouchables favouring conversion to Buddhism.

The general ferment reached its peak in Ludhiana. Dalits liked Ambedkar's approach with regard to solving the problems of untouchables. As a result of all this, a large number of Dalits embarrassed Buddhism.[85] This changed the whole attitude of Dalits towards Hinduism in general and Buddhism in particular. Conversion to Buddhism was considered as a great victory by the Dalits.

Rajasthan: Mobility and Religion

In the past and in the present, many untouchables have attempted to escape the stigma through conversion to other religions which espouse equality e.g. Islam, Christianity, Sikhism and most recently Buddhism.

The most recent effort has been the movement led by Dr Ambedkar for conversion to Buddhism. Despairing of ever achieving equality within the Hindu fold, he led a crowd estimated at 3,00,000 to 6,00,000 people in a mass conversion ceremony in October 1956 – shortly before his death.[86]

In the process of mobilization, the next step of the Bhangis was a further move in the direction of separation from caste Hindu. The vast majority of the Bhangi community continued to live as before in Jodhpur. Their lot, however changed, for it was here that 'Ambedkar study Kendras made their efforts and got success. The first Bhangi conversion was made in 1973. Through an initiation ceremony, Bhanwarlal Pandit,[87] a matriculate Bhangi from Bhagar Basti, was the first to be converted to Buddhism. He took the 'dhiksa' in an All India Buddhist Maha Sammelan held in Ramlila ground New Delhi in 1973. The Sammelan was presided over by Dalai Lama. Soon after this, three more persons, Himmat Ram Jodha (Meghwal by caste), Om Prakash Jawa and Chenprasad Pandit (Both Bhangis) took the 'dhiksa' in Rajasthan Buddhist Sammelan held at Ajmer in 1973.[88]

As early as 1948 and again in 1974, conversion to Christianity was initiated. The initiative was taken by Narsingh Dev Gujarati – a dynamic and powerful person who was the architect of Dr Ambedkar Kendra, on 8 September 1974[89] embraced Christianity at Jodhpur. Suffering severe social and economic disabilities as a defiled caste, the Bhangis sought escape from the hierarchy of ritual purity in Buddhism and Christianity. They saw Buddhism and Christianity as protectors and in them, they saw the possibility for socio-economic changes and advancement. Many sought to abandon the arduous occupation which had degraded them in the eyes of those of high castes. In Jodhpur, if their social position has not greatly improved, Christianity and Buddhism have given the Bhangis hope of a release from their suffering under the dominance of upper Hindu castes. M. Glen and Sipra Bose Johnson comment:

> 'This sense of self esteem may indeed be an extremely important resource for people attempting to better their lot in society'.[90]

It is important to note here that in recent years particularly after Independence, individual mobility has become possible for the Bhangis, but there are no signs of group mobility. In case of Bhangis the reasons for this can be well explained in the words of M. Glen and Sipra B. Johnson.

They pointed out:

> 'Conversion seems to have occurred in castes, which have already achieved, in comparison to other untouchable castes in India, a degree of mobility and some access to the resources of wealth, education and privilege.[91]

Ban on Migration of the Bhangis From Pakistan to India, 1947 and Ambedkar

While Ambedkar was in the process of organizing Bhangis across the country to fight for their rights, he also took lead in raising certain questions to national leaders pertaining to the Bhangis in public meetings and conferences. For instance, after the Partition of the country in the year 1947, Ambedkar went to

Bunta Mandi, Jalandhar, to address a huge public meeting. On 27 October 1951,[92] while addressing the gathering, Ambedkar was grieved by the non-cooperative and negative attitude of national leaders towards the Bhangi issues and this led to increasing frustration among the Bhangis. Ambedkar said that Pakistan government by issuing orders had banned the migration of Bhangis to India. The direct effect of this order on the Bhangis was that they could not leave Pakistan. Ambedkar urged Pandit Jawaharlal Nehru to talk with the Pakistan government. It is the paramount duty of the government to interfere with Bhangis' issue. Are Bhangis not Hindus? Very few people know that Ambedkar was the first Dalit leader who raised these questions publically. At the official level, India did not raise these uncomfortable issues. But Ambedkar's raising issue was intended to send that message to Pakistan. From an account of the events in Ambedkar's life given by one of his biographers, Dr Rajendra Mohan Bhatnagar[93] narrated the issue as follows:

> '27 अक्टूबर 1951 को डॉ. अम्बेडकर ने बूटामंडी, जालंधर में लाखों लोगों को संबोधित करते हुए, सधे हुए शब्दों में कहा था कि यदि वे चाहते तो हाईकोर्ट के न्यायाधीश बन सकते थे और सुखमय जीवन व्यतीत कर सकते थे, परन्तु उन्होंने लोकसेवा के कठोर पथ का चुनाव किया। पं. नेहरू बराबर एक ही बात दोहराते रहते हैं कि उनकी पार्टी कांग्रेस ने अछूतों के लिए बहुत काम किया। उनका यह कहना गलत है। इसके लिए एक उदाहरण पर्याप्त है। पाकिस्तान सरकार ने आदेश जारी करके अछूतों पर पाकिस्तान छोड़ने के लिए अंकुश लगा दिया था। अछूत पाकिस्तान नहीं छोड़ सकते थे। क्या अछूत हिन्दू नहीं है? अछूत चले गए तो सफाई का काम कौन करेगा। उन्होंने पं. नेहरू से इस संबंध में प्रार्थना की थी और कहा था कि वे पाकिस्तान से बात करें। कई बार पाकिस्तान से भारत ने बातचीत भी की थी परन्तु उन्होंने यह मुद्दा उसके साथ नहीं उठाया। पाकिस्तान अछूतों पर अमानुषिक अत्याचार कर रहा है। पर कांग्रेस चुप है, सरकार मौन है। यह कैसा सितम है? फिर भी वे क्या निराश है? क्या वे मंत्री पद पाकर शांत हो जाएं, यह उनका कर्तव्य होगा? इसलिए उनका कहना था कि पिछडे वर्ग के लिए राज्य शक्ति पाना बहुत आवश्यक है। बिना राज्य शक्ति पाए उनके वर्ग का उनयन असंभव है।'

The Pakistani Bhangis have been living in the present Islamic republic region in a miserable condition even today. Dev Kishan Gund,[94] 65, a resident of Hanumanji-ki-Bhakri, Jodhpur, and retired Chief Sanitary Inspector, Jodhpur Nagar Nigam, who had been to Pakistan several times, while talking about Pakistani Bhangis in May 2013, said that Pakistan had failed to provide justice and security to Bhangis. In fact, Ambedkar[95] was offered the judgeship of Bombay High Court, but he declined and preferred to continue in public life to serve his people for their upliftment.

Similarly, the issue of Pakistan's Bhangis did come up before Gandhi, which was so oppressive to them. Gandhi in his speech said:[96]

> 'मैंने कल एक बयान में देखा था कि मण्डल साहब और पाकिस्तान कैबिनेट के कुछ दूसरे मैम्बरों ने यह तय किया है कि हरिजनों से ऐसे बिल्ले लगाने की आशा रखी जायेगी, जो उनके अछूत होने की निशानी हो। उन बिल्लों में चांद और तारे की छाप होगी। यह फैसला हरिजनों का दूसरे हिन्दुओं से फर्क दिखाने के इरादे से किया गया है। मेरी राय में इसका लाजमी नतीजा यह होगा कि जो हरिजन पाकिस्तान में रहेंगे, उन्हें आखिर में मुसलमान बनना पड़ेगा। दिली विश्वास और आत्मा की प्रेरणा में लोग धर्म बदलें, तो उसके खिलाफ मुझे कुछ नहीं कहना है। अपनी इच्छा से हरिजन बन जाने के

कारण मैं हरिजनों के मन को जानता हूं। आज तक भी हरिजन ऐसा नहीं है, जो इस्लाम में शामिल किया जा सके, इस्लाम के बारे में वे क्या जानते हैं? न वे यही समझते हैं कि वे हिन्दू क्यों हैं। हर धर्म को मानने वालों पर यही बात लागू होती है। आज वे जो कुछ भी हैं वह इसीलिये है कि वे किसी खास धर्म में पैदा हुए हैं। अगर वे अपना धर्म बदलेंगे, तो सिर्फ मजबूर होकर या किसी लालच के शिकार बनकर, जो उन्हें धर्म बदलने के लिए दिखाया जायेगा। आज के वातावरण में लोग खुश होकर धर्म बदलें, तो भी उसे सच्चा या कानूनी नहीं मानना चाहिए। धर्म को जीवन में भी ज्यादा प्यारा और ज्यादा कीमती समझना चाहिए, जो इस सच्चाई पर अमल करते हैं वे उस आदमी की बनिस्पत ज्यादा अच्छे हिन्दू हैं जो हिन्दू धर्म शास्त्रों का जानकार तो हैं, लेकिन जिसका धर्म संकट के समय टिका नहीं रहता।'

While consisting of some good points in Gandhi's speech at Prathna Sabha on Pakistan's Bhangis, it was truly disappointing. The Bhangis had hoped that Gandhi would take up the issue of Pakistan's Bhangis and would ensure safety of them, for Pakistan's Bhangis, who wanted to migrate to India were not allowed. On migration of Pakistan's Bhangis, we do not see Gandhi's full political weight, who spoke not of untouchables but in terms of actual problems faced by marginalized Bhangis.

Notes

1. Dhananjay Keer, *Dr Ambedkar: Life and Mission*, Bombay, Popular Prakashan, Reprinted 1995, p. 347.
2. Bhagwan Das, In Pursuit of Ambedkar: A Memoir, New Delhi, Navayana, year not mentioned, p. 27.
3. Ibid., p. 27.
4. Ibid., p. 27–28
5. Ibid., p. 28. Also see Bhagwan Das 'बाबा के चरणों में', नई दिल्ली, दलित प्रेस, 2004, पृ. 17.
6. डी.डी. कल्याणी, बाबा साहेब डॉ. अम्बेडकर की वाल्मिकी जातियां अर्थात सफाई काम करने वाली जातियों के प्रति देन, नई दिल्ली, मूल निवासी पब्लिकेशन ट्रस्ट, 2002, पृ. 16.
7. देवी दयाल, डॉ. बाबा साहेब भीमराव अम्बेडकर की दिनचर्या, लखनऊ, उत्तर प्रदेश दलित टुडे प्रकाशन, 1989, पृ. 24.
8. वही, पृ. 24.
9. वही, पृ. 25.
10. वही, पृ. 3.
11. Bhagwan Das, In Pursuit of Ambedkar. A Memoir, New Delhi, Navayana, year not mentioned, p. 28.
12. राजेन्द्र मोहन भटनागर, 57 अम्बेडकर: चिंतन और विचार, दिल्ली, जगतराम एंड संस, 2006, पृ. 210.
13. भगवान दास, बाबा साहेब भीमराव अम्बेडकर : एक परिचय, एक संदेश, वही, 1998, पृ. 55-56.
14. वही पृ. 56-
15. वही पृ. 56.
16. राजेन्द्र मोहन भटनागर, 57 अम्बेडकर: चिंतन और विचार, दिल्ली, जगतराम एंड संस, 2006, पृ. 210.

17. भगवान दास, बाबा साहेब भीमराव अम्बेडकर और भंगी जातियां, लखनऊ, उत्तर प्रदेश, दलित टुडे प्रकाशन, 1996, पृ. 34–35.
18. Bhagwan Das, In Pursuit of Ambedakar: A Memoir, New Delhi Navayana, p. 29.
19. Ibid., p. 20.
20. भगवानदास, वही 1996, पृ. 37.
21. वही, 1996, पृ. 38.
22. वही, 1996, पृ. 36.
23. वही, पृ. 36.
24. वही, पृ. 36.
25. वही, 1996, पृ. 36.
26. डी.डी. कल्याणी, वही, 2002, पृ. 16.
27. भगवानदास, 1996, वही, पृ. 36–37.
28. भगवानदास, 1996, वही, पृ. 36–37.
29. Bhagwan Das, In Pursuit of Ambedakr, A Memoir, ibid., p. 23.
30. Ibid., p. 29.
31. Ibid., p. 29.
32. Ibid., p. 29–30.
33. Ibid., p. 30.
34. Dhananjay Keer, Dr Ambedkar : Life and Mission, Bombay, Popular Prakashan, 1995, p. 297. यह भी देखें गजानन सुर्वे (अनुवाद), डॉ. बाबा साहब अम्बेडकर: जीवन चरित, पॉपूलर प्रकाशन, 2006, पृ. 284–285.
35. Ibid., p. 298
36. Ibid., p. 298.
37. डी.डी. कल्याणी, वही, 2002, पृ. 10.
38. वही, पृ. 10.
39. वही, पृ. 10.
40. The most important sources for early movement and the situation of the Bhangis in Delhi and other regions is भगवान दास, सफाई कर्मचारी दिवस, 31 जुलाई, नई दिल्ली बीसी-1/एचडीडीए फ्लैट, मुनीरका, प्रकाशन, वर्ष अंकित नहीं है।
41. वही पृ. 12.
42. भगवान दास, बाबा साहेब भीमराव अम्बेडकर : एक परिचय - एक संदेश, लखनऊ, दलित टुडे प्रकाशन, 1996, पेज 56.
43. Chandan Mal Naval, 2010, 'Garibo-ke Masiha Dr Bhimrao Ambedkar' Jodhpur, Minerva Publications, Bhagwati Colony, p. 105–106.
44. B.R. Sampla was quoted by Chandan Mal Naval, in his recently published book 'Garibo-ke Masiha Dr Bhimrao Ambedkar' Jodhpur, Minerva Publications, Bhagwati Colony, 2010, p. 104–105.
45. Ibid, p. 104–105, यह भी देखें, राजेन्द्र मोहन भटनागर, डॉ. अम्बेडकर : चिन्तन और विचार, दिल्ली, जगतराम एंड संस 2006, पृ. 115.
46. डी.डी. कल्याणी, वही, पृ. 17–18.
47. डी.डी. कल्याणी, वही, पृ. 18, यह भी देखे - भगवानदास, वही, 1996, पृ. 41.
48. भगवानदास, 1996, पृ. 41.

49. भगवानदास, वही, 1996, पृ. 41.
50. Chandan Mal Naval, 2010. ibid., p. 105–106. Also see Rajendra Mohan Bhatnagar, 2006, op. cit., p. 115.
51. विस्तृत जानकारी के लिए देखें, भगवान दास, सफाई कर्मचारी दिवस : 31 जुलाई ibid., p. 28.
52. वही पृ. 28.
53. Chandan Mal Naval, 2010, ibid., p. 106.
54. भगवान दास, सफाई कर्मचारी दिवस : 31 जुलाई, वही पृ. 17. For more details also see, Col. 6171, 30–7–1957, Lok Sabha Proceedings, 1957.
55. Dhananjay Keer, 1995, p. 252.
56. Ibid., p. 252.
57. Ibid., p. 252.
58. Ibid., p. 253.
59. Ibid., p. 253.
60. भगवानदास, वही, 1996, पृ. 41.
61. वही, पृ. 34.
62. वही, पृ. 34.
63. पूरणमल, अम्बेडकर और दलितोद्धार आन्दोलन, जयपुर, आविष्कार पब्लिशर्स, डिस्ट्रीब्यूटर्स, 2009, पृ. 190.
64. वही, पृ. 190–91.
65. वही, पृ. 191.
66. वही, पृ. 191.
67. Adele Fiske, Scheduled Caste, Buddhist Organisations 'In the Untouchables in Contemporary India, J., Michael, K. Mahar (ed.), Jaipur, Rawat Publications, Indian edition published, 1998, p. 113.
68. भगवानदास, सफाई कर्मचारी दिवस 31 जुलाई, वही, पुस्तक का अंतिम पृष्ठ देखें, यह भी देखें 'बाबा साहेब अम्बेडकर और सफाई कर्मचारियों की समस्याएं' इन बाबा साहेब भीमराव अम्बेडकर, एक परिचय : एक संदेश , लखनऊ, दलित टुडे प्रकाशन, 1998, पृ. 55.
69. भगवानदास, 1996, वही, पृ. 16–17. यह भी देखें, धनई राम (सम्पादक) बाबा साहब डॉ. अम्बेडकर की चुनी हुई कृतियां, वाराणसी, डॉ. अम्बेडकर साहित्य एवं कला केन्द्र, 2011, पृ. 16–17.
70. भगवानदास, 1996, वही, पृ. 16–17.
71. वही, 1996, पृ. 40.
72. वही, 1996, पृ. 38.
73. वही, 1996, पृ. 44.
74. वही, 1996, पृ. 44.
75. अगने लाल और राहुल राज, 'उत्तर प्रदेश में दलित आंदोलन' दिल्ली, गौतम बुक सेंटर, 2011, पृ. 22.
76. वही, पृ. 22–23.
77. वही, पृ. 23.
78. वही, पृ. 24.
79. वही, पृ. 23–24.

80. वही, पृ. 25.
81. वही, पृ. 203.
82. भगवानदास, बाबा के चरणों में, नई दिल्ली, दलित प्रेस, 2004, पृ. 73–74.
83. वही, पृ. 74.
84. वही, पृ. 74.
85. वही, पृ. 74.
86. Shyam lal, Caste and Political Mobilization: The Bhangis, Jaipur, Panchsheel Prakashan, 1981, p. 118.
87. Ibid., p. 118.
88. Ibid., p. 118.
89. Ibid., p. 118.
90. Ibid., p. 119.
91. Ibid., p. 119.
92. Chandan Mal Naval, ibid., 2010, p. 95.
93. वही, 2010, पृ. 95. For more miserable conditions, also see, 'Asylum-seeker left behind in fant in Pak'. In the Times of India, Jaipur, Monday, 8 April 2013, 'Pak Hindus must be honoured' in The Times of India, Jaipur, Monday, 17 June 2013, 'Pak Hindus in Paldi Meena don't want to return' in The Times of India, Jaipur, Saturday, 22 June 2013.
94. Talk with Dev Kishan Gund, 65, Hanumanji Ki Bhakri, Jodhpur, 15–18 May 2013.
95. Sheshrao Chavan, Gandhi and Ambedkar: Saviour of the untouchables, Mumbai, Bharatiya Vidya Bhavan, 2001. p. 23.
96. बृजकृष्ण चांदीवाला, पाक के हरिजन, गांधी की चेतावनी, इन गांधीजी की दिल्ली डायरी, खण्ड-3, पृ. 344.

6

Bhagwan Das: Ambedkarite Scholar and Dalit Rights Activist

In post-Independence India, we have hardly any record of the several men and women, who played key roles in Dalit movements across the country, especially those who donned the roles of the 'intellectuals and chroniclers of the movement'. *Bheem Patrika*, the monthly journal founded by L.R. Balley, celebrated 50 years of existence in 2008. Balley has produced scores of books on the Dalit movement and Ambedkar.[1] Bhagwan Das, to whom nothing mattered more than his association with Ambedkar,[2] has produced scores of books on Ambedkar movement, but his views on Bhangi caste, etc. rarely find mention in the post-Independence histories of India. They are neither feted nor remembered.[3]

I shall discuss in this chapter Bhagwan Das's first meeting with Ambedkar and that meeting changed the trajectory Bhagwan Das's 'life'.

Bhagwan Das was born on 27 April 1927 in Jutogh cantonment, in Shimla, the modern-day capital of the State of Himachal Pradesh. His father Ram Ditta, whom they called Abba, belonged to a well off family.

In Class VII, Bhagwan Das stood second and was chosen for admission to the Sanatan Dharam School. The topper was taken by the Dayanand Anglo Vedic School, Shimla. He also received his education in Urdu, Mathematics, Hindi, etc. from his father.

A crucial role in his education was played by the European families[4] living in their neighborhood. In the Cantonment area people belonging to scavenging communities were employed for jobs like baby sitting, cooking, etc. For instance, the Andrews from England (Alexander and Edith Andrew) were like a second family to him and it was from them that he learned enough among other things. He used to read the Bible. This helped him a lot. After completing his matriculation in 1942, he opened a night school for unlettered adults in Shimla. After attending typing classes in Shimla, Bhagwan Das spent an hour or two with Baidwan helping him write letters. Rest of the time he spent reading in public library. During this period, Bhagwan Das came to know about Babasaheb Ambedkar.

His father was also fond of writing and reading books. Copies of the urdu monthly magazines '*Mastana Jogi*' and '*Hamdard-e-Sehat*' were available at home. They also used to borrow from their friends various newspapers and magazies such as the '*Madina*' newspaper published from Bijnaur, '*Pratap*', '*Milap*' and '*Zamindar*'. Bhagwan Das used to enjoy reading political articles in the weekly newspaper '*Riyasat*' edited by Sardar Diwan Singh Maftoon.

These newspapers used to publish a lot of things about Gandhi, Jawaharlal Nehru, Abul Kalam Azad, Subhash Chandra Bose and Mohammad Ali Jinnah, but hardly a thing about untouchable communities. These leaders belonged to the upper castes but, being an untouchable, Bhagwan Das used to wonder, who is our leader. He asked his Abba about this, and Abba replied, 'Ummedkar', the one who brings hope, which is how Abba saw Babasaheb Ambedkar.

Bhagwan Das and Ambedkar, 1943

Bhagwan Das passed his matriculation examination in 1942 and was in acute need of some government job. While he was wandering here and there, somebody advised him to meet Ambedkar Saheb, who was then the Labour Minister, Government of India. Babasaheb first came to Shimla as Labour Minister in 1943. He went to meet Ambedkar at his bungalow at Shimla and waited there nearly for 6–7 hours. At last he succeeded in meeting Ambedkar Saheb.[5] Hon'ble Minister asked him the purpose of his visit. In response to Hon' ble Minister's question, he very humbly urged for a job. The conversation took place in English and lasted for a few minutes. Hon' ble Minister was so much impressed by his answers that he assured him help. Thus, for the first time Bhagwan Das met Dr. Ambedkar at Shimla. Ambedkar's slogan 'Educate organize, Agitate' had clearly inspired Bhagwan Das. It was meeting with Ambedkar that defined the tragetory of Bhagwan Das's life in his single-minded pursuit of Ambedkar's ideals. Soon after this meeting, formal orders were issued. The credit of his appointment as LDC in the Labour Department, Shimla, goes to Ambedkar. The orthodox Muslims in the office treated Bhagwan Das as low caste untouchable Bhangi and, therefore, they (Muslim employees) harassed, tortured and humiliated him. Bhagwan Das in his personal conversation with the author said that amidst strenuous tension, he left the job.

Soon after this Bhagwan Das joined the military. The recruiting officer was from Kangra and belonged to a Rajput caste.[6] He told Bhagwan Das that if he had been Sikh, Muslim or Christian, he would have had no problem enrolling him, but now he would have to first talk with his Chief in Ambala. The recruiting officer asked Bhagwan Das to come back after two days and checked all his documents. After his medical examination and other formalities Bhagwan Das was given railway pass and some cash to go to recruiting office in Jalandhar. The recruiting officer asked him a few questions on English and Mathematics and very sympathetically advised him to join the Air Force instead of the Navy. Bhagwan Das followed his advice and attended a training camp at the Jalahalli

Air Force station in Bangalore. After he finished training in Jalahalli, he was sent for radar training to the Adgodi Royal Force (RAF) training centre near Belgaum.

Kranti, from Lahore was the only Urdu Magazine that used to report on Babasaheb's speeches and publish them in Urdu translation. Kranti's editor Sant Ram born in a backward caste family was a progressive thinker and writer.

After joining the Air Force in 1944, Bhagwan Das started his writings, such as short stories and essays to highlight the pitiable conditions of the untouchables. His first essay, entitled 'Achut Aur Aajaadi',[7] was published in a paper called *Kranti* in 1944 which was then edited by Sant Ram and published from Lahore (now in Pakistan). This article attracted a lot of attention and through it he developed a friendship with Sant Ram. A series of stories and essays centreing around various untouchable issues were published in leading newspapers and magazines such as *Milap* and *Naya Jamana*, both published from Lahore. Bhagwan Das continued his writing on untouchables' issues and also wrote in a Communist Party's paper published from Bombay. He also translated a few English Books into Urdu language. For instance, Lyndon Johnson's book *My Hope for America* was translated in Urdu which was later published in early 1950 from Delhi.

After spending a few days with his family in Shimla, Bhagwan Das reached Calcutta. Here he started working in the unit of the South East Asia Command of RAF. Wherever he went, he always made an effort to visit untouchable colonies and associate with Babasaheb's group. This way, he met many Ambedkarites in Bangalore, Mysore and Belgaum.[8] From Calcutta, he was posted to Chittagong, Buthidaung and another RAF unit near Akyab. After a few months, he was sent back to Calcutta and then to Bombay.

Bhagwan Das was stationed at Air Force camp in Cotton Green near Sivri in Bombay. There was an Excise officer[9] in that colony who became his friend. He was very surprised to find his intense interest in and knowledge of Babasaheb's life struggle and teachings. Bhagwan Das regularly went to Babasaheb's house in Dadar to meet him and visited his library. It had too little space and too many books. Here Bhagwan Das used to meet Babasaheb.

Meanwhile, he was chosen for the Air Force Commission for which he would have to go to England for training. But mandatory ₹ 5,000 fee deposit[10] was too big an amount for him. So he got relieved from Air Force and returned home.

Bhagwan Das and his Works

Bhagwan Das was highly influenced by Ambedkar's personality, character and, above all, his dedication against discrimination and exploitation of the Dalits which had always been a great source of inspiration for him. He was a staunch follower and supporter of Ambedkar. Since 1943 he had been in touch with Ambedkar. He actively worked for Ambedkar and was engaged in carrying out the constructive work of Ambedkar.

After serving in the Royal Indian Air Force as a radar operator during the Second World War, Bhagwan Das[11] worked with Ambedkar as a research assistant in the last years before Ambedkar passed away in 1956. Six years later, Bhagwan Das began to compile and edit Ambedkar's speeches in the four volumes, *Thus Spoke Ambedkar*.

After four decades of dedicated activism, Bhagwan Das supported by a coalition of Dalit organizations, testified on untouchability in 1983 before the UN Sub-Commission on Human Rights in Geneva, much against the wishes of India's official delegation to the Conference.[12] He played a pivotal role in International Dalit Convention, 1998, held at Kualalumpur, Malaysia, a precursor to the World Conference against Racism, held in Durban, South Africa.

Bhagwan Das himself had attained mastery over Ambedkar ideology and had written[13] more than 50 books on Buddha Dharam, untouchables and untouchable castes and nearly 500 essays and short stories had been published. The most notable work is 'मैं भंगी हूं', 'बाबा साहब अम्बेडकर एक परिचय एक सन्देश', 'दलित राजनीति और संगठन', 'बाबा के चरणों में', 'डॉ. अम्बेडकर के विचार', 'सफाई कर्मचारी दिवस 31 जुलाई', 'डॉ. अम्बेडकर और भंगी जातियां', 'रिपब्लिकन पार्टी ऑफ इंडिया: वर्तमान राजनीति की आवश्यकता', 'वाल्मीकि जयंति और भंगी जाति', 'महर्षि वाल्मीकि'. Similarly in English, '*Thus Spoke Ambedkar*' (Vol. 1–4), '*Ambedkar on Gandhi and Gandhism*', '*In persuit of Ambedkar: A Memoir*', '*Revival of Buddhism in India and Role of Dr. Babasaheb B.R. Ambedkar*', '*Slavery and Untouchability*' (edited).

Besides writing books, Bhagwan Das made extensive tours, propagating Ambedkar's new message, delivered Ambedkar Memorial lectures in Nagpur University, Nagpur and Marathwada University, Aurangabad. He also attended World Council for Religion and Peace Assembly held at Kyoto, Japan (1970), Washington, USA (1979), Asian Conference on Religion and Peace (1981), Nairobi Lenya (1984), Seoul, Korea (1987) and participated in Executive Committee of ACRP Mellboum, Bangkok (1989). He also delivered a lecture on the Problems of the Untouchables and Caste System in Northfield College, Minneapolis, USA.

Bhagwan Das and the Congress

Every sociologist, anthropologist, political scientist and cultural historian, who has ever worked on Dalits/anti-Dalit movement had visited at Bhagwan Das's flat in Munirka, New Delhi, as he[14] had been 'a store house of insight and information generous with his time and knowledge for anybody willing to stop by and ask'. Some of the eminent scholars[15] who met Bhagwan Das and discussed with him several issues were: Eleanor Zelliot, Mark Juergensyer, Owen Lynch, Marc Gallanter, R.K. Kshirsagar and Sukhadeo Thorat down to younger scholars like Vijay Prakash, Nicolas Jaoul and Maren Bellwinke Schempp.

Despite many achievements, Bhagwan Das led a lonely life. He was afraid that very few had shown interest in the kind of work he had done[16]. He was also not satisfied that in spite of pool of educated Dalits with an aptitude for research is meagre, especially of Dalits who have a felicity with the English language, the chronicling of Dalit history has seriously suffered.[17] He was grieved to see that quite a few Congress-influenced caste fellows treated him as anti Congress. This fact is very clear from the statement given when he said:

> As someone born in a sweeper community, as untouchable among untouchables, 'he is not very popular among sections of the Valmiki community that have been Hinduised under influence of Gandhi, the Arya Samaj and other Hindu organisations'.[18]

The attitude of Gandhi Congress towards Bhagwan Das was hard and biased. Before Maharashtra State Government's education department began to publish Ambedkar's writings and speeches in 1971, Bhagwan Das had edited, compiled and produced four volumes between 1963 and 1980. It was the first professional effort to publish Ambedkar's writings in one place. Bhagwan Das had direct access to Ambedkar.

Fifteen years after Ambedkar's death, in 1971, the Maharashtra Congress[19] Government 'decided to edit and publish his writings and speeches. It was because of their close association with Ambedkar that the editorial committee, constituted by the Maharashtra Government to put together Ambedkar writings and speeches, excluded Bhagwan Das and L.R. Balley of *Bheem Patrika* as they were the men who had pioneered the publication of Ambedkar's writings and speeches.[20] As Bhagwan Das in a typical manner, recalls in his memoir:[21]

> '... Maharashtra Government decided to edit and publish his writings and speeches and formed a committee for the same under the Chairmanship of Vasant Moon. Membership to committee was limited to Maharashtra's politicians and intellectuals'.

In another notable instance during 1993-1994, Bhagwan Das was to be nominated to the National Commission for Safai Karamcharis. And this was neglected for the second time, resulting in Congress-Bhagwan Das clashes.

Bhagwan Das along with L.R Balley and Harish Chahande, the proponent of Samta Sainik Dal (SSD) in Punjab, led the SSD movement. They encouraged the Dalits of Rajasthan to initiate SSD activities. The leadership of the movement achieved significant gains by 1988 when Dalits of Rajasthan organized, for the first time, a two-day national conference of SSD at Pali Town Hall on 14 February 1988.[22] The national conference was inaugurated by Bhagwan Das and L.R. Balley presided. The local sainiks also took lead in spreading Ambedkar's ideology.

Long back on reading Bhagwan Das's book 'मैं भंगी हूं', published in Hindi, 1976, the author decided to see and listen to him one day. When the news of the conference was widely publicized, the author decided that it was a golden opportunity for him to see a scholar like Bhagwan Das. So the author reached Pali from Banswara and met him in the hotel. This was his first meeting with Bhagwan Das, with the intention of sharing and exchanging of views on various aspects of Dalits in general and Bhangis in particular. Since then, the author had met Bhagwan Das several times at his flat in Munirka, New Delhi. We also met in seminars and *sammelans*. His flat at New Delhi has been a mandatory stopover for the author as he was working on Dalit/Ambedkar movement/Anti-Caste movement, in general and Bhangi caste in particular. The author was highly impressed by his writings and views. The author paid rich tributes to Bhagwan Das although he differed from him on certain issues.

The Congress was not pleased with Bhagwan Das. When the National Commission for Safai Karamcharis came into existence in 1993, during P.V. Narsimha Rao regime, Congress leaders and Sardar Buta Singh, the then President All India Safai Mazdoor Congress, once again vehemently opposed his nomination as a member in the Commission. Bhagwan Das spoke about this incident to the author at his Delhi residence long back.

It is true that the Bhangis have made very little progress in the field of higher education and employment in public services. The contrast becomes all the more obvious if one considers the progress made by Jatavs of Agra, Chamars of Dehradun, Mahars of Maharashtra and Nadars of Tamil Nadu in all fields. The reason for their progress was following Ambedkar teachings.

Bhagwan Das strengthened and expanded the views of Ambedkar among the Bhangis. His association with Babasaheb Ambedkar was an asset to the Bhangi caste. He struggled to raise the socio-economic and educational level of the community, but he faced opposition from his own men.[23] There were many factors which contributed to such a situation. The Bhangis were/are not particularly interested in the economic, educational and the political programmes of the caste as a whole, but were attracted by the social reformation programme of Gandhi and Gandhi Congress.

Bhagwan Das was active as socio-religious reformer, in 1943. He died on 18 November 2010. During a period of about 67 years the kind of changes he ushered in and the work carried out were remarkable.

Notes

1. Bhagwan Das, *In Pursuit of Ambedkar: A Memoir*, translated from Hindi by Isha, New Delhi, Publication year not mentioned. p. 10.
2. Ibid., p. 10–11.
3. Ibid., p. 10.
4. Ibid. p. 19.
5. Shyam Lal, *Ambedkar and Dalit Movement*, Jaipur, Rawat Publications, 2008, p. 89.
6. Bhagwan Das, *In Pursuit of Ambedkar*, p. 31.
7. Shyam Lal, *Ambedkar and Dalit Movement*, 2008, p. 89–90.
8. Bhagwan Das, *In Pursuit of Ambedkar*, p. 33.
9. Ibid., p. 34.
10. Ibid., p. 35.
11. Ibid., p. Back portion of the book.
12. Ibid. p. Back portion of the book. also see, p. 11 of the same book.
13. For more details, see particularly last page of book 'बाबा के चरणों में', नई दिल्ली, दलित प्रेस, 2004, also see, 'बाबा साहेब भीमराव अम्बेडकर : एक परिचय - एक संदेश', लखनऊ, दलित टुडे प्रकाशन, 1998, 'दलित राजनीति और संगठन', नई दिल्ली, दलित वर्ल्ड लाइब्रेरी, 2002, 'सफाई कर्मचारी दिवस 31 जुलाई', नई दिल्ली, श्रीमती रमादास.
14. Bhagwan Das, *In Pursuit of Ambedkar*, p. 12
15. Ibid., p. 12

16. Ibid., p. 11 .
17. Ibid., p. 11
18. Ibid., p. 12.
19. Ibid., p. 8.
20. Ibid., p. 8.
21. Ibid., p. 8.
22. Shyam Lal, *Ambedkar And Dalit Movement*, 2008, p. 90.
23. Bhagwan Das, *In Pursuit of Ambedkar*, p. 11, For more details, see *Special Issue on Bhagwan Das: Life and Mission*, published by Aapexa, Vol. 8, No., 26, New Delhi, January-March 2009.

7

Interaction between Ambedkar and Bhagwan Das

As stated earlier, Bhagwan Das was employed in Shimla, with the office of the Controller and Auditor General, which kept accounts of Government transactions and expenditure. After some time, this office, like many others, was shifted to Delhi. The Delhi office was located at Kapurthala House on Mansingh Road.

Opposite Kapurthala House was another office building, where there was a library. Bhagwan Das used to go there after work. Here he used to read books and journals that were not available anywhere. Later, the Backward Classes Commission (BCC) office also opened in the same building. Once Bhagwan Das was reading, sitting in the verandah when a BCC member saw the book Bhagwan Das had. It was about Babasaheb Ambedkar. He asked Bhagwan Das why he was reading that book. Bhagwan Das replied, 'He was very interested in knowing more about Untouchables and Babasaheb'. He then took Bhagwan Das to his room and introduced himself as Shiv Dayal Singh Chaurasia.[1] Chaurasia belonged to a backward caste of Lucknow and worked as lawyer in Lucknow Court. Chaurasia took Bhagwan Das to Ambedkar at his 26 Alipur Road residence.

Babasaheb Ambedkar asked him his name and enquired about the kind of work he had done before. Then Babasaheb said, 'Yes, I need an assistant. Nanak Chand Rattu is good at typing but he is not qualified enough for other work'. Bhagwan Das told Babasaheb, 'I live very far away. After my office work, I can come thrice a week to assist you.' The conversation took place in English and with it began the period of his closest acquaintance with Dr Ambedkar.

By the time Bhagwan Das began working with Babasaheb in 1956, Babasaheb's health was declining. Babasaheb worked in his library for most of the time. Around 7 pm, he used to sit in verandah with a few books. He also met visitors there. Once Bhagwan Das was sitting with Ambedkar and he had a copy of Charles Darwin's *The Origin of Species* in his hand. Just then Ambedkar took the book from him and after formal questions, Ambedkar switched on to the main topic.

A conversation between Bhagwan Das and Babasaheb Ambedkar[2] which appeared in the book *In Pursuit of Dr. Ambedkar: A Memoir* by Bhagwan Das is given below:

Ambedkar: 'Darwin came up with the theory of the survival of the fittest, but I don't agree with it.'

Bhagwan Das: I politely sought Babasaheb's permission to interject and said, 'Darwin did not come up with the theory of the survival of the fittest. He only wrote that species that fail to make adjustments with the changing environment become extinct.

Ambedkar: Have you done MA in anthropology?

Bhagwan Das: No, I could not go to any university or college.

Ambedkar: Have you have done a PhD?

Bhagwan Das: Sir, I could not study after matric. I had family responsibilities. And there was no college in Shimla before Independence.

Ambedkar: It does not matter. I have got bundles of degrees, what matters is the knowledge one has and the ability to use it.

Bhagwan Das: I remembered another such incident. When Chaurasia went to meet Babasaheb regarding the Backward Classes Commission report and his Note of Dissent, a political discussion on Buddhism was going on in the room. Sohanlal Shastri and other leaders from Dalit organizations in Delhi were also present.

Shiv Dayal Singh Chaurasia told Babasaheb that he (Bhagwan Das) was writing a book on Safai Karamcharis.

Ambedkar : Oh, sweepers came into existence only after the Muslims came to this country.

Bhagwan Das: Almost everyone there seemed to agree, I realized they had fallen victim to the propaganda of many Hindu politicians, religious leaders and writers.

I gathered the courage to interrupt. Babasaheb was a world renowned intellectual and the others present were either Sanskrit experts or Arya Samaj followers. I said, 'If it is true that sweepers came into existence after the coming of the Muslims how is it that we find them mentioned in Buddhist text?'

Ambedkar: Which texts?

Bhagwan Das: I didn't mention Fa- Hien and Hsuan Tsang (also spelt Yuen Chwang) the obvious names, though they have written about the caste system and untouchability. I referred to 'I Tsing, whose work made detailed observations about cleanliness, sanitation and sweepers.

A little irritated, Babasaheb said, 'No Chinese with the name Iching ever came to India.'

Bhagwan Das: I said apologetically, 'probably my pronounciation is not correct, but his name is written like this: 'I' followed by an apostrophe and 'Tsing'.

Ambedkar: Oh you mean, I' Tsing. Show me what he has written.

Bhagwan Das: I could not show him the text right then, but I knew the book was in the Central Secretariat Library. I later took it to him and showed him where I' Tsing had written about toilets and how to keep them clean.

For the information of readers, I am presenting all the relevant texts below. Fa-Hien visited India to study Buddhism in the 14th century CE and wrote about Chandalas and untouchability in his travelogues:

'The Chandalas are named "evil men" and dwell apart from others, if they enter a market place, they keep beating a piece of wood in order to separate themselves, then men, knowing who they are, avoid coming in contact with them. In this country, they do not keep swine or fowl, and do not deal in cattle; they have no wineshops in their market places. In selling, they use cowrie shells. The Chandalas only hunt and sell flesh.

The other prominent Chinese scholar, who came to India in the 7th century was Huan Chwang. Babasaheb has cited him in his book, *The Untouchables.* Huan Chwang referred to the practice of untouchability and the conditions of low caste people in his travelogue:

> The shops are on the highways and booths (or inns) line the roads. Butchers, Fishermen, Public performers, Executioners and Scavengers have their habitations marked by a distinguishing sign. They are forced to live outside the city and they sneak along on the left when going about in the hamlets.

But what I' Tsing has written about toilets is different from what his predecessors had discussed. What is notable is that he does not write that people from a specific caste used to come to clean the Buddha Vihara, the monastery:

> I shall now describe, in brief the rules concerning evacuation. One should put on a bathing skirt for the lower part of the body, a Sankashika robe for the upper part. One should then fill up a jar (Lit 'touched jar') with water for the cleaning purposes, go to the lavatory with hat jar, and shut the door in order to hide oneself. Fourteen balls of earth are provided and placed on a brick plate, or sometimes on a small board, outside the lavatory (varkas kuti). The size of the brick or board is one cubit long and half a cubit wide. The earth balls are to be ground into powder and made into two rows, the powder of each ball being placed separately. There must be an additional ball placed there. One should take three other balls in the lavatory, and put them aside. Of these three, one is to be used in rubbing the body, another in washing the body. The manner of washing the body is as follows: one should wash the body with the left hand and again purify with the water and with the earth. There is still one ball left, with which one should roughly wash the left hand, once. If there is a piece of card (or peg), it is well to bring it in, but when it has been used, one should throw it away outside the lavatory. And if an old paper be used, it must be thrown away in the urinal. After the purification has been done, one should put down (i.e. adjust) the clothes, put the other jar on one side, open the door with the

> right hand, and come out holding the jar in right hand. Again embracing the jar in the left arm by closing the left hand, one should shut the door behind him with the right hand, and leave the urinal. One should now come to the place where earth balls are kept and squat down on one side, if one uses a mat, one should place it accordingly. The jar should be placed on the left knee, and be pressed down with the left arm. First the seven earth balls nearby should be used one by one in order to wash the left hand, and then the other seven one by one to wash both hands.
>
> The surface of the brick and wood (board) should be clearly washed. There is still another ball with which the jar, arms, abdomen and feet (soles of feet) are to be washed, when all are pure and clean, one may go away according to one's desire. The water in the jar is not fit to be put into mouth. ... When one has touched the jar after having been to the lavatory, one should again wash the hands and rinse the mouth, and then one is fit to touch other utensils. Such are the rules concerning the voiding of the bowels. To save trouble a priest always washes himself, but he who has a page can let the latter wash him.
>
> After having been to the lavatory, one should in any case wash one's hands with one or two earth balls, for purity is the foundation of paying honour. True, there are some who consider these points a very small matter, but there are strict prohibitions in the Vinaya.

Babasaheb was very happy to read these passages. He looked at Bhagwan Das lovingly and said, 'Very good! You complete this book and bring it to me, I shall write its preface'. His words encouraged Bhagwan Das a lot and he became even more involved in writing the book.

When all went out of the room, Ambedkar said to Chaurasia, 'Where had you kept this boy hidden until now'.

The conversation thus ended in a pleasant atmosphere. Ambedkar was the leading figure of Dalit politics, the intellectual and the uncrowned king of Dalit masses who were dazed and electrified by his dynamic action. To answer Ambedkar back was to incur permanent displeasure and to create undying bitterness. But the conversation sounded the well beginning between Bhagwan Das and Ambedkar.

In this connection, it should be noted that in his introduction to *In pursuit of Ambedkar: A Memoir*, S. Anand[3] made the following observations praising Bhagwan Das:

> '... his formal education amounted to nothing more than Matriculation when he worked for Ambedkar, who had a clutch of degrees and two doctorates from Columbia University (It was only in the mid-1970 that Das acquired degrees in political science and Law). Yet, what draws Ambedkar to Das was his command over the English language and his hunger for books and research.

Issue of Conversion

Another notable incident, which is associated with conversion to any other religion, Bhagwan Das described thus.

Dharam, Mazhab and religion are used interchangeably in everyday life, but their meaning and implications are different. Born in the lowest of the low untouchable family, Bhagwan Das often saw his father reading Ramayana, Gita, the *Japji Saheb* and the Bible. They celebrated Diwali, Holi, Dussehra and also Baisakhi and Christmas, but they never entered in a temple or mosque to offer prayers. It was only in the churches that they were allowed entry.

His family members enjoyed a lot of freedom in food. Meat was a part of their daily menu. Fresh beef, pork, etc. were commonly eaten. Goat's meat was double the price of beef. Hindus used to hate them.

History tells us that many attempts had been made from time to time to reform Hinduism. These attempts proved futile or sometimes led to the formation of new caste groups. The Hindu religion is like a *jungle* in which new plants keep growing even if some become extinct. It is not possible to control or shape a jungle.

In order to get rid of discrimination and exploitation, Ambedkar realized the importance of conversion. Thus, in 1935 Babasaheb Ambedkar in his Yeola speech used one or two teachings of Buddhism. Though he talked about having decided to quit Hinduism, he did not advocate conversion to any specific religion to his followers. His speech led to numerous discussion and debates across the country. Untouchables were wondering which religion could offer them freedom from discrimination and exploitation, so they could move towards progress and dignity.

Babasaheb Ambedkar made many attempts to organize, educate and uplift the untouchables. There were many branches of political parties in various provinces of India, but they also fell victim to casteism. Many people belonging to the Namashudra caste, for instance, joined the Scheduled Castes Federation in Bengal, but the other untouchable castes of Bengal were ignored. It is, thus, very difficult to organize untouchables as long as they remain Hindu.

Bhagwan Das had some doubts about religion. He studied the Hindu religion, Arya Samaj literature Satyartha Prakash, Rigveda Bhumika, the Bible, the Quran-e-Sharif, Mirza Ghulam Ahmad's new religion, Bahaullah's new religion, Sikh literature, etc. He began reading about Buddhism after reading Babasaheb's speeches and writings.

One day Bhagwan Das was sitting in Babasaheb's verandah after work and had some preliminary discussion with Ambedkar about conversion. Bhagwan Das urged:

> 'Babasaheb, I want to ask you a few things about Buddhism. You are in favour of adopting Buddhism. You have sent parts of your work on Buddhism to England, Germany and France for expert comments. I am from Shimla and many Buddhists live there. I have seen them not allowing untouchable castes to enter their temples. Bhikkhus and lamas enjoy themselves, drink chhang (home brewed liquor) and idle the time away. When I was on the Burma front during my Air Force years during the Second World War, I also got a chance to observe Buddhists Viharas in cities like Chittagong. But I could find no positive difference in their life-style or behavioural patterns. Do you feel sure that Buddhist Dalits will not end up becoming a separate caste like untouchable Christians or Muslims?

Babasaheb thought for a while and said, 'It will not be so this time'.[4]
His conviction was so strong that Bhagwan Das did not enquire further.

This was not, however, the first time that Bhagwan Das's questioning had caused a stir in Ambedkar's mind. Some time later Babasaheb Ambedkar converted to Buddhism in 1956, Bhagwan Das followed in his footsteps and in 1957 embraced Buddhism along with his family. While the formal association of Bhagwan Das with Ambedkar ended in 1956, however in his individual capacity, he remained as one of the leading propagators of Ambedkar ideology. His indebtedness to Ambedkar can be summed-up in his own words thus:[5]

> 'I can never forget what I learnt from him and I am greatly indebted to him. I continue to derive inspiration from his life struggle and character even today.'

Notes

1. भगवान दास, 'बाबा के चरणों में', नई दिल्ली, दलित प्रेस, 2004, पेज 27-28. Also see, अंगलेलाल एवं राहुल राज, एडवोकेट शिवदयाल सिंह चौरसिया, 'इन उत्तर प्रदेश में दलित आन्दोलन', दिल्ली, गौतम बुक सेंटर 2011, पृ. 34-37.
2. भगवान दास 'बाबा के चरणों में', first written in Hindi and published in 2004 by Dalit Press, New Delhi, p. 33–42, was later translated into English by Isha. The translated book, *In Pursuit of Ambedkar: A Memoir* was published by New Delhi: Narayana. Pubication. Year not mentioned, p. 44–48. For more details, see above referred books.
3. For more details, see, Introduction by S. Anand in *In Pursuit of Ambedkar: A Memoir*, ibid. p. 9.
4. See 'Babasaheb's Approach to Buddhism' in *In Pursuit of Ambedkar: A Memoir*, ibid., p. 58–59.
5. Ibid., p. 65.

8

Thus Spoke Bhagwan Das* on Untouchability in UN

I am grateful to the chairman of the sub-committees for granting me an opportunity to present the case of the untouchables living in India and the neighbouring countries that came under the influence of the Hindu religion and culture. I am giving this testimony on behalf of Secretary General (Dr Homer A. Jack) World Conference on Religion and Peace (WCRP). I also speak on behalf of various untouchables and Buddhist organizations of India, namely All India Samata Sainik Dal (Volunteers for equality), an organization founded by Dr Bheem Rao Ambedkar, Indian Buddhist Council Ambedkar Mission Society. Ambedkar Mission Incorporated (Canada) and Dr Ambedkar Mission Society, Bedford, UK.

I take this opportunity to mention here that WCRP in its first conference held at Kyoto, Japan, in 1970, discussed the problem of the discrimination including the practice of untouchability. In its third conference held at Princeton (USA), the problem of the untouchables in India and BuraKumin of Japan was discussed and mentioned in the declaration in the Asian Conference of Religion and Peace held at New Delhi. The problem of untouchability and discrimination against the Buddhist converts was taken up and recommendations made in the declaration issued at the end of conference. The Human Rights Commission of ACRP decided to set up an office is New Delhi and an office is now functioning is New Delhi with the help of the Japanese committees of WCRP under the title Asian Centre for Human Rights.

Untouchability is a phenomenon peculiar to Hinduism and it is an integral part of their religion. It took birth in India and it is from India that this abominable practice spread to other religions and countries. No religion in India is free

* Testimony by Bhagwan Das, Chairman, All India Samata Sainik Dal and Ambedkar Mission Society in the 36th Session of Human Rights Sub-Commission on Prevention of Discrimination and Protection of Minorities, held at Geneva in August 1983.

from this contamination, not even those who loudly preach from housetops the fatherhood of God and the brotherhood of man.

Hindu society is divided vertically and horizontally on the basis of caste. Christianity and Islam have allowed caste to exist in their society. Lower caste Christians especially in southern states of India are meted out discriminatory treatment in the matter of burial in the cemeteries, appointment of parishioners priests, etc. and matrimony. Upper caste Christians seldom marry a girl from the lower caste Christians. Islamic society is also modelled on the pattern of Hindu society. It is divided into three or four groups namely 'Ashraf' upper caste, Moghuls, Turks Afghanis etc. Ajalaf converts from upper castes of Hindus and at the lowest rung of ladders sit the lowly Arzal butchers, tanners, shoemakers, sweepers, Scavengers, etc. Sikhs, who claim to be more progressive and egalitarian, have also not been able to keep their society free from caste system and untouchability. Even in a country like Britain, they rigidly follow caste system and practise untouchability and discrimination against the untouchables (Ramdaasia and Mazhbis) living in England. A 'jat' Sikh shuns the company of the untouchables and avoids going to the pubs patronized by the Valmikis and Ravidassis, two untouchables castes of Punjab. An upper caste Sikh (Jat, Khatri, Arora), trading communities of Punjab, never miss an opportunity if he can offer an untouchable by referring to the castes.

Untouchables in Various Countries

Nepal

Nepal is predominantly Hindu state and 89 per cent people either wrote their religion as Hinduism or are registered as Hindus in the census. Barely 7 per cent of the Nepalese are Buddhist. Proselytization is prohibited. Hindu society is divided into as many as 59 castes and several artisan and other castes, such as Paura (sweepers and Scavengers), Damais (smiths), Sarakis (leather workers), goldsmiths in hilly regions are treated as untouchables. Even though there is free education, very few among those castes can take the benefit owing to the practice of untouchability. In the Nepalese Panjyat (Panchayat), not more than one or two members of this community can get elected owing to the deep-rooted prejudices against these people whose only fault is that they perform useful duties. Their exact numbers is not known because, unlike India, Nepal census reports do not register caste. Owing to the dominating upper castes Hindus, even Buddhists avoid contact with the untouchables in Nepal. These communities suffer from numerous disabilities arising from untouchability. So far as I have been able to ascertain, they have not been able to organize themselves for struggling against discrimination. Those who come in contact with these people were neglected by the authorities and only after paying the fine and performing some ceremonies they could be re-admitted in the society.

Pakistan

Pakistan, with 97 per cent of its population owning Islam as their religion, is divided into numerous castes, tribes, etc. Hindus constitute about 2 per cent of the population and are listed as Caste Hindus (2,98,837) and Scheduled Castes (6,03,369). Scheduled Castes is the statutory title given under the Government of India Act 1935 to the untouchables. Most of them earn their livelihood as sweepers, Scavengers, cobblers, weavers, etc. Muslims also treat them as untouchables, like Hindus, throughout the world. Pakistan also has a Christian population numbering about 9,08,000. Christians are divided into three groups, Europeans and Anglo-Pakistanis, Eurasians like Goanese, converts from upper castes of Hindus and Muslims and people belonging to upper stratum of society. At the bottom sit the most despised sweepers and Scavengers who are known as Christian Punjabi Sweepers (CPS). They are the descendants of the members of Chuhra community, traditional sweepers, who embraced Christianity to escape the tyranny of Hinduism and the stigma of untouchability but the partitioning of the country compelled them to revert to the traditional occupation of sweeping and scavenging. Although they are economically better than the rural workers so far as the wages are concerned, yet they are compelled to live in segregated localities and are treated as untouchables. Like their counterparts in India, CPS are the most despised people in Pakistan. They suffer from numerous disabilities arising from untouchability.

Sri Lanka

Sri Lanka is predominantly Buddhist (Population 85,37,000, 67.3%) with Hindus constituting the second largest religious group (22,39,000) divided into clean and unclean castes. Among the Sinhalese, Goyigama is the highest caste and those engaged in occupations like butchers, drum-beaters, toddy tappers, sweeping, etc. are considered hina jati hina SIPP People. Discrimination in the matter of marriage is practised among the Sinhalese. Siame Nikaya, a Buddhist sect, does not admit the members of the lower castes as Bhikkhus but the other two Nikayas admit men belonging to the lower castes if they desire to join the order. But among the Tamilians, caste system is rigidly followed and untouchability practised in the Jaffana area which is predominantly Hindu (Tamilian). Society is divided into two major groups, namely clean castes and unclean castes. Among the unclean castes are included Palla (potter), Seneer (weaver), Parriyar, Kadaiyan (Lime burner), Chikkalayan (leather worker and sweeper), Yunnan (washer man) and Thurmba, etc. Upper castes (Vellala, Brahmin, Chetty etc.) treat them as untouchables. Present conflict has temporarily obliterated the differences but after the trouble has subsided caste feelings will again revive.

Bangladesh

Bangladesh is predominantly Muslim (80%), with 49,26,448 (20% Hindus divided into two groups namely Caste Hindus – Brahmin, Kayasthas, Baidyas etc. and Namoshudras Kaibartas, Hadis, Mochis etc.). Many of the Muslims are converts from among the untouchables and Buddhists. Yet discriminatory treatment is meted out to the untouchables in Bangladesh. Our informants have stated that the Hindus of upper castes are treated as equal but the lower castes are discriminated in the matter of housing employment, etc.

All these countries were part of greater India until 1947 and were influenced by the Hindu religion in the matter of rituals and customs.

Untouchability in India

Untouchability has not been defined by the sociologists or the legislators. At the time of discussion of Untouchability Offence Act in the Parliament, when a question was raised about definition, the law Minister said: 'There is no need to define untouchability. Every body knows it'. He was trying to avoid definition but he was telling the truth that everybody knows whom to avoid, whom to persecute. Untouchability is deeply embedded in the minds of Hindus and regulates their behaviour with other people. Stratification of society and restrictions on inter-marriage between different classes or groups are not unknown in other societies or cultures, but to use the words of Dr G.S. Ghurye, a renowned sociologist: 'Hindu system is unique only in this that it classified some groups as untouchable and unapproachable. Other religious groups only copied them. Since Hindus treated the Scavengers, sweepers, cobblers, basket makers, weavers, etc. as untouchables, Christians, Muslims, Sikhs also treated them as lowly, despised, degraded people. Since untouchability had religious sanction behind it, all efforts made by social reformers failed. Hindus avoided discussion and foreigners did not want to take up the cause of the untouchables for fear of antagonizing the Hindus. They were also taken in by the propaganda carried out by the followers of Gandhi. Dr Ambedkar had rightly observed':

> The old orthodox Hindu doesn't think that there is anything wrong in the observance of Untouchability. To him it is normal, natural thing. As such it neither calls for expiation nor explanation. The new modern Hindu realises the wrong but he is ashamed to discuss it in public for fear of letting the foreigner know that Hindu civilisation can be guilty of such a vicious and infamous system or social code as evidenced by Untouchability.

Mass conversion of untouchables to Christianity and Islam and growing importance of number in the politics of India occupied with criticism of Hindu society by Western writers, sociologists, travellers, etc. led Hindus to introduce certain changes in their social system. While they wanted to remove untouchability, they did not want Hinduism and caste system to suffer in any way because Hinduism is sustained by caste system. If caste system goes, Hinduism cannot survive for long. On the other hand, Hindus have developed a vested interest in untouchability and caste system. More than 75 per cent population of India is illiterate and people sincerely believe that caste is God-made and there is no hope or scope for change. Any laws made by men are interference in the God's work. Hindu law-makers had made elaborate laws and rules to keep untouchables in degraded condition perpetually. Economic measures were adopted to perpetuate degradation, segregation and poverty while laws were framed and strictly enforced to keep them divided, dispirited, poor, ignorant, illiterate and physically weak. They were not allowed to acquire wealth; higher interest was charged on loans, good wholesome nutritious food proscribed so that they may not grow strong. Right to possess arms was denied so they may never revolt. Low wages and excessive work was prescribed so they may have no leisure. Identity marks and symbols were prescribed so that in any event by mistake, pure Hindus may not eat or drink with them. This system was rigidly followed by the Hindus for centuries. Even Muslims did not disturb it. British especially after the Sepoy Mutiny of 1857, for fear of antagonizing the Hindus, tried to maintain those laws and enforce them through courts of law.

Progressive Western educated Hindus, however, felt uneasy and promised to bring about changes after attaining Independence. Accordingly provisions were incorporated in the Constitution abolishing untouchability and certain ameliorative provisions were made, such as reservation in legislature, services of Union Government and states, educational institutions, etc. Untouchables were subjected to some inhuman laws like forced labour in rural area. A provision to abolish slavery of this kind was made in the Constitution, but the law was enacted in 1976. Millions of rupees were provided for the economic upliftment of the untouchables in the Five Year Plans.

In spite of these laws the untouchables suffer from numerous disabilities in smaller towns and villages of India. Untouchables do not have a well in thousands of villages and upper caste people do not allow them to dig wells. Untouchables have to beg for water from a distance lest their shadow should pollute the upper caste Hindus. Sometime the water pipes are laid and stopped a few yards short of the Untouchable locality. The present writer struggled for seven years to get a public hydrant installed in a village of Himachal Pradesh while every Minister or even the Chief Minister had announced that water had been provided.

If the untouchables demand higher wages in villages, the caste Hindus pour filth or kerosene in the wells so as to starve them of water. Untouchability is widely practised. A mild and harmless law which was neither educative nor a deterrent was enacted in 1955 under the title Untouchable Offences Act 1955. This proved to be ineffective. This law was amended and passed as Protection of Civil Liberties Act 1976 containing a provision of minimum punishment. Owing to the illiteracy of majority of untouchables who live in the rural areas, very few cases are reported and a very small number reaches the courts of law. Untouchability in its worst form is practised in the Hindi region but the largest number of cases are registered in the state where the Scheduled Caste people are awakened and better organized.

Of all the countries where untouchability is practised, India has the best of laws and the most generous provisions in its Constitution. The British had introduced quota system with a view of giving share in administration to all religious groups and other minorities. Untouchables were, however, denied a share on the plea that there were no educated men available. Through the efforts of Dr B.R. Ambedkar, undisputed leader of the untouchables, reservation in services was introduced for the untouchables in 1943 during the term of Viceroy Lord Linlithgow. Later on provision was made for the Scheduled Castes and Scheduled Tribes but reservation in favour of other minorities was abolished.

During the early years, there was little resistance because very few qualified people were available to fill up the reserved seats. Resistance was offered by non-implementation of government orders, or by declaring that suitable candidate was not available or if available not found suitable and also through courts of law by filing writ petition. Since 1974, organized resistance is being offered by the upper caste employees who have been enjoying monopoly of all government jobs. Private sector does not employ the Scheduled Castes people excepting in the lowly, low paid and degrading situations. The following statistics give some idea of the success in the part of the opponents of the reservation.

Quota Reserved: 15 per cent

Reservation given in: Class I = 4.95 per cent, Class II = 8.54 per cent, Class III = 13.44 per cent, Class IV=19.46 per cent.

Discriminatory treatment is being meted out to the Scheduled Caste people in the matter of recognition of their unions on the plea that it is the policy of the Government that 'communal' organizations of the employees will not be organized. On the other hand, organizations of the Hindu employees who are opposed to the reservation have the support and blessing of administration as well as the political parties, especially of those who have their base among the middle classes of Hindus.

Scheduled Caste (statutory title of the untouchables) is an artificially created minority under the Constitution. Names of castes can be deleted or added by the President. Pressure is mounting now through press to delete the names of more awakened and better organized castes. Majority of the untouchables (about 76%) live in 5,68,000 villages of India. In some places they are allotted land by the government. Dr Ambedkar demanded nationalization of land with collectivization of allotment on cooperative basis. The Government favoured the creation of small holdings and peasant proprietors. Fragmentation of land is non-productive but the untouchable farmers, who never owned land because of the laws prohibiting possession of land in some states, desired to own land. The landholding dominating upper castes do everything possible in their means to obstruct distribution of land. Even if land is allotted, the upper caste landlords do not allow the untouchables to take the fruit of their labour, if untouchables demand higher wages or even the minimum wages prescribed by the Government, the upper caste landlords indulge in murders, torture, arson rape, etc. to terrorize the poor ignorant untouchables. Thousands of men are employed as bonded labourers and kept away from the cities, police, etc. Hundreds of women are forced into prostitution by exploiting their ignorance, poverty and superstitious belief and sold into the brothels of Bombay, Calcutta, Madras, Kanpur and Delhi.

Untouchables are becoming increasingly convicted that the Hindus hate them not because they perform unpleasant duties but because their religion teaches them to hate certain castes. Many embraced Christianity and Islam. Dr Ambedkar, who saw no hope of Hinduism reforming itself, exhorted his people to renounce Hinduism and embraces Buddhism which he had revived in 1956. Millions of people responded to his call and embraced Buddhism. The Government of India immediately issued order that if an untouchable renounces Hinduism and embraces any religion other than Sikhism, he will become disentitled to concessions and grants allowed to the Scheduled Castes. When a few hundred untouchables in Madras embraced Islam because the Hindus harassed and humiliated them and did not allow them even to wear shoes or loincloth which went below the knee. Hindu militant organizations turned notorious and burnt the huts of untouchables and molested their women. Even the then Prime Minister, Indira Gandhi, forgetting that she was the head of a secular government showed no concern and delivered speeches discouraging the conversion of untouchables. Some States enacted laws, making conversion difficult. Those renouncing Hinduism had to obtain a certificate from the Magistrate that the person desiring conversion to Islam or Christianity is doing it voluntarily. The police is dominated by the upper landholding castes of Hindus and is generally hostile towards the untouchables. The Indian Penal Code contains certain provisions under which the police has power to arrest and detain a person if he has no ostentatious means of livelihood. This in a country where majority of the people have no employment, house or shelter of any kind. The Police abuses its powers especially against the Untouchables and many people are killed or incapacitated through torture in police custody.

Hinduism has closed the doors of armed forces to the untouchables for ever. Untouchables were admitted to the armed forces of Islam after embracing Islam which many did. During early decades of their rule, the British recruited untouchables in their armies, but after some time they began to close the doors especially in central India and Bengal under pressure from the high castes of Hindus. They introduced the pernicious theory of martial races and non-martial races. Later on they disbanded the untouchables' armies and raised class regiments recruiting men belonging to upper castes. The Indian Government has not completely abolished the class regiments a ıd has officially removed the ban on recruitment. But the Government has not taken any measure to change the mode of recruitment. Recruiting officers, mostly belonging to peasant castes, owing to deep-rooted prejudices based on caste, and their medical officers invariably ask a man's castes and reject him on medical grounds. Untouchables have little share in the officers (0.44%) cadre and 10.62 per cent in other ranks in the army, 7.63 per cent in other ranks and 0.156 per cent in officers cadre of navy and 2.568 per cent in other ranks.

Untouchables have the equal right to vote and contest elections; 79 seats are reserved in the House of the People (Lok Sabha) out of the total number of 542. Out of a total strength of 3,997 members in the State legislatures and Union Territories, 540 belonging to the Scheduled Castes. On paper, the number appears to be very impressive but owing to the election system of the country it is the majority community which elects the representatives from among the candidates. In the rural areas, the untouchables can not exercise their right to vote freely and independently. Very often police protection has to be provided. After the election, heavy price has to be paid to the untouchables, if the members of higher castes owning land feel that they did not get the support of the untouchables.

Violation in Villages

Scheduled Castes in the rural areas demand land, better wages, right to wear clothes according to their liking and assert the rights granted under the Constitution. Hindus, on the other hand, want to maintain status quo in all fields. Tensions arise and often result in confrontation. Landlords have raised armies of trained men released from army and police to terrorize the untouchables, landless labourers. Police protects the strong against the poor. The Government, through its machinery and religious polices, strengthens casteism and superstition because it helps the ruling classes. Leaders of struggle are picked up and either involved in false criminal cases or murdered by the police in encounters. Men, women and the children have been massacred and burnt alive whenever they put up resistance against oppression. Men have been killed for offering Ganges water in a shrine. A man was killed in Aligarh (UP) for affixing the word Chauhan to his name. Women's toes were crushed for wearing rings. Men were killed for twirling moustaches. In Meenakshipuram, where mass conversion to Islam took place, men were not allowed to sit beside the upper caste men in the state buses, nor allowed to walk through the streets, women were punished for wearing sandals. In Kafalta, 11 persons were done to death for riding a horse in marriage procession and for using palanquin. The incidents of violence in the villages had shown an upward trend in the period from 1976 to 1980:

Year	*No. of Incidents of Atrocities*
1976	6,197
1977	10,879
1978	15,055
1979	15,070
1980	13,341

Recent figures are not available but the then Home Minister N.R. Laskar during a session had stated that the number was showing an increase but during the Monsoon session of last week he said that number of incidents has fallen considerably. Figures furnished by the Government do not represent the fact. These represent only a tip of the iceberg because many of the cases remain unreported. Untouchables feel very insecure owing to the growing resentment against the declared policies and programmes of the government which are very rarely accompanied by implementation. Bureaucracy is being blamed for non-implementation but it is the government which lacks the political will to take action against those who flout the government authority.

This weakness is evident from the fact that even a simple and harmless demand by the Scheduled Caste legislators in the Parliament to have a portrait installed in the Central Hall of Parliament where Dr Ambedkar played a very important and historical role both as a member of the Executive Councillors in the Viceroy's Executive Council (1942–46) and as first Law Minister and Chairman of the Constitution Drafting Committee (1947–51) had been rejected. The government had been resisting this demand on some pretext or the other. Similarly in recognition of the great services rendered by Dr B.R. Ambedkar in the field of education, a unanimous decision was taken in the Maharashtra Assembly to change the name of Marathawada University to Ambedkar University. This university came into existence chiefly owing to the establishment of three colleges by Dr Ambedkar in the most backward region of Marathawada of Maharashtra. Orthodox Hindus in the region felt offended and instigated the illiterate and ignorant villagers that now Ambedkar, an untouchable will enter your houses in the form of degrees and diploma certificates and you will have to repeat his name. As a result many houses of Buddhist converts were looted, women molested, old men insulted, buildings demolished or set on fire and some people killed. Hundreds of men were forced to leave their villages and seek shelter in the towns, railway platforms, footpaths, etc. The Government could not implement its decision and the oppressor won the field. Untouchables and Buddhists continue the agitation with unshaken determination.

In spite of the fact that the Indian Constitution has the most liberal provision, the Government has failed to implement its own declared programmes and policies for the removal of untouchability and upliftment of the deprived and disadvantaged section of society. Prejudices cannot be removed merely through legislation. Religious policy of the government is discriminatory and is based in favour of Hinduism and Sikhism and prejudicial to the religion like Buddhism, Christianity and Islam. The Government in accordance with the wishes of the orthodox Hindus has used coercive measures to check the conversion of untouchables to Buddhism lest they should unite and organize themselves for struggle. Present policy of the government appears to be based on the tenets of Hinduism. Methods may have changed but the aim of the Hindu lawmakers and religious leaders have not changed. Anything which the untouchables consider good for them is vehemently resisted and opposed. Whatever goes to make them weak, dispirited and dependent is encouraged.

Proposals

1. A commission should be set up to investigate and submit a report on the practice of untouchability in the countries wherever it is practised.
2. Action should be taken against countries and institutions who encourage this practice in the name of religion and custom.
3. Government should be asked to check discrimination against the despised and segregated groups in the matter of freedom of religion.
4. To set up a commission to monitor the activities of government and religious groups in the countries where untouchability is practiced.

5. Government of the countries where the Hindus and Sikhs have migrated and practice untouchability and discrimination against the untouchables should be approached to enact laws to discourage the practise.
6. A separate office should be set up to receive cases of untouchability and disability and the states concerned should be asked to report what measures they have taken to eliminate discrimination to their respective countries.

Part III

Gandhi and Ambedkar

9

Gandhi and Ambedkar: Some Thoughts and Views of Two Saviour of Bhangis

Gandhi and Ambedkar are appreciated in India for their great determination towards the 'cause of uplift' or 'emancipation of the Dalit'. They are appreciated because their hearts bled for the suffering of people particularly untouchables and they desired to deliver the untouchables from the slavery of centuries, although their paths were different. Both Mahatma Gandhi and Dr Ambedkar, the two great leaders and visionaries of the 20th Century, have now conventionally been regarded as arch rivals.[1] There were many issues on which the two greats did not agree for the obvious reasons. Gandhi wanted to reform and end injustice while Ambedkar demanded rebellion for the annihilation of caste system itself. O. Chinnappa Reddy[2], former Judge, Supreme Court of India, in his foreword writes:

> Because of his birth (Ambedkar) because of his courage, because of his integrity, he emerged as a great, but misunderstood intellectual. So he continued till the end and so he continues after death.

After Independence, both Indian and foreign scholars have written volume on Gandhi, controversy on untouchables/Dalits in general but the thoughts, views and feelings of Gandhi and Ambedkar to the cause of uplift of the Bhangi caste in particular have not been explored till today.

In this chapter, I have endeavoured my best to place before the readers the thoughts, views and feelings of Gandhi and Ambedkar on a few selected issues of Bhangis particularly, which they had chosen and pursued differently during the pre-Independence period.

Socio-Political Background

It is necessary to briefly look at the socio-political background of both Gandhi and Ambedkar before delving into their roles and commitments for the uplift and empowerment of untouchables. Both Gandhi and Ambedkar hailed from two different caste backgrounds and were born as Hindu, though the latter embraced Buddhism and attained his Nirvana (death) in December 1956. Being born in a traditional Bania caste at Porbandar in Kathiawad of Saurashtra peninsula (now a part of Gujarat state), Gandhi as a child was brought up in the conservative Hindu tradition. In fact, his family was deeply entrenched in the neo-Vedantic religious faith of the 19th century and in the devotional path of the Bhakti tradition of the medieval period which also helped Gandhi to imbibe 'compassion for humble and care for poor'. It is this tradition which enabled him to proceed later in politics, with implicit social criticism of the (caste) hierarchy, social distance (between rich and poor or between high caste and low caste) and exclusively of Brahmanic Hinduism.[3]

However, with traditional socio-cultural movings, Gandhi had completed his matriculation in 1887 and gone to England in the subsequent year to pursue the legal study for his LLB degree. During his stay in England he largely retained with him the values and cultural traditions that he had inherited since his childhood. Anyway, Gandhi became a Barrister in June 1891.

Then after carrying out social reform of some kind in his own region, Gandhi went to South Africa for pursuing a legal suit and stayed there, at first distance for three years, i.e. up to 1900, where he became aware of the racial discrimination and apartheid against the Blacks. After returning to India, he participated in the Annual Conference of INC held at Calcutta in 1901. He again went to South Africa and began his political activities there in 1906. But he soon returned to India and ultimately took charge of the Indian National Movement in 1920 and devoted 28 full years of his life in launching Satyagrah, mass mobilization and fast unto death. Finally, he was assassinated on 30 January 1948 and thus disappeared for ever from the Indian political scene, though he had already been transformed into Mahatma.

Two points need to be mentioned here about Gandhi's childhood experiences. The first is related to his knowledge about untouchability and his temporal social boycott. The latter being milder than the former, it could easily be removed after the required purification and fulfilling the caste or community obligation. As a child, he touched the untouchable – the Bhangi boy who had accompanied his parent as a domestic servant appointed to clean the latrine in his house. He had also touched another untouchable boy while playing with him. On both occasions, he was rebuked and punished by his mother and other members of the family and was asked to undergo the purification process. Secondly, he entered politics and joined the INC at a time when it was almost 30 years old and carrying out some activities for the removal of social disabilities under the rubrics of social reform.

The views expressed by Gandhi from time to time on Hinduism untouchability are summarized below.[4]

> 'I have regarded untouchability as the greatest blot on Hinduism. I was hardly yet twelve when this idea had dawned on me. A scavenger named UKA, an untouchable used to attend our house for cleaning latrines. Often I would ask my mother why it was wrong to touch him, why I was forbidden to touch him. I accidentally touched

UKA. I was asked to perform ablutions and touch. I naturally obeyed, it was not without smilingly protest that untouchability was not sanctioned by religion, that it was impossible that it should be so. I was a very dutiful and obedient child and so far as it was consistent with respect for the parents. I often had tiusles with them on this matter. I told my mother that she was entirely wrong in considering physical contact with UKA was sinful.'

'While at school, I would often happen to touch the untouchables and as I would never conceal the fact from my parents, my mother would tell me that the shortcut to purification after the unholy touch was to cancel the touch by touching any Musalman passing by. And simply out of reverence and regard for my mother, I would do so. I do not pretend that this thing had crystallized as a conviction in me at the age of twelve, but I do say that I did then regard untouchability as a sin.'[5]

On the contrary, Ambedkar had emerged from a very modest family background of an untouchable (Mahar) caste of Maharashtra. Born in Mhow (Military House of the War), a small military town, now in Madhya Pradesh, where his father served as a teacher in the British army and retired as a Subedar Major. Ambedkar was brought up in Satara, Maharashtra, as his father had settled there after retirement. He, then, with his father moved to Bombay and lived in two small rooms in a chawl at Parel from where Ambedkar completed his matriculation in 1907 and BA in 1912.

In July 1913, Ambedkar, a young boy of 20 years and perhaps the first Indian untouchable, went to Columbia University, New York (USA), on a scholarship from the Maharaja of Baroda to pursue the higher studies. He obtained his MA and PhD degree from this University in 1915 and 1916 respectively. He also earned his M.Sc. and D.Sc. degrees from the London School of Economics in 1921 and 1923. In addition, he obtained his Bar at Law from the Gray Inn, London in 1922. Thus, there cannot be any parallel between Gandhi and Ambedkar not only in terms of their academic credentials, but even in theoretical empirical articulation as the latter had much superior intellectual acumen than the former.

Ambedkar was born in a family which, like Gandhi's family, was also religious but had deep faith in the saintly tradition of Bhakti period as the proponents of this tradition had condemned the caste system and rejected its rigidity. He not only revolted against any form of Hinduism but completely rejected it and embraced Buddhism.

In spite of his father being educated, a soldier in the army and having deep religious faith in Hinduism, Ambedkar and his family members, like his castemen, could not escape the various forms of untouchability practised by the caste Hindus. As a school boy both in Satara and Bombay, he faced untouchability and other forms of untouchability on many occasions including in classroom. Even as a young graduate and a lieutenant in the Baroda State forces, he was discriminated against by his peon and colleagues. Besides these incidents, there were numerous occasions on which untouchability and other forms of discrimination were practised against him. A vivid account of all this has been given by Dhananjay Keer[6], his biographer. Ambedkar was also well aware of the horror of untouchability practised day and night against his castemen and other untouchable castes in the Maharashtra and other states in the country.

Like Gandhi, Ambedkar also took up the leadership of the untouchables at a time when, in Maharashtra and elsewhere in the country, they had already formed a number of organizations and started agitation for their socio-religious uplift and political rights. Many of these organizations were supported either by the Indian National Congress and a few other political parties or by caste Hindu organizations. These lacked independent articulations and strong assertions in getting rights and justice to be granted to the untouchables.

It is at this juncture that Ambedkar[7] took up their leadership in the early 1920s and in less than 10 years became the undisputed champion of their assertion for social uplift and political rights. With his high academic credentials and much superior intellectual and rational argumentation, he succeeded not only in getting the Indian untouchables accepted as district and separate political minority, but also their right of political representation accorded first in the separate and later in the joint electorate system. He also played a crucial, instrumental role in getting special provision enshrined in the Indian Constitution and enacting policy of reservation in favour of Scheduled Castes and Scheduled Tribes.

Gandhi and Ambedkar: Thoughts, Views and Feelings of Two Saviours of Bhangis

In the light of such a frame of socio-political background of both Gandhi and Ambedkar, I will discuss here their thoughts of *Chatur Varna-vivyastha*, caste based occupation of Bhangi, and strike by them and to examine their views and feelings (both Gandhi and Ambedkar) expressed on these issues.

Chatur Varna or Caste System

Sociologically speaking, caste is a traditional institution deeply entrenched in Indian society, specially in the Hindu social system which has originally divided the entire Hindu population into thousands of castes, sub-castes vertically arranged with their superior and inferior ranks or statuses in a well knit hierarchy. That is why Ambedkar has called it a system of graded order or inequality based on division of labours and not of labour – a thesis pursued by caste Hindu social scientists and others. Hinduism imposed numerous forms of social and religious disabilities on untouchables. Since it put millions of low untouchable castes into sub-human conditions, it drew major concerns of both Gandhi and Ambedkar.

As stated earlier, Gandhi had witnessed the act of untouchability in his early childhood with a rebuke from his family members. Gandhi's limited experiences with untouchability sensitized his social and moral conscience to take up a vow to remove the evil of untouchability from this land. Between 1920 and 1932, he continuously wrote articles and issued statements in journal – *Harijan* and *Young India*, accepting untouchability in 1920 as a moral sin to god humanity and Hinduism.

Gandhi wrote in *Young India* on 10 June 1921:

> 'I am a sanatani Hindu. I believe in varnashram dharma, I believe in protection of Cow.'[8] ...

On one occasion Gandhi expressed[9]:

> 'I have declared times without number from various public platforms that it is the prayer of my heart that if I should fail to obtain moksha in the very birth, I might be born a Bhangi in my next birth. I believe in varnashrama both according to birth and moksha. But I do not regard Bhangi as in any sense a low order'.

Yet on another occasion Gandhi expressed:[10]

> I do not want to attain moksha. I do not want to be reborn. But if I have to be reborn, I should be born an untouchable, so that I may share them sorrows, sufferings and this affronts leveled at them and that, I may endeavour to free myself and them from miserable condition. I, therefore may that if I should be born again, I should do so not as a Brahmin, Kshatriya, Vaishya or Shudra, but as an Atishudra. I also pray that if am I of the untouchable unfinished, with my Hinduism unfulfilled, I may be born again amongst the untouchable to bring my Hinduism to its fulfilment.

Once Mahatma Gandhi, the Father of the Nation, said:

> 'आचरण रहित विचार कितने अच्छे क्यों न हों, उन्हें खोटे मोती की तरह समझना चाहिये।' (दैनिक भास्कर, जयपुर, शनिवार, 7 नवंबर 2015)

Sorry, he is fully wrong, Bindeshwar Pathak argues, our Father of the Nation, who is known as one of the saviour of Dalit and campaigner against untouchability by the people of India than Jyoti Rao Phule and Ambedkar – all put together. This is why it is important to point out ignorance and falsehoods in his claims. For example service to the cause of removal of untouchability as well as upliftment of the untouchables by Mahatma Gandhi have become proverbial. A majority of scholastic discussions with respect to SC and ST masses, however, suffer from one serious flaw. The drawbacks in the Gandhian approach to the untouchables are carefully and cautiously overlooked or avoided. A critical appreciation of the totality of the contribution with all its pros and cons is not attempted. There is the seed and danger of deification. His total personality is not presented to the public. Nothing except encomiums about Gandhi is tolerated whereas a balanced approach calls for weighing both the plus and minus, weak and strong points in the character and actions of the great man. Some of the actions and utterances of Gandhi are commonly not known. Those teachings and/or thoughts of the Mahatma are not in sync with his popular image. Historical facts, incompatible with the image built by hype, are shut out of public view. Else, there cannot be any doubt, some of the sayings and utterances of Gandhi, if presented, will create disbelief, if not consternation in common man because of its strong bias for maintaining the Indian caste pyramid characterized by graded inequality, in fact, unscratched.

Fine Exposition of Human Feelings

But can we depute an inspector to ascertain if and where the great Mahatma has taken rebirth, if at all. Neither an auditor can be drafted to compile a balance sheet as to the performance vis-á-vis promise made by the great son of India for the untouchables. The Hindu belief in rebirth is a convenient ploy to perpetuate one's status, social, religious, economic, etc. This ensures that *savarna* shall reign at the top and *avarna* slog at the bottom. It hurts more viciously the low-born by showing them the prospect of better life and endless bliss and happiness in next birth against selfless servitude towards high castes in present birth. They will, therefore, bear stoically the sufferings and wrongs done to them in present birth for millennium of happiness in next world: M.N. Roy[11] puts succinctly:

> 'The belief in transmigration fosters fatalism, destroys initiative. Spiritualist culture has taught the Indian masses to be resigned. The spirit of revolt is unknown in them. But they must revolt, otherwise, instead of saving the world with the message of their spiritual culture, they will themselves follow the other ancient peoples into oblivion. To conquer the future, the past must be shaken off. The people of India must have the conviction that man makes his own destiny. Karma, fate, transmigration, un-attachment, immortal spiritual essence, providential ordinance all these are ghost of the past. Let the past bury its dead, so that the people of India may live in future brighter than the present'.

Those who have not suffered the pangs of deprivation and social humiliation and injustice, have the knack of romanticizing the life and sufferings of the untouchables. Gandhi's refusal for moksha and desire for rebirth as Atisudra actually falls in this category of romantic reverie and blabbing. Those who genuinely appreciated the pangs of sufferings of the disadvantaged, had, like Abraham Lincoln, the President of USA, faced the bullets of assassin valiantly.[12] The great President did not hesitate to wage a civil war against his own countrymen. Putting off for tomorrow or next birth something that merits to be addressed here and now is only a convenient ploy to suppress the contours of the ultimate motive. Abraham Lincoln did not wait for next birth nor did he want to be a Black on rebirth. He fought against formidable odds, risked his life and achieved what he firmly believed at considerable cost both to the nation as well as to himself.

The kind of romanticization referred to above gives a golden escape route from the harsh realities of life, suspending infinitely the vital interests of the underdogs for remote future to the tender mercies of others. To live a life as an untouchable in the Hindu fold and to suffer the hatred and indignity bears no parallel under the sun. Their state of mind and feelings can perhaps be articulated in the words of Patrick Tamayo[13], a Black poet of America who gives vent to his anguish and excruciating pain thus:

> 'Step into my shoes, wear my skin
> See what I see, feel what I feel
> And then you shall know,
> Who I am, who I am, and why I am'.

Mahatma Gandhi had to face, for the first time, discrimination and ill treatment in South Africa where he went to earn a living. A few instances may be enumerated in his own words:

On his way to Pretoria, soon after his arrival in South Africa, he was denied the right of travelling in the first class train compartment though he held a ticket. In his own account[14], let us relate the incident:

> The train reached the capital of Natal at about 9 pm. Bedding used to be provided at the station. A railway servant came and asked if I need one. 'No, said I, I have one with me'. He went away. But a passenger came next and looked me up and down. He said that I was a coloured man. This disturbed him. Out he went and came in again with one or two officials. They all kept quiet, when another official came to me and said, 'Come along, you must go to the van compartment.'
>
> But I have first class ticket, said I.
>
> That doesn't matter, rejoined the other. I tell you, you must go in van compartment.
>
> I tell you I was permitted to travel in the compartment at Durban and I insist on going on in it.
>
> No, you won't, said the official. You must leave this compartment, or else I shall have to call a police constable to push you out.
>
> Yes, you may. I refuse to go out voluntarily.
>
> The constable came. He took me by hand and pushed me out. My luggage was taken out. I refused to go to other compartment and the train steamed away.'
>
> On a third, occasion[15] he was physically assaulted by a white man while travelling in a coach to Johannesburg. As an Indian, he was considered as coloured and a coolie. Gandhi was not allowed a proper seat in the coach though he had a ticket for the intended journey. He was being insulted by being asked to vacate his seat for the facility of smoking by a white co-traveller. He was offered a piece of dirty sack 'which was spread on the footboard' and was shown with the direction thus 'Sami you sit on this'. He refused to obey, whereupon the man came down upon him and began heavily to box his ear. 'He seized by the arm and tried to drag me down. I clung to the brass rails of the coach box and determined to keep my hold even at the risk of breaking my wrist bones ... He was strong and I was weak'.

Insult on a foreign land by members of the alien ruling race was sure to have its far reaching consequences on Gandhi. Should not it surprise many why he did not see discrimination and hatred in India which is the highest temple of inequality sanctified by Hindu religion before his assault in South Africa. How did the Shudra and untouchables, who in those days, as it is today, used to be given ignominious and barbarous treatment by the Hindus in the name of caste and religion without any compunction and feelings of sympathy escape the notice of the Mahatma? The Mahatma was in South Africa for a part of his life, spanning over 22 years. This was little over one-third of his life that he spent in foreign land. But the initial couple of months or so, as per his autobiographical accounts, were encountered by insults and indignities. That was the period of bitter memories for the Mahatma. On the other hand, he had his moments of victory as well as joy on that land.

Has anybody ever imagined what does it mean to be insulted, incarcerated and repressed in one's own home for whole life? There is a gulf of difference between insult abroad and outrageous treatment at home before the eyes of one's own relations and neighbours. Over thousands of years, millions of untouchables have been subjected to insult, humiliation and indignity in their own motherland. Gandhi was insulted when his near and dear ones were not witness to it. The untouchables, on the other hand, have been traditionally brutalized and stigmatized in their own home before the eyes of their parents, wives, children, neighbours and friends ages after ages. This not only demoralizes the victims, but the whole kith and kin are, as a result, terrorized and traumatized. Since caste is the basis for barbaric treatment, all the untouchable castes face demoralization, and fear and feeling of persecution grips them. Sustained humiliations and aggression on the dignity robs them of the sense of self-esteem, confidence, independent judgment and judicious decision, it produces in them fatalism, and insensitivity to torture, it emaciates their vigour and vitality, and kills their spirit and initiative as well as aspiration for better life. They are despondent, lifeless and listless. Helpless, rudderless and aimless, they become men of relaxed frames of no creative activities. They cannot undertake any enterprise with courage and determination. They are not imaginative nor do they have initiative.

As victims of fatalism, they set their eyes and hearts to the next world. Due to motivated propaganda unleashed by cunning people, they are convinced that the other world is the realm of all happiness for them. The next birth will take them to their dreamland. The next world for them is green. To make it greener still they turn their present birth into deserts of self-inflicted injuries and unhappiness. The scriptural teachings induce them to think that the more the self-negation, self-deprivation and self-surrender, the greater is the store/treasure of bliss and happiness on their rebirth. This they can achieve by making the present totally sour and unbearable against which they shall not utter a word. They should not aspire for anything for themselves here and now but perspire for others as beasts of burden, regardless of every hardship and sufferings. They will safeguard their next world by destroying their present. As a game plan and strategy, it is superb. The cruel minds and ugly faces of the people who designed it were without parallel.

They are to be aided by others. They are controlled by others. Their existence is pathetic and life pitiable. They feel and start believing too that they are inferior even to animals. It generates inefficiency, affects productivity, increases wastage and retards economic growth. Such a situation ultimately arrests the progress of the nation. But they, nevertheless, are not burden on others. On the contrary, others have been burden on them for centuries. They have carried on their heads and shoulders heavy and unbearable burden of whole of the Aryans.

Little gesture of sympathy makes them grateful. An insignificant show of mercy makes them forget all oppression. Little piety brings tears to their eyes and glow on their face. Suddenly they are transformed into lively men/women.

These people are the most faithful. They never challenge the authority. They rather obey the authority, even if tyrannical. In a state like this, rebellion by the oppressed is out of question. Fatalism is so deeply ingrained through orchestrated propaganda that the victim takes insults and indignities as pre-ordained. Therefore, nothing is done against such divine dispensation. The state of the oppressed is beyond human interference or intervention. The oppressor too considers that there is nothing wrong to hurt and outrage the dignity of the low because he is ordained to do it. Hindu conscience is not roused. No Hindu felt ashamed. They are proud of and engrossed in their religion and the theory of pre-ordination. Even if stirred out of sympathy, nothing has been done to end a remorseless and highhanded system. Rather it has been supported and reinforced.

A worm even turns.[16] A dog barks at someone he considers inimical and chases his attacker. The untouchables never raised a voice against his oppressor nor they stood up against tyranny. The question is who did emasculate them? Maltreatment on the foreign land made Gandhi rebellious. He held the British rule in India as satanic and vowed to end the Raj. He came to the firm conclusion that British rule in India was not in the interest of Indians. It was against her economic and political interest. The alien rule was against the growth and development of Indian mind and intellect. The British rule offended the culture of India. The insult and humiliation at the hands British in South Africa dawned on him this realization which actually propelled him to a long and successful political odyssey that terminated in the transfer of power from the British to the Indians. Here is a valuable lesson. A treatment marked by compassion and courtesy would have perhaps delayed the ultimate political freedom of India from foreign yoke. To Gandhi the end of foreign rule in India was sacred duty and ultimate goal of Indians.

Untouchability sanctified by Hinduism offended the Atisudras or the low castes.[17] It was not in their interest to suffer socio-cultural, economic and religious disabilities That was in the interest of the upper caste Hindus. To keep the untouchables under the heels was to yield enormous economic gains to the touchables. The moral and intellectual development, and economic prosperity of the former was arrested and stunted by caste system. The caste system is as much satanic for *avarnas*, as the British rule for India. Caste is against overall interest of the untouchables in the same manner as the British rule harmed the interest of the nation. Hence, Gandhi was against alien rule. He went against it because he was insulted by the racial ruling class and their hirelings. That roused in him a sense of abhorrence and antipathy against the British. It was quite natural for any man with self-esteem. The contrary is unnatural and unexpected. The domination of the low castes by the high castes is equally satanic and against the interests of the *avarnas*. Gandhi's struggle against the foreign rule was patriotic movement, the struggle of the SCs and STs against the upper caste hegemony is equally patriotic as the less fortunate will be liberated from the bondage. It will ultimately benefit the country, though the high caste few may not like it.

It is seen that a picture was painted by Gandhi himself as if he himself associated with Bhangi and claimed as their friend and colleague. In his own words:[18]

> 'I count myself a Harijan and it pleases me to call myself a "Bhangi" among them, because that is the lowest caste of Harijans. When I stayed recently in the sweeper's quarters in the Delhi the Harijans there too complained against the use of the word "Bhangi". They suggested Mehtar'.

Whatever the origin of the word may be, Bhangi is in my opinion another name for Shivaji – whether you call a sweeper, a Mehtar or Bhangi, like Shivaji' he brings health to man. The one brings it by keeping the home clean, the other cleanliness than man.[19]

As stated earlier, Gandhi was staunch supporter of Varna Dharm. He wanted that a person should not change his traditional occupation which his forefathers were following. He went to the extent of asserting that change of occupation primarily meant as violation of Varnadharm. That is why Gandhi intended for a person to follow hereditary calling. In other words, Gandhi was bent upon to keep Bhangis within the Hindu fold. In this context, the words of Gandhi are pertinent. He has said:[20]

> '...That a person creates confusion of caste when he leaves his hereditary calling is obvious. When a Brahmin begins to earn his bread by say, following the profession of a barber or engineer, he does create confusion of caste, as much as when a barber or an engineer to impart religious instructions as means of livelihood. In the Gita, the adjective used in reference to women is wicked. It has therefore, reference probably to promiscuous intercourse rather than the off – spring born of the sacred tie of marriage.'
>
> The law of Varna prescribes that a person should for his living follow the lawful occupation of his forefather.[21]
>
> A Bhangi who does his work willingly and faithfully will find favour with God.[22]

Again in his paper 'Harijan', in reply to a question Gandhi reiterated:[23]

> 'What I meant is, one born a scavenger must earn his livelihood by being a scavenger and then do whatever is as worthy of his hire as a lawyer or your President. That according to me is Hinduism'

He concentrated his attention on its removal by suggesting three specific modes or strategies for the purpose:[24]

(i) The inter-caste drinking and dinning.

(ii) Throwing open Hindu temples for untouchables.

(iii) In 1946, the inter-caste marriages specially between the untouchables and caste Hindus.

But all those Gandhi left to the persuasion and change of the heart of the caste Hindus to render of their motion not as a matter of patronage, but as a matter of duty.[25]

When the idea of declaring himself as a 'Harijan' by Gandhi in promoting the cause of untouchables was declared then it was criticized bitterly. Gandhi then wrote a letter to P.N. Rajbhoj, pleading for removal of discrimination against untouchables in socio-religious and educational spheres. This letter did evoke response from Rajbhoj, although, it was condemned, Rajbhoj questions Gandhi[26]:

> '... गांधी जी अपने आपको लाख हरिजन कहें, पर स्वयं उनके कहने या मानने से कोई उन्हें हरिजन समझेगा या किसी ने समझा हो, ऐसा हमें कोई विवरण नहीं मिलता। किसी ने उन्हें जाति के आधार पर (हरिजन के रूप में) दुत्कारा हो, अपने घर में प्रवेश न करने दिया हो, मंदिर में प्रवेश करने, कुएं पर चढ़ने से रोका हो या उन्हें देखकर कोई सनातनी दूर भागा हो, ऐसी जानकारी भी हमें नहीं मिलती। बावजूद इसके गांधी कुछ हरिजनों में प्रिय थे वे उनके नेता थे, कांग्रेस पार्टी की ओर से तो दलित मतों के लिए विशेष अभियान भी चलाया गया था जिसके सूत्रधार या अगुआ चाहे जो कहें, स्वयं गांधी थे हालांकि अधिकांश राजनीतिक प्रापेगंडा था, जिसकी आड़ में गांधीजी दलितों में नंबर वन बनना चाहते थे।'

Bhangis were sure that Gandhi would make them one of his main priorities, even though during his dramatic stay at Valmiki Mandir from 1946–1948, Bhangis issues were barely discussed. Somehow Gandhi had given the impression that merely staying in a Bhangi Basti would be enough to make Bhangis feel more happy on all fronts. The question of physical contact with Bhangis was, of course, his number one concern. Bhangis wanted Gandhi to intervene and announce fresh programme to improve their socio-educational and occupational conditions and inhuman treatment by caste Hindus. When those continued unabated, it was clear Gandhi and the Congress party were not paying much attention to their miserable conditions.

Even in other areas, despite Gandhi's talking long and hard about basics like removal of untouchability, progress on removal of night-soil had been negligible, so far. Bhangis still have to remove night-soil across the country and their children still do the same as they were doing several decades ago.

Gandhi and the Congress promised a lot, but actually gave very little. Bhangis are the backbone of our country. They have suffered for centuries. Today, they are hurt and disappointed. Gandhi had promised Bhangis that they meant a lot to them. It is a symbol of trust. Promise has to triumph over despair for the Bhangis of India. Yes the scenario is grim.

Contrary to Gandhi's treatment of untouchability, Ambedkar had traced the root of untouchability in the caste system which is an offshoot of the *varna* system and of an elaborate system of the Vamashram Dharma.

And now look at the what Ambedkar said about Hindus and Hinduism. In his own words:[27]

> It must be borne in mind that those who like Mr. Gandhi accept the Chaturvarna as an ideal form of society, either do not know the history of the mutual relation of the four variance or cherishing an illusion conjuring up of a vision for the purpose which they are out to service. For the fact is that the four varnas never formed a society based on co-operation efforts. The four varnas were animated by nothing, but a spirit of animosity towards one another. There would not be the slightest

> exaggeration to say that social history of the Hindus is a history not merely of class struggle but class war fought with such bitterness that even the marxist will find it difficult to cite parallel cases to match.

Caste system for Ambedkar enjoys religious sanction of the Hindu Dharmshastra. In this respect, it is not much different from *varna* system, which in Ambedkar's opinion was not divine in its origin but was legal and penal. Ambedkar had expressed this view on *Varna* system. Ambedkar said:[28]

> The established order is a hereditary order, both in status as well as in function, once an untouchable, always untouchable. Once a Brahmin, always a Brahmin. Once a sweeper, always a sweeper. Under it, those who are Baru high remain high, those who are low, remain low. In other words the established order is based on an in exonerable law of Karma or destiny which is fixed once and for all and can never be changed. This destiny has no relation to the merits of the individuals living, under it. An untouchable, however superior he may be mentally, is below a touchable in rank, no matter how inferior he may be morally. An untouchable, however poor he may be, must always take rank above an untouchable, however rich he may be.

> The Bhangis do unclean jobs. The main task is sweeping and scavenging, sweeping streets, cleaning drains and severs, removal of human excrete and animal waste, raising pigs, etc are their jobs. Since latrines in most cities do not have flush, the Bhangis have to carry buckets of human excretas on the head. The jobs that Bhangis do are not only undesirable, polluting and hard, but are also low paid.

Both untouchability and caste system have caused tremendous harm for the progress of the untouchables in India.

Completely supporting the caste system, Gandhi asked all Hindus, including the untouchables, to stick to their traditional duties or caste callings by eulogizing the occupation of scavenging, Gandhi[29] wrote in *Young India* on 17 November 1927:

> The law of Varna (system) ... prescribes that a person should, for his living, follow the lawful occupation of his forefathers ... A sweeper has the same (Occupational) status as a Brahmin.

This, he mentioned believing in traditional ordering of the Hindu society for preserving the social harmony and growth of the soul and also by accepting all traditional caste callings or occupations equally honourable in the social esteem.[30] But a question is often from the Dalit perspective that why the forefathers of Gandhi, also Gandhi himself did not stick to their traditional caste occupation of petty business. This question still remains unanswered.

Ambedkar, on his part, fought throughout his life for the socio-economic and political empowerment of the Dalits. His main dictates to his men were to educate, take up white collar employment and achieve power through the democratic means or the Parliamentary democracy. Needless to say that since his entry into active politics in the 1920 up to Viceroy's Cabinet as member to the dawn of the Independence, Ambedkar relentlessly fought and succeeded in getting formally incorporated in the Indian Constitution, a number of socio-economic and political concessions in favour of Dalits in general and

Bhangis in particular, as stated earlier. Even he sent R.R. Bhole, immediately after the constitution of the Commission for Safai Karamcharis, to Philadelphia from India to present the socio-economic conditions of Bhangis in the International Conference on Labour. For, Ambedkar felt necessary for apprising the world about socio-economic conditions of Bhangis in the British India and for the social uplift and betterment of Bhangis and the poorest of the poor. Thus, Ambedkar effectively influenced the Bhangis in pre-independent India as he remained in Viceroy Cabinet only for a brief period (1942–1946) and he had almost his lone voice.

Ambedkar said that Gandhism is no different from Hinduism. It is a refined form of Hinduism. It has removed and polished the sharp edges of the Hinduism. According to Ambedkar:[31]

> What is there in Gandhism which is not to be found in orthodox Hinduism? There is caste in Hinduism, there is caste in Gandhism. Hinduism believes in low of hereditary profession, so does Gandhism. Hinduism enjoins cow worship, so does Gandhism. Hinduism upholds the law of karma, predestination of man's condition in this world, so does Gandhism. Hinduism accepts the authority of Shastras. So does Gandhism. Hinduism believes in avatars or incarnation of God. So does Gandhism. All that Gandhism has done is to find a philosophic justification for Hinduism and its dogmas. Hinduism is held in the sense that it is just a set of rules which bears in its face the appearance of crude and cruel system. Gandhism applies thc philosophy which smoothens its surface and gives it the appearance of decency and respectability and so alters it and embellishes it as to make it even attractive. What philosophy dose Gandhism propound to cover the nudity of Hinduism? The philosophy can be put in a nutshell. It is philosophy which says that all that is in Hinduism is well, all that is in Hinduism is necessary for public good.

Whatever stands[32] in the way to self-esteem and self-development of the low and the neglected the sufferers should stand up and raise voice against it. Any thing that promises, provokes and finally perpetuate interest of the high-born and milinates against the low and the neglected should be demolished with disdain it merits. It will promote national interest and happiness. If they fail in raising their voice, the harmful system will be endowed with longer life much against the interest of the sufferers. Sufferers can accept, thus, at their own peril. There goes a great moral.

> 'It may be your interest to be our masters, but how can it be ours to be your slaves?'[33]

In 1946, Gandhi's two decades long activism for the untouchable rights was severely criticized by B.R. Ambedkar (What Congress and Gandhi have done to the Untouchables), by J.E. Sanjana (in the pages of *Rast Rahbar* – a Gujarati newspaper and in his 'caste and outcaste').[34] Besides, the sweepers union also played an important part in criticizing Gandhi's drama of Bhangis in Delhi.[35]

When Gandhi mistfully spoke of being reborn a sweeper, Sanjana pointed out in his writings, 'Caste and Outcaste', that:[36]

'He (Gandhi) can easily and promptly (be, reborn) in this very life by going and living among, say, Bhangis – who do admit outsiders into their caste and becoming one of them, instead of generously wishing to do so in the next problematic incarnation'.

Critique questioned Gandhi's claim. The fact is that there have been severe criticism or attack on Gandhi in India in past and in recent years. The critique asserted that the reality is that it was just issuing statement after statement like to be reborn, say Bhangis. These were just slogans. Shame on Gandhi for not becoming Bhangi in this very life. This is a shameful hard selling of Gandhi-Bhangi agenda.

When I heard in my childhood days about the social philosophy of Gandhi towards Bhangis, I was overjoyed and impressed. Because he desired to be reborn as Bhangi like me. Because he cleaned his own toilet like my mother and sisters cleaned the public latrines. But during my university days (as student) when I read Ambedkar literature about Gandhi I was shocked and disappointed by nasty political theories that surrounded the issue of the untouchables in general and Bhangis in particular. My supposed sins include my being a long time Gandhi admirer and I had put too much faith in the good sense of Gandhi. After a few years, I rejected the shameful narrative of Gandhi trust and respect that Congressmen, *netas* and leaders had created. It was a slap, a tight slap, since I was an educated Bhangi youth in the face of upper caste Hindus hate mongers like Gandhi. I tell you, I have never been so proud of being a Gandhi admirer as I was at that moment. After I graduated, I began to appreciate the intellectual virtues of Dr B.R. Ambedkar.

Gandhi made an attempt to overcome their socio-educational and religious disabilities. However, this did not create any enthusiasm among the masses. In early 1990s, radical Balmikis said in a statement:[37]

'Gandhi has killed our caste', ... which refers to the Balmiki tendency to work within system of power rather than in opposition to the established state of privilege'.

This was manifestation of anger of Bhangis with Gandhi.

The First Non-Violent Strike in India by Chandalas[38] (1873)

It is important to discuss the first non-violent strike in British India by Chandalas based on article written by A.K. Biswas, a retired IAS officer and also former Vice-Chancellor, Ambedkar University, Muzafarpur, Bihar, which appeared in *Outlook* (English edition), 29 August 2016. According to him, the first non-violent strike in 1873, by Chandala (also known as Bhangi), is barely recognized in historiography. Gandhi was infant then and Tolstoy's writing on non-violence which so influenced him came out only in 1896. Since the Chandalas of Bengal and in other parts of India were generally placed at the bottom of the untouchables, the term 'non-violent', was first used during the 1873 strike by the Chandalas but it was ignored. Thus, most of the writers, scholars, researchers, historians, sociologists intellectual elites and others refers to Gandhi as initiator of term 'non-violent' in the sphere of politics during the national movement. In fact, 1873 proved to be the year of non-violent movement. This year was the first manifestation of the feeling of the Chandala subjects of Bengal caused by denial to their rights. Thus, the Chandalas were not given the credit.

It is said that history repeats itself. For instance, in 1873 the Chandalas of Bengal, from region to region the name of Chandalas caste varies, but the common name for caste/community across the country is the Bhangi, the lowest of low untouchables, who in 1911 were officially redesignated as Namasudhra, called for a strike in Faridpur district (now in Bangladesh) refusing to work for other Hindus and Muslims. It is vividly detailed in a book published very recently in 2015 by West Bengal's Department of Backward Classes, '*The 1873 Movement for Dignity and Equality Before Law*'. The strike brought normal life to a standstill. Significantly, this was when Bengal was witnessing a 'renaissance' which was quite unmindful of the suffering of untouchables.

It all began in Amgram village, where a rich Chandala, Choron Sapah, invited 10,000 men to a feast as part of his father's Shraddh ceremony. He invited people of all castes, including Brahmins and Kayasthas. The Kayasthas reportedly instigated others, and they 'refused to accept the invitation, couching their refusal with taunts and reproaches'. Eat with men who permit their women to go to the market and who are employed as Mehtars in jails for removing filth and every thing unclean? What next 'was the refrain'.

This was reported after an inquiry conducted by the Superintendent of Police, W.L. Owen. He noted:

> 'The women of the poorer Chandals attend hauts and bazars for buying and selling purposes, on which account they have been depised by Hindus of higher caste, who consider them only little better than beasts'...

The insult of their women did not go down well with Chandala community leaders. The aggrieved Chandalas leaders, therefore, adopted in a meeting three momentous resolutions.

One, Chandala woman must not visit future hauts (haats) and bazars,

Two, Chandala men and women would not join any 'Service' with other castes.

Thirdly, food prepared by any caste other than Brahmins would not be partaken.

The strike drew the attention of the colonial administration. In a letter on 18 March 1873, Owen speculated on the impact:

> If the second resolution is literally carried out, much injury will be sustained by other castes ... at present fields belonging to Mohammedans and other castes are cultivated by Chandals; these would remain unfilled. Boats are built and manned by Chandals, those belonging to other castes would cease to ply and trade will be paralysed. Agricultural and domestic tools of iron would not be repaired.

The Faridpur Chandala strike was joined by their caste brother's of adjoining Buckergunge (now Barisal) and Jessore district. But the strikes did not resort to violence, peace and order remained undisturbed.

The district Magistrate of Faridpur, W.S. Wells, reported to the Government:

> 'A large body of Hindus and Mohommedans came up to complain to me of the ruinous effects arising out of the action of the Chandals'.

He recorded:

> 'The fields remained untilled, houses unthatched and not a Chandal was in the service of any Hindu or Mussulman. The Magistrate warned that they (Chandals) have always been united and this movement may become very serious'.

At its root was the government compelling Chandala prisoners to work as sweepers and clean prison toilets. The district officer, in a letter on 22 April 1873, admitted:

> 'It is a most humiliating reproach, which should be removed. Under our law men are equal, but Chandals have no such equality if they alone are obliged to perform the most degrading duties'.

The Chandalas asked:

> 'Why were Brahmins, Kayasthas, Sudras and Mussulmans exempted from the dirty work in Jails'? The strike of 7,54,323 Chandals in three districts continued for six months'.

Lieutenant Governor of Bengal Sir George Campbell issued orders to the effect that:

> 'The Chandals in jail should not be forced to do the work of the sweepers'. (vide Letter No. 523 T., 7 June 1873)

Dalits and tribal communities form over 23 per cent of India's population, though they are denied justice and dignity by Hindu elite castes. Their refusal to dispose carcasses and clean streets is a potential nightmare. Together, this makes a formidable force that promises the road for their emancipation.

Bhangi's Strike and New Face of Gandhi Congress

Col. Saleeman,[39] an Englishman, was an officer in East India Company. In 1834, when the Bhangis of Oudh had gone on strike and after 1834' s strike, Saleeman wrote a book entitled *Ramblings in Oudh*. One of the unique features of Saleeman's book is to discuss the Bhangis strike activities in different parts of Oudh and it also appeared that he was fed up and very much perturbed about the strike. The book, thus, became the first and chief source of information/activities of the Bhangis strike in India.

The Bhangis normally do not go on strike. As regards their wage, dress, broom, soap, accommodation, sanitation tools and other facilities, they often met the authority. This approach, however, have not adversely effected the public life. On the contrary, the refusal of the authority compelled them to go on strike.

The use of strike by poor is an old one. During British rule and later, Bhangi community was denied opportunities of various kinds which they acquired after a series of intense agitations. Thus, Bhangis used strike even before the Marx. This is the story of genesis and growth of Bhangis strike over a period of nearly 181 years. The questions that arise now are: during British rule Gandhi observed several times fast, staged dharnas, went on strike and also started the Disobedience Movement against British rule. Besides, Gandhi even went on indefinite hunger strike (fast) in Yeravada Jail, Poona (Pune) against the separate electorates for untouchables or Communal ward. Gandhi justified all these strategies for political gain. But he was dead against the Bhangi's strike. In 1946, when Bhangis of Bombay and Lucknow went on strike, Gandhi not only vehemently opposed it but also criticized it bitterly, why? We shall address these questions in the section that follows.

During the British rule both caste Hindus and the untouchables accepted Gandhi as their God. One thing had to be admitted, had Gandhi expressed a few words of sympathy to Bhangi strike, this would have roused the consciousness of the British Government and would have given the greatest impetus to the strike for the uplift of the Bhangis, the poorest people. But Gandhi not only condemned and criticized the Bhangis' strike, he also pointed out that Bhangis must not go on strike for their demands. The news shocked the Bhangi Samaj like an earthquake.

It may be reproduced what Gandhi expressed in his book *Removal of Untouchability* relating to Bhangi's strike. In his own words:[40]

> My opinion against sweepers strike dates back to about 1897 when I was in Durban. A general strike was mooted there and the question arose as to whether the scavengers there should join it. My vote was registered against the proposal.
>
> Therefore, I was perturbed when I read about the sweepers' strike in Bombay. Fortunately, it has *come to an end. I understand however, that the sweepers, both men and women refused to submit their case to arbitration.
>
> In spite of my close attachment to sweepers, better because of it, I must denounce the coercive methods they are said to have employed. They will thereby be losers in the long run. City folks will not always be cowed down. If they were, it would mean the collapse of municipal administration. Coercion cannot but result in the end in chaos. An impartial tribunal for settling disputes should always be accepted. Refusal is a sign of weakness. A Bhangi may not give up his work even for a day. And there are many other ways open to him of securing justice.

And now look at what Ambedkar said about Bhangis and their strike. In an attempt to suppress the strike, Safai Karamcharis were harassed, tortured and were also cruelly beaten. This news was widely published. The attitude of political parties, including Gandhi Congress and others towards the strike of Safai Karamcharis was non-supporting and non-cooperative and this led to increasing frustration among them. However, it may be noted here that Ambedkar not only made a statement attacking Bombay and Lucknow governments, but also supported Safai Karamcharis' agitation. His support had a direct effect on the strike as he was trying to establish a dialogue with authority and Safai Karamcharis leader to solve the deadlock.

Having discussed one instance of Bhangi strike in pre-Independence India, I shall now discuss another instance of Bhangi strike in post-Independence India. The main issue before Safai Karamcharis of Delhi in 1957 was agitation for increase of salary and other facilities, for the Bhangis were paid less. In 1957, Bhangis submitted a memorandum to the officers and the authority and staged a dharna. As we shall note later this way was very much similar to the stand adopted by Gandhi in 1945.

The character of the Congress changed with Pandit Jawaharlal Nehru becoming the first Prime Minister of India in 1947. Thus, the Congress which was pro-Dalits in pre-Independence, now in the post-Independence era moved away. This development should also be seen in context of continuing moving away from pro-Dalits. Thus, the Congress changed its attitude towards Bhangis and this time, Pandit Nehru expressed the similar views of 1945 relating to Bhangis strike. With the ruling party becoming hostile in its stand, it was likely that both administration and police became more hostile. As a result of all this, on 31 July 1957,[41] the police opened fire at Panchkuia Bhangi basti (colony) in Delhi during the strike. Police lathi-charged, them cruelly. Discussing this incident in his book, Bhagwan Das wrote that one Safai Karamchari was shot dead and 11 were injured seriously. Since 1957, every year in memory of their dead man, Bhangis in Delhi, celebrated 31 July as 'Safai Karamchari Divas'. This day is as important as 'May Day' for labour class.

On 26 July, speaking in Prarthna Sabha, Gandhi did not support Bhangis' strike, he considered the strike as harmful to people. He stated:[42]

> 'मैं चाहता तो यही हूं कि एक बैरिस्टर को जितना जैसा मिलता है उतना ही एक भंगी को भी मिले, परन्तु यह बात कहने में जितनी आसान है करने में उतनी ही मुश्किल है। दूसरे, ये सब बातें हड़ताल करने से पूरी नहीं होती। वेतन कमीशन की सिफारिशों से जो वेतन बढ़े हैं पहले हमें उन्हें हजम करना चाहिए और फिर बाद में अपने पक्ष में लोकमत तैयार करना चाहिए। हड़ताल का भी एक शास्त्र होता है, यों ही हड़ताल कर बैठने से कोई लाभ नहीं।
>
> आज तो हिन्दुस्तान में हड़तालों का एक वातावरण सा बन गया है जहां लोगों की अपनी हकूमतें हैं, वहां भी हड़ताल होती है। जब हमारे यहां अंग्रेजी हकूमत थी तब, जहां तक मुझे याद है, इतनी हड़तालें नहीं होती थी। आज कलकत्ते से तार आया है और अखबारों में भी छपा है कि वहां एकाउंटेंट जनरल ऑफिस के कर्मचारियों ने कलमबंद हड़ताल कर दी है। इस ऑफिस में डाक और तार घर शामिल हैं जो किसी एक आदमी की खातिर नहीं, बल्कि सब लोगों की भलाई के लिए चलते हैं। यह माना कि उनमें बड़े-बड़े अमलदार भी हैं जिन्हें काफी पैसा मिलता है। फिर छोटो ने क्या गुनाह किया है कि उन्हें थोड़ा पैसा मिलता है। आखिर इतना बड़ा अन्तर क्यों रहता है? अंग्रेजों ने यह आदत डाली, मगर हमको भी वह मीठी लगी और उसे हम जारी रख रहे हैं, परन्तु इस तरह से यदि लोग कलमबंद करके बैठने लगे तो हिन्दुस्तान का क्या होगा? हड़ताल के जरिए दबाव डालकर यदि कुछ पैसे उन्होंने बढ़वा भी लिए तो उससे क्या हुआ? मगर यह तरीका तो गलत है और इससे हिन्दुस्तान का सत्यानाश होने वाला है।
>
> इसके अलावा हड़ताल का तो मैंने शास्त्र बना रखा है। दक्षिण अफ्रीका में पहले पहल हमने इसकी आजमाईश की थी। वहां हिन्दुस्तानी कुली और मजदूर समझे जाते थे। वहां उनका हड़ताल करना कुछ मानी रखता था क्योंकि और तरह से वहां उनकी बात कोई सुनने वाला नहीं था। अतः वह आदमी जो हड़ताल का शास्त्र जानता है वह उन लोगों से जो कि आज इधर-उधर हड़ताल कर रहे हैं वह सूचना

देना चाहता है कि जो तरीका उन्होंने अपनाया है उससे वे अपना ही खात्मा कर लेंगे। हमारे देश के दो टुकड़े तो हो गए, मगर अब भी अगर हमारे आपस के झगड़े इसी तरह जारी रहे तो ईश्वर ही जानता है कि हमारा क्या हाल होने वाला है। अब तो हमारा यह धर्म हो गया है कि हम अपना काम करते जायें, क्योंकि वह हकूमत का काम है।

'बम्बई में, हाल ही में, मजदूरों की एक नाममात्र की हड़ताल हो चुकी है। वहां की सरकार ने एक-दो करोड़ रूपया तो मजदूरों को दिया, मगर उससे भी उनको संतोष नहीं हुआ और अपनी ताकत जाहिर करने के लिए उन्होंने एक नाममात्र की हड़ताल की। उन्हें चाहिए तो यह था कि जो कुछ मिल गया उसे तो हजम करते और उसके बाद अपने पक्ष में लोकमत बनाते। इसके बजाय उन्होंने हड़ताल करके पैसे बढ़वान का मार्ग अपनाया। कांग्रेस में भी आज जितनी पार्टियां बन गई है और उनमें से ही एक पार्टी का इस हड़ताल में हाथ है, ऐसा मुझे बताया गया है। मगर इस नाममात्र की हड़ताल में तो चाहे वह दो घंटे के लिए ही क्यों न हो, एक तरह का घमंड भरा रहता है। उससे वह पार्टी यह सिद्ध करने की कोशिश करती है कि उसकी मजदूरों में कितनी चलती है अन्यथा इस नाममात्र की हड़ताल का क्या उद्देश्य हो सकता था? मुल्क का इस प्रकार की हड़तालों से कोई भी भला नहीं हो सका। इसलिए वहां के मजदूरों ने जो कुछ किया वह मुझे अनर्थ लगा है।'

Ram Vilas Sharma also narrated in his book 'गांधी, अम्बेडकर लोहिया और भारतीय इतिहास की समस्याएं', published in 2000, that Gandhi was against the strike. More particularly Gandhi never supported Bhangis strike. On the contrary, he criticized it bitterly. Sharma wrote:[43]

'... हड़ताल पर सफाई मजदूर जाएं, यह तो उन्हें बिल्कुल स्वीकार ही नहीं था इसके लिए गांधीजी ने कहा, कुछ काम ऐसे हैं जिनके बारे में हड़ताल वर्जित होनी चाहिए। भंगियों का ऐसा ही है यानि भंगियों को किन्हीं भी परिस्थितियों में हड़तालें नहीं करनी चाहिये। यह गांधी की राय थी।'

No need to go far to seek demonstration of this fact. When Gandhi came to know through newspapers about the strike of Bhangis of Bombay, his immediate reaction was:[44]

'... जब मैंने बम्बई के सफाई कर्मचारियों की हड़ताल के बारे में पढ़ा तो मुझे मानसिक परेशानी हुई। एक भंगी को एक दिन के लिए भी अपना काम नहीं छोड़ना चाहिए।'

The conditions that prevailed at that time were such that nobody took courage to go against Gandhi's wishes. However, in 1921, a Congress leader from Andhra Pradesh wrote a letter to Gandhi, pleading for strike. Congress leader said in his letter:[45]

'हड़ताल को आपने गलत कदम बताया है लेकिन मुझे यह कहने की अनुमति दीजिए कि हड़ताल के इन चंद दिनों में गुंटूर में जो जन जागृति हुई है वह वर्षों के परिश्रमपूर्वक किये गये प्रचार कार्य से भी नहीं हो सकती थी। इसके सिवाय इस स्वरूप काल में लोगों में संयम और आत्म निर्णय के गुणों का भी बहुत अच्छा विकास हुआ है।'

This letter did evoke response from Gandhi, although it was not encouraging. Gandhi said in his endorsement:[46]

'कार्य समिति की अनुमति लिए बिना हड़ताल करने के खिलाफ मेरा जो विरोध है वह तो इसके बाद भी कायम है।'

Whenever the labour went on strike, including the Bhangis' strike, who supported the agitation and strike? Bhagwan Das has tried to answer this question. A brief description, given by Mohandas Naimishrai, from Bhagwan Das's writings clearly showed Ambedkar backing Bhangi's strike. Bhangis had been associated with Ambedkar. If we analyse the socio-political relationship between Ambedkar and Bhangis, we feel that Ambedkar always promoted Bhangi leaders and social activists to agitate and fight against social injustice. Therefore, Ambedkar had publically supported Bhangis strike in Bombay, says political analyst Bhagwan Das.

Besides, many a time, even Ambedkar[47], along with his colleagues of Bombay legislators, had a hot discussion with Congress legislators on Bhangi issues. Thus, Bhangis were lucky to have been supported Ambedkar.

Gandhi and Bhangis Dinning

The first and foremost characteristic of Gandhi was that he called himself a Bhangi. On every trip to Delhi, Gandhi used to visit Bhangi colony and live with them and show a will to live among them. It means sharing happiness and sorrows and in sharing, the basis was love. So it was a formalistic, fraternal social order. This togetherness was the first necessity to win the hearts of the Bhangis in particular and untouchables in general. In this sense Gandhi's cause be termed as revolutionary. Gandhi wanted to change the hearts of *sarvarnas* so that untouchability could be abolished.

From the Dalit perspective, certain sets of pertinent questions were raised. Did Gandhi accept cooked food, touched water and took fruits from the hands of residents of Bhangi colony? Whenever Bhangis offered fruits, Gandhi never accepted and indicated them to give it to the she goat. He will drink her milk – Why? While in Delhi, Gandhi insisted on living in the Bhangi colony, where all dignitaries, British or Indian had to go to Bhangi Basti and meet Gandhi and where many momentous meetings of Working Committee of Congress were held. Were all these meetings held within five star facilities? Was Gandhi living in the same social environment in which Bhangis were living?

These questions demanded immediate answers from Gandhi or from the Gandhians. Such questions need to be addressed seriously with adequate replies, else in the absence of these all the concerns and strategies of Gandhi or of Gandhians may appear to be mere political rhetoric as presently termed by Dalits in the country.

Gandhian Studies have not elaborated these aspects/issues or taken courage to look into it, while much was made of Gandhi's visit to the Bhangi Basti, Gandhi's supporters or followers used Gandhi as a symbol of Bhangi saviour. However, after more than five decades, the first attempt was made by Bhagwan Das in 1996, when he addressed these issues. Thus, Bhagwan Das revealed the truth.

In this context, the observations of Bhagwan Das and others are pertinent. Bhagwan Das said that removal of untouchability had become a part of Gandhi's life. While living in the Bhangi Basti in Delhi, Gandhi also made it a point not to accept food and water from the hands of Bhangis. Bhangis Das wrote:[48]

'गांधी जी न किसी के हाथ का छुआ पानी पीते थे और न उसके घर में पका खाना खाते थे। अगर कोई व्यक्ति फल आदि उन्हें भेंट करने के लिए लाता था तो वो कहते थे कि मेरी बकरी को खिला दो उसका दूध मैं पी लूंगा।'

Thus, discrimination against the Bhangis was practised by Gandhi, the extent of which it is impossible for an outsider to imagine. It was of most virulent type.

I agree with Bhagwan Das , the eminent writer on Bhangi's issue, that all this Gandhi propaganda should be stopped. Bhagwan Das was a literate Bhangi and had come in contact with Ambedkar. Of course that influenced Bhagwan Das. Bhagwan Das was intelligent enough to influence Ambedkar too.

Gandhi's curiosity may well have been genuine and not governed by any thing sinister. However, not accepting any thing from the Bhangi has opened speculations over Gandhi's stay in Bhangi Basti.

The story, as it has unfolded over the years, is sad and it is understandable that many people are convinced that there was a conveniently ignored real truth about Gandhi's fight against untouchability.

Gandhi was confused because he did not know what he must do with Bhangis, whether to elevate Bhangis or marginalize them. He had to answer the people. It is to be seen whether Gandhi's politics supported the eradication of untouchability which meant for the upliftment of the poor Bhangis or it continued on the traditional Hindu line and opposing for the sake of opposition.

That was the first time in Indian politics that an important leader of a political party, such as Gandhi himself, created such an anxiety that the sensation level went so high that people dared to question Gandhi on not accepting things from Bhangis' hands and the stay in Bhangi Basti by Gandhi to eradicate untouchability had not borne fruit due to rigid following of Santani Dharma.

This was the wrong way forward. The right way forward must include inter-dinning with Bhangis to remove the restriction imposed on inter-dinning. Simply living in a Bhangi basti is just an outwardly exercise. Gandhi had proved conclusively that he lacked the motivation to succeed. The Bhangis are untouchable amongst untouchables, poorest of the poor and lowest of the low. Everybody agrees that Bhangis are the greatest sufferers and the worst victims of untouchability than other untouchables. Why then there was not inter-dinning with Bhangis? The answer is that Gandhi wanted the uplift but not strongly enough to launch agitation.

Gandhi, who launched agitation against untouchability for more than three decades, no longer talked about inter-dinning with the Bhangis. Campaign against untouchability had become a Gandhi slogan. Gandhi had no answer. So silence was his best policy.

The higher classes are the higher castes of India and they are free from the blot of illiteracy. The lower strata of the Hindus, on the other hand, furnish the overwhelming majority of the world's 50 per cent illiterates. Caste has promoted as well as contributed to illiteracy contrary to the Gandhian claim. Light is to darkness what education is to caste and obscurantism.

'I believe inter-dinning and inter-marriages are not necessary for promoting national unity. That dinning together creates friendship is contrary to experience. If this was true there would have been no war in Europe. Taking food is as dirty an act as answering the call of nature.'[49]

> 'In India children of brothers do not intermarry. Do they cease to love because they do not intermarry.'[50]

In the second decade of the 20th century certain organizations, namely Indian National Congress, Hindu Mahasabha, Arya Samaj, Muslim Organizations, Christian Missionaries and Dalit Organizations, were active and attempts were made by them to fight for their rights. By 1927, Gandhi's influence was widespread. Ambedkar and Periyar, enlightened Dalit leaders, were fighting because of indignities and humiliation heaped upon untouchables by caste Hindus. While Gandhi, supporting the Hindu four-fold system, emphasized on Dalit emancipation, Savarkar and Hindu Mahasabha wanted to keep untouchables in the grip of caste Hindus at any cost. These attempts, however, did not acquire the character of a movement and it was only with propagation of Ambedkar's agitation that it emerged as a widespread movement.

Pandit Nand Kishore Tiwari, editor of *Chand* – a monthly magazine (Hindi) which Ramrakh Singh Sahgal had started in 1922 from Allahabad, UP, published a special issue called 'अछूत अंक' in 1927 depicting the atrocities committed by caste Hindus on untouchables through cartoon. At that time caste Hindus in general and Brahmins in particular maintained the social distance with untouchables and did not touch them. But Pandit Nand Kishore Tiwari, the then editor of issue, 'अछूत अंक', supported the untouchables' cause. For instance, on front page of the magazine a photograph of Pandit Nand Kishore Tiwari and Banshi Lal Kori (Chamar) having food in the same *thali* was shown and published. In Feburary 2005, Virendra Yadav, a noted writer, wrote an essay 'चांद का' अछूत अंक: दलित विमर्श की पूर्व पीठिका in 'तद्‌भव' (अंक 12, फरवरी 2005, पृ. 84–99) criticized Gandhi and others bitterly. The essay carried the following story:

> 'धर्म, पाप और प्रायश्चित की इस पदावली और हिन्दू धर्म पर आसन्न संकट से आक्रांत होने के बावजूद 'अछूत अंक' के दलित सरोकार गांधी व सुधारवादी हिन्दू संगठनों से भिन्न थे। पत्रिका के मुखपृष्ठ पर इस अंक के सम्पादक पंडित नन्दकिशोर तिवारी व प्रेस के ललित कम्पोजिटर बन्शीलाल कोरी (चमार) का साथ एक ही थाली में भोजन करते हुए एक चित्र प्रकाशित है। आज से आठ दशक पूर्व एक सरयूपारीय ब्राह्मण का चमार जाति के व्यक्ति के साथ एक ही थाली में भोजन करते चित्र छपवाना कितना दुस्साहस पूर्ण रहा होगा इसका सहज ही अनुमान लगाया जा सकता है। विशेषकर तब और भी जब गांधी सरीखें अछूतोद्धारक भी अपने अंतिम वर्षों तक दलितों के साथ भोजन करने का आत्मबल नहीं जुटा पाये थे। इस संबंध में गांधी के दिल्ली की भंगी कॉलोनी के निवास के दिनों की अप्रेल 1946 की घटना को याद करना प्रासंगिक होगा जब गांधी ने दलितों के साथ भोजन करने से इंकार कर दिया था।' (पृ. 86–87)

In another instance, narrated in Vijay Prasad's book *Untouchables Freedom* published recently from the Oxford University Press also played an important part in removing mask of Gandhi. The attitude of Gandhi towards the emancipation of Bhangis to overcome their socio-religious disabilities were not positive and this led to increasing frustration among Bhangis. Some scholars began to question the sincerity of Gandhi for overcoming their religious and civic deprivations. In his essay, Virendra Yadav quoting, Vijay Prasad, elaborated it in detail thus:

> 'ऑक्सफोर्ड यूनिवर्सिटी प्रेस से प्रकाशित अपनी पुस्तक 'अनटचेबल फ्रीडम' में विजय प्रसाद ने इस घटना का खुलासा कुछ यूं किया है – 'दलितों के लिए गांधी का प्रयास उस भेदभाव को अनुभव करने का अवसर था जो सवर्ण हिन्दू नेतृत्व को उनसे अलग करता है। जाहिरा तौर पर सबसे बड़ी बाधा साथ खानपान की थी। 3 अप्रैल 1946 को जब वाल्मीकि समुदाय के लोगों ने गांधी को खाने पर अपने घर बुलाया तो उन्होंने संकोच के साथ कहा कि 'अच्छा हो कि जो धन आप मेरे भोजन आव भगत में खर्च करेंगे उसे एक हरिजन बच्चे की शिक्षा पर करें। आप मुझे बकरी का दूध दे सकते हैं लेकिन उसका भुगतान में करूंगा। यदि आप चाहते हैं कि आपके द्वारा पकाया हुआ भोजन ग्रहण करूं तो आप मेरे यहां आकर मेरे लिए भोजन बना सकते हैं। उन्होंने बाल्मीकि समुदाय द्वारा आवभगत के इस प्रस्ताव से किनाराकशी करते हुए इस अवसर को दुर्व्यवसनों (शराब पीना, जुआ खेलना व वेश्यावृत्ति करना) पर बेकार के खर्चों के मशविरे में बदल दिया। बाल्मीकियों के बुजुर्ग आज भी गांधी के इस पाखंड की चर्चा किंचित असहजता के साथ करते हुए बताते हैं कि जब उनमें से एक ने गांधी को सूखे मेवे खाने को दिये तो उन्होंने उसे अपनी बकरी को यह कहते हुए खिला दिया कि बाद में वे इसे बकरी के दूध के रूप में ग्रहण कर लेंगे। गांधीजी के लिए उन दिनों भोजन व खाद्य सामग्री बिरला हाऊस से आती थी, वे इसे दलितों से नहीं ग्रहण करते थे।' (पृ. 87)

Virendra Yadav further highlighted that Gandhi was not good at heart and in thought regarding Bhangis and their occupation and inter-dinning. When he started his reform movement in India, Gandhi intentionally confined it to temple entry, school admission only. But he never discussed the economic idea of reform. It is a misconception that Gandhi did good in the past. Yadav made a statement attacking Gandhi:

> 'गांधी अपने दलित सरोकारों में सहभोज व अन्तर्जातीय विवाह के युक्त पक्षधर नहीं थे। चांद के अछूत अंक में ही अन्त्यजों का प्रश्न शीर्षक गांधी की एक टिप्पणी प्रकाशित है जिसमें उनका मत है कि 'सहभोज आदि आंदोलनों को धक्का देने की आवश्यकता नहीं है। इस आंदोलन से वर्णाश्रम धर्म का लोप नहीं हो सकता। इसका उद्देश्य उसके अतिरिक्त या ज्यादती को निकाल कर उसकी रक्षा करना है। इस आंदोलन के पुरस्कर्ताओं की यह भी इच्छा नहीं है कि भंगी आदि अपने-अपने काम छोड, दें, किन्तु उन्हें यह दिखा देना है कि मल, गंदगी आदि साफ करने का उद्यम आवश्यक और पवित्र है'। इस संबंध में इतिहासकार सुमित सरकार का सटीक निष्कर्ष है कि 'गांधीजी ने जानबूझ कर हरिजन आंदोलन को सामाजिक सुधार (हरिजनों के लिए सामाजिक कुआं, सड़कें और विशेष रूप से मंदिरों को खुलवाना, साथ में मानवतावादी कार्य) तक सीमित रखा था और किसी भी प्रकार की आर्थिक मांगों से अलग रखा था (यद्यपि अनेक हरिजन खेतिहर मजदूर थे), साथ ही उन्होंने समग्र रूप में जाति व्यवस्था की भर्त्सना करने से इंकार कर दिया। उन्होंने रोटी बेटी के व्यवहार में सावधानी बरतने की सलाह दी और मूल वर्णाश्रम धर्म की हिमायत की, जिसका परिणाम हुआ कि अम्बेडकर ने 'साप्ताहिक हरिजन के लिए यह कहते हुए संदेश देने से इन्कार कर दिया कि 'जाति व्यवस्था को नष्ट किये बिना अछूतों का उद्धार संभव नहीं है।' (पृ. 87)

The message is clear for the Bhangis, who had accepted Gandhi as saviour of Dalits in general and Bhangis in particular in the past. Since then, dissent has been festering among the Dalits. It also exposed Gandhi's Bhangi emancipation agitation that he had claimed. When Gandhi started his stay at Bhangi Basti

Panch Kuian, New Delhi, then food for Gandhi came from Birla's House and so he did not accept cooked food from Bhangis. This incident makes it clear that Gandhi's non- acceptance was in reality motivated by caste superiority.

In the matter of facilities, this is indeed a very glaring paradox. What is the explanation of this paradox? There is only one explanation of this paradox. It is that social environment had been against all the dignitaries: British or Indian had to go and meet him. Many momentous meetings of the Working Committee of Congress were held. As the socio-economic surroundings of Bhangi Bastis did not provide suitable atmosphere, the Congress provided five-star facilities to regard Gandhi as VVIP for leadership. It may not be an exaggeration to say that it was a good fortune of Gandhi.

Experience and traditions regarding untouchability tell us that despite the campaign against untouchability, a great deal of untouchability was observed in Bhangi Basti. The real fight against untouchability lies elsewhere. Talk to those aged Bhangis who were the eyewitness of the incidents and they will tell you that Gandhi never accepted food in the Bhangi Basti. Bhangis were being lured to believe that Gandhi's presence signalled their (Bhangis) acceptance on equal terms at the social level. But if campaign against untouchability truly worked, logic demands that at least Gandhi must have accepted food from the hands of Bhangis. As pointed out by some writers, there had been no such instance from Gandhi despite living in Bhangi Basti. In reality, living in Bhangi Basti had only created privileged sympathetic layer within untouchable communities.

This illustrates the point that campaign against untouchability had less to do with logic than to keep Bhangis together with the Congress. In other words, Gandhi wanted Bhangis to come into the Congress camp to take them away from Ambedkar's Dalit movement. But Gandhi failed to convert his stay in Bhangi Basti into anti-Ambedkar agitation. Gandhi may have attempted to change the wind but the harsh truth is that he had little impact.

Gandhi stayed in Bhangi Basti, but he denied to accept anything from Bhangis. Only a courageous leader could take up the cause. We think Gandhi had it in him to do so, but he could not. What we find difficult to explain is the motive behind not accepting food, etc. To me Sanatani influence could have been a legacy. That appears logical, I believe. What Bhangis find devious is Gandhi's apparent friendliness with residents of Bhangi Basti. Gandhi stayed at the Bhangi Basti during his visit to Delhi. It may also be claimed that pressure from Gandhi and successive Congress regimes had forced Congressmen to ignore it despite removal of untouchability being his pivotal agenda in his campaign. A little was done to eradicate untouchability over the years. It was Ambedkar who dealt the final blow and forced caste Hindus to legally abolish this discrimination. Ambedkar was not only a leader of one particular group/ underprivileged as a whole but of the country.

Having discussed the Gandhi and Bhangi inter-dinning issue, I shall now discuss Ambedkar and Bhangi inter-dinning in pre-Independence India.

One of the most significant events of Ambedkar movement was to promote inter-mixing between untouchable castes/communities and between Bhangis and other untouchables. All untouchable castes considered the Bhangi as most degraded untouchables and, therefore, had no commensal relations with them. Ambedkar realized the contradiction in that while Dalits were fighting against pollution as practised by the castes above them, they were themselves treating the Bhangis as most untouchables. Ambedkar advocated casteless society and started a programme of inter-dining. The credit of having started a movement of self-correction among the untouchables goes to Ambedkar. B.K. Gayakwad, the closest colleague of Ambedkar, narrated in D.D. Kalyani's book:

> 'Whenever Ambedkar visited Nasik some caste Hindus and Brahmins met him and invited him to have food with them'[51]

However, it may be noted that Ambedkar used to visit his friend's home. Rambhau Palajimaro and stayed there. Here Ambedkar used to take food. Ambedkar called for equality of citizenship, movement for removal of restriction regarding inter-dinning. It should be noted that Rambhau Palajimaro was born in a family of Bhangi.[52] Some of his Dalit followers played an important role in publicizing Ambedkar's inter-dinning and inter-marrying campaign in Nasik. D.D. Kalyani[53] wrote:

> 'उन्हीं (अम्बेडकर) की शिक्षा को क्रियात्मक रूप देने के लक्ष्य से नासिक में महारों और भंगी जाति में परस्पर अनेक शादियां हुई।'

Similarly, the charismatic influence of Ambedkar pleaded for removal of restriction regarding inter-dining. For instance, according to Devi Dayal[54], 'उनका सबसे प्यारा, मेहतर उनको खाना खिलाने का भी काम करता था और तेल मालिश भी करता था।'

We have noted earlier Ambedkar's attempt to organize the untouchable castes/ communities to carry on his agitation and this did create enthusiasm among the masses which made them realize that unity of masses was essential for progress in a socially, economically and educationally backward communities and, therefore, decided to work under Ambedkar leadership.

From an account of the events in Ramratan Janorkar's life given by Vasant Moon,[55] a noted Dalit writer of Maharashtra, wrote an essay titled 'Climax? The Encounter of Dalits and Hindus' in Subhadra Mitra Channa and Joan P. Mencher (ed.) *Life as a Dalit: Views from the Bottom on Caste in India* (2013), it will be seen that in Nagpur the Dalit movement had been a Mahar movement. At a time when most of the Bhangis and Chambhars were in the Congress, some of the Bhangis and Chambhars took part only as individuals. For instance, Ramratan Janorkar, born in a poor Bhangi family, in his earlier days, he was directly inspired and impressed by Ambedkar. Thus, Ramratan Janorkar under Ambedkar's influence took lead and dedicated his life to Ambedkar movement. He took active interest in bringing a socio-political awakening among the Bhangis. As a staunch follower of Ambedkar, he did much to expand the Buddhism all over Nagpur. Therefore, by 1956 he also became a Buddhist. However, it may be noted in this connection that 'Buddhist Community in turn took Ramratan Janorkar[56] as one of their own and made him the mayor of Nagpur Corporation'.

Similarly, apart from Ramratan Janorkar, there was Mahadevrao Chakole, a Chambhar, another great social worker and Ambedkar follower. Whenever Ambedkar came to Nagpur, he inquired about him. *'It is said that Ambedkar once visited the chakole House. Naturally the Buddhists praised his courage for this'.*

Notes

1. For more details see, Nandu Ram, 'Gandhi, Ambedkar and the Dalits: Retrospect and Prospects' in *Social Exclusion: Essays in Honour of Dr Bindeshwar Pathak*, A.K. Lal (ed.). New Delhi, Concept Publishing Company, 2003, Vol. I, p. 301.
2. See, 'foreword' by Hon'ble Justice O. Chinnappa Reddy in *Ambedkar and Nation-Building*, Shyam Lal and K.S. Saxena (ed.). Jaipur, Rawat Publications, 1998, p. 8.
3. Nandu Ram, Gandhi, *Ambedkar and the Dalits: Restospects and Prospects*, ibid., p. 304.
4. Sheshrao Chavan, *Gandhi and Ambedkar: Saviours of Untouchables*, Mumbai: Bharatiya Vidya Bhavan, 2001, p. 216–217. Also see, B.R. Ambedkar. *Mr Gandhi and the Emancipation of the Untouchables*, Jullunder: Bheem Patrika Publications, year not mentioned.
5. Ibid., p. 217.
6. For details, see, Dhananjay Keer, *Dr Ambedkar: Life and Mission*, Bombay: Popular Prakashan, 1985.
7. Nandu Ram, ibid., p. 207.
8. For details see: Markandey Katju. 'Mahatma Gandhi was a British Agent, say Katju' in *The Times of India*, Jaipur, Wednesday, 11 March 2015.
9. Sheshrao Chavan, ibid., p. 224–225.
10. Ibid., p. 225.
11. For more details, see particularly A.K. Biswas, 'Of Human Dignity: Indian Scenario' in Social and Cultural Vision of India, Delhi: Pragati Publications, 1996, p. 166.
12. Ibid., p. 166–167.
13. Ibid., p. 167.
14. Ibid., p. 167–168.
15. Ibid., p. 168.
16. Ibid., p. 170.
17. Ibid., p. 171.
18. M.K. Gandhi, *Removal of Untochability*, quoted by Dhagwan Das in Ambedkar and Bhangi Jatia, p. 29.
19. Ibid., p. 29.
20. Ibid., p. 30.
21. Ibid., p. 30.
22. Ibid., p. 30.
23. M.K. Gandhi, *Removal of Untochability*, p. 125.
24. Nandu Ram, ibid., p. 308.
25. Ibid., p. 308.
26. Mohan Das Naimishrai, *Bharatiya: Dalit Aandolan Ka Itihas-2*, New Delhi: Radhakrishan Publications, 2013, p. 159.

27. Sheshrao Chavan, ibid., p. 225.
28. Ibid., p. 228.
29. Nandu Ram, ibid., p. 311.
30. Ibid., p. 311.
31. Ibid., Biswas, p. 175.
32. Ibid., p. 175.
33. Ibid., p. 175.
34. Vijay Prashad, *Untouchable Freedom: A Social History of Dalit Community*, New Delhi, Oxford University Press, 2000, p. 136.
35. Ibid., p. 136.
36. Ibid., p. 136.
37. Ibid., p. 137.
38. See, for a systematic social movement, A.K. Biswas, 'A Chandal's Rage', in *Outlook* (English edition), 29 August 2016, p. 30. Also see, *The 1973 Movement for Dignity and Equality Before Law*, published by West Bengal's Department of Backward Classes, Kolkata, 2015.
39. विस्तृत जानकारी के लिए देखिए, भगवान दास, सफाई कर्मचारी दिवस, 31 जुलाई, पृ. 11, यह भी देखें, बाबा साहेब भीमराव अम्बेडकर और भंगी जातियां, लखनऊ, दलित टुडे प्रकाशन, 1998 पेज 31, यह भी देखें बाबा के चरणों में, नई दिल्ली, दलित प्रेस, 2004.
40. Ibid., p. 31–32.
41. विस्तृत जानकारी हेतु देखें, भगवान दास, सफाई कर्मचारी दिवस, सफाई कर्मचारी दिवस, 31 जुलाई, पृ. 1, नई दिल्ली, बीसी 1/एच, डीडीए फ्लैट मुनीरका, यह भी देखें भगवान दास, बाबा साहेब अम्बेडकर और भंगी जातिगां, वही, पृ. 31. बाबा साहेब भीमराव अम्बेडकर एक परिचय : एक संदेश, लखनऊ, दलित टुडे प्रकाशन 1998, पृ. 54–55.
42. ब्रजकृष्ण चांदीवाला, 'हड़ताल का भी एक शास्त्र', इन गांधीजी की दिल्ली, डायरी, खण्ड–3, पृ. 233–234.
43. Mohandas Naimishrai, *Bharatiya Dalit Aandolan Ka Itihias-2,* New Delhi: Radhakrishan Publications, 2013, p. 145.
44. Ibid., p. 163.
45. Ibid., p. 145.
46. Ibid., p. 145.
47. Ibid., p. 163.
48. भगवानदास, बाबा साहेब अम्बेडकर और भंगी जातियां, लखनऊ, दलित टुडे प्रकाशन, 1998, पृ. 27.
49. Ibid., Biswas, p. 159.
50. Ibid., p. 159.
51. विस्तृत हेतु देखें, डीडी कल्याणी, बाबा साहेब डॉ. अम्बेडकर की वाल्मीकि जातियों अर्थात सफाई का काम करने वाली जातियों के प्रति देन 'नई दिल्ली, मूल निवासी पब्लिकेशन ट्रस्ट, 2002 पृ. 10.
52. वही, पृ. 10.
53. वही, पृ. 10.
54. देवी दयाल, डॉ. बाबा साहेब भीमराव अम्बेडकर की दिनचर्या, लखनऊ, दलित टुडे प्रकाशन, 1998, पृ. 3.
55. Vasant Moon, 'Climax? The Encounter of Dalits and Hindus' in Subhadra Misra Channa and Joan P. Menecher (ed.), *Life as a Dalit: Views from the Bottom on Caste in India*. New Delhi, Sage Publications India, 2013, p. 297.
56. Ibid., p. 297.

10

How Gandhi Lost his Social Relevance?

Acknowledging that untouchability is a black spot on our society, Gandhi, who is popularly referred to as the 'Father of Nation' spoke, wrote and published several slim and expensive volumes containing essays on untouchables and untouchability. Gandhi had started the campaign the against untouchability. He, along with his staunch supporters, remained with the members of Bhangi community who used to work as manual Scavengers in Panch Kuai Bhangi Basti, New Delhi. Their relationship or specifically the relationship between Gandhi and Bhangis has been marked by both bitter conflict and a most non-productive, i.e. useless, activities.

To pick holes in the essay I would highlight the new fact of debate. Here and there is a hint of Gandhi's arrogant condescension toward untouchables in general and Bhangis in particular. His achievement seems to leave him cold footed.

Poona Pact: Gandhi's Evil Design Denying Political Power to the Untouchables

On 17 August 1932, Ramsay MacDonald[1], the then Prime Minister, announced his decision on the communal question. Soon after this, on 13 September 1932, newspapers all over India, carried a sensational announcement: Gandhi, still a prisoner in Yervada Jail, has decided to fast unto death from 20 September as protest against the grant of separate electorate to the depressed (untouchables) classes in the new Constitution.

Jawaharlal Nehru, who was in jail, said:[2]

> '... the British premier and his advisers were unable to appreciate Gandhi's deeply emotional and religious approach to the problem. Their first impulse was to sense a political motive in the fast. Gandhi ji was trying to stunt to recover the prestige he had lost through the decline of civil disobedience ...
>
> 'Then came the news of tremendous upheaval all over the country[3] ... "Rabindranath Tagore[4] dressed in black clothes, addressed a large gathering on significance of Gandhi's fast."'

Also observed was:[5]

> 'The Hindu Leaders' Conference met at Bombay on 19 September. The leaders who included Madan Mohan Malaviya, Tej Bahadur Sapru, M.R. Jayakar, Rajagopalachari, N.C. Kelkar, Rajendra Prasad and Moonje were anxious for quick solution'.

On the eve of the conference, Ambedkar[6] issued the following statement to the press:

> 'I need hardly to say that I was astounded to read the correspondence between Mahatma Gandhi, Sir Samuel Hoare and the Prime Minister Ramsay MacDonald which were published recently in the papers in which he has expressed his determination to starve himself up to death till the British government on its own accord or under pressure of public opinion revise opinion and withdraw their scheme of communal representation for the depressed classes. The unenviable position in which I have been placed by the Mahatma's vow of self-immolation can easily be imagined'.

However, on the other side, threats to murder began:[7]

> 'Scores of letters written in blood started pouring in his office, threatening to do away with him if he persisted in his demand and did not yield to the will of Gandhiji.'

Ambedkar[8] himself said:

> I have been getting letters threatening my life. They are not paid. I have been telling my secretary that in law when we hang a man we do not inflict a fine on him. Why should these assassins fine me by sending not paid letters in addition to taking my life.'

> 'There was a flurry of hectic activity among the top leadership. Their anxious concern was to devise some solution so that Gandhi's life could be saved. Madan Mohan Malaviya appealed to both the Hindu and the depressed class leaders to bury their differences and come to a settlement which would be acceptable to Gandhiji. Sapru and Jayakar, immediately stirred themselves and carried on behind the scene conciliation moves.[9]

> 'A deputation with Sapru among others met Gandhi more than once to discuss a new scheme based on joint electorate with adequate safeguards to depressed classes. Sapru, Jayakar, Birla, Rajendra Prasad and Rajagopalachari explained the new scheme to Gandhi.[10]

As a result of all[11] this:

> 'Both the caste Hindu and depressed class leaders rose to their fullest stature by coming to an agreement and the terms were reported to Gandhi. He accorded his approval. Sapru drafted a cable to the Prime Minister to that effect urging him to withdraw the separate electorates for the depressed classes'.

The agreement was signed by Pandit Madan Mohan Malaviya, M.R. Jayakar, Tej Bahadur Sapru, Chunilal Mehta, B.R. Ambedkar, M.C. Rajah, P.G. Solanki, Rajagopalachari, G.D. Birla and 20 others. Rajaji and Ambedkar exchanged the pens with which they had signed the agreement.[12]

For the first time two leaders, Gandhi and Ambedkar, agreed to a certain set of demands. Thus, 'Poona Pact' was signed on 24 September 1932. Ambedkar won for untouchables a guaranteed percentage of seats in any future legislature among other safeguards that would ensure they were not perpetually voted out by the Hindu majority.

Opinions of Dalit *Netas*, Social Activists, Organizations on Gandhi's Fast unto Death Against Communal Award to Untouchables in India

As soon as the then British Prime Minister, Ramsay MacDonald's decision on Communal Award was announced on 17 August, 1932, Gandhi declared fast unto death from 20 September 1932. This also drew the attention of socio-political organizations, Dalit *netas*, social activists, MLCs, etc. They realized that communal award would be helpful for their empowerment. So the enlightened among Dalits criticized and condemned Gandhi's fast unto death. It also caused multiple reactions.

The then British Prime Minister, Ramsay MacDonald, once again appealed to Gandhi: 'अछूतों के विरुद्ध इस प्रकार का खतरनाक पग न उठाए'.[13] Similarly many Europeans also condemned Gandhi[14], saying: 'दूसरे से आजादी मांगने से पहले स्वयं अछूतों को अपने चंगुल से मुक्त करो'

On 20 September 1932, a statement was issued by the Dalit *netas* from Lahore (now in Pakistan). The statement said:[15]

> 'गांधीजी ने अपनी ताजा घोषणा से स्वयं को एक नए रूप में प्रकट किया है। वह सदा अछूतों की मित्रता का दम भरते हैं। परन्तु यह मित्रता एक नए प्रकार की है। जो लोग उन्हें बहुत प्रिय हैं उन्हें परिषदों में देखना पसंद नहीं करते। हम ऐसी मित्रता को धन्यवाद सहित अस्वीकार करते हैं। गांधीजी अछूतों को हिन्दुओं का दबैल बनाए रखने के लिए जान बूझकर भूखे रहकर स्वयं को मार रहे हैं हालांकि जिस व्यवस्था के बनाए रखने के लिए ऐसा कर रहे हैं उसके आधीन करोड़ों अछूत भूखे मरते हैं। हमें डा. अम्बेडकर के नेतृत्व में पूर्ण विश्वास है।'

Likewise Swami Achhutanand[16], another Dalit leader from UP, while addressing a huge public meeting in Allahabad, criticized Gandhi bitterly and said:

> गांधी का यह मरण व्रत अछूतों के राजनीतिक अधिकारों के पनपते पौधे को जड़ से उखाड़ फैंकने का षड्यंत्र है। हम किसी भी स्थिति में संयुक्त चुनाव स्वीकार नहीं कर सकते। हिन्दू उस समय कहां थे जब नासिक मंदिर के सत्याग्रह के समय अछूतों को पीटा गया। अब हिन्दू ढोंग रचाने के लिए अछूतों पर मंदिरों के दरवाजे खोल रहे हैं। हिन्दुओं के साथ संयुक्त चुनाव अछूतों के लिए खतरनाक है। हम यह खतरा मोल नहीं ले सकते।

Manuswami Palle MLC[17], speaking on this issue at the sammelan of 'Dalit Jati Sangh' held at Otakmand, said:

> भारत के अछूत शताब्दियों से हिन्दुओं के अत्याचारों का शिकार बने हुए हैं। अब जबकि उनके अधिकारों की घोषणा हुई है तो गांधीजी ने उनके विरुद्ध मरण व्रत शुरू कर दिया है। गांधीजी का मरण व्रत अत्याचार की आग को बढ़ाने के समान है। यह मरण व्रत अछूतों की उन्नति रोकने का एक यत्न है। राजनीति में धर्म को जबरदस्ती लाकर गांधीजी अपने आपको

सदा के लिए कलंकित कर रहे हैं। मैं हिन्दुओं को अच्छी तरह जानता हूं और जोर के साथ कहता हूं कि संयुक्त चुनाव अछूतों को मौत के घाट उतार देंगे।

Himanshu Rao wrote:[18]

गांधीजी जो स्वयं को दलितों का हितेषी सिद्ध करने में कभी पीछे नहीं रहते थे और अपनी शरारतपूर्ण बातों से बाबा साहेब जैसे सच्चे कर्मयोगी को झुठलाने का प्रयास करते थे पृथक निर्वाचन के निर्णय से विचलित हो गए। गांधी के इस अनशन से सारे हिन्दुस्तान में एक तूफान सा खड़ा हो गया था। जहां हिन्दुओं ने अछूतों को डराया व धमकाया वहां अछूतों ने भी अपनी दृढ़ता का प्रमाण दिया। हिन्दुस्तान के कोने-कोने से डॉ. अम्बेडकर के पक्ष में बयान प्रकाशित हुए, सभाएं हुई और जुलूस निकाले गए।

In Punjab, saint Brahmdas[19] toured from village to village and warned Dalits against Gandhi's fast unto death:

पंजाब में सन्त ब्रह्मदास ने गांव-गांव घूमकर अछूतों को गांधीजी के मरण व्रत से सावधान रहने का उपदेश दिया। सन्त जी ने अछूतों को संगठित होकर अपने अधिकारों के लिए लड़ने को कहा उन्होंने डॉ. अम्बेडकर को अछूतों का मुक्तिदाता बताया।

From the very beginning he had adopted a critical attitude towards Gandhi. His criticism was mainly directed against fast to death. Later on Ambedkar[20] issued a statement in which he criticized Gandhi's policy.

मैं इस प्रकार की राजनीतिक बेहूदगियों की परवाह नहीं करता। मि. गांधी ने जो यह धमकी दी है कि वे भूखे रहकर मर जाएंगे तो यह कोई नैतिक लड़ाई नहीं है बल्कि केवल राजनीतिक बेहूदगी है। यदि गांधीजी ने हठ किया तो वह कुदरती मौत की बजाये बनावटी मौत मरेंगे। मैं निरोधियों को सद्भावना के लिए कहता हूं। परन्तु मैं इस प्रकार की बेहूदगियों से प्रभावित होने वाला नहीं हूं। मेरा फैसला अंतिम है और यदि गांधीजी हिन्दुओं के अधिकारों के लिए अपनी जान पर खेलना चाहते हैं तो अछूत भी इस बात के लिए मजबूर हो जाएंगे कि अपने अधिकारों की कीमत पर संयुक्त चुनाव को स्वीकार नहीं करेंगे और न ही पृथक चुनाव के अधिकार को छोड़ेंगे। इससे यदि स्थिति बिगड़ती है तो बिगड़ती रहे।

Rajni Kothari[21], a noted Indian political scientist, while writing in his essay 'गांधी के सवाल और गांधी के जवाब', had observed:

अहिंसक और विकेन्द्रीकृत समाज व्यवस्था बनाने के अपने प्रयासों में गांधी ने हिन्दू समाज के हरिजन वाले मुद्दे पर कई बार उचित ध्यान नहीं दिया। वे अछूतों के साथ शताब्दियों से हो रहे अन्याय के प्रश्न पर व्यापक हिन्दू समाज को नहीं ला सके। गांधी हरिजनों को स्वयं अपना रास्ता तालश करने और भविष्य का निर्माण करने का मौका देने को तैयार नहीं हुए। आज इस बात पर बहस हो सकती है कि अगर अछूतों को अलग मतदाता मण्डल बनाने की इजाजत मिल जाती तो उन्हें समाज के हाशियें से हटकर मुख्य धारा में आने के संघर्ष में फायदा होता या नुकसान, लेकिन इस तथ्य से इन्कार नहीं किया जा सकता कि व्यवस्था के अंदर अछूतों को संघर्ष करने की गुंजाइश दिए जाने की तब भी जरूरत थी।

Bhagwan Das[22], an eminent Buddhist and Dalit scholar, worte:

गांधी अछूतों के आरक्षण को लेकर मरने जा रहे थे, यह कहना तो मुश्किल है, लेकिन हिन्दु पत्रकारों ने ऐसा माहौल पैदा कर दिया कि वे सचमुच मरने जा रहे हैं।

More than 83 years ago, Gandhi in response to the Ambedkar's Presidential Address, wrote three essays to his paper *Harijan*. The prime target of Gandhi's fury was Ambedkar. An apprehensive Gandhi said,[23] 'डॉ अम्बेडकर हिन्दू समाज के लिए एक चुनौती है।'

1918 Agitation and Collective Mobilization

During the national movement across the country, non-Brahmin and backward classes agitation which was over 97-year-old movement of historic and cultural significance was another significant event especially for the down trodden.

According to recently published book, entitled 'भारतीय दलित आन्दोलन का इतिहास' (2013), by Mohandas Naimish Rai, the non-Brahmin and backward classes people demanded some seats or their representation in Vidhan Sabha in 1918.[24] This was the first set of event which sparked off a mass movement. The demand of representation would benefit the vast majority of backward classes, but this attracted the attention of trio extremist group consisting of Lal-Bal-Pal and were strongly resisted by vested interests who were better organized and carry a great degree of political clout. Take India's extra ordinarily rigid orthodox people who opposed and criticized bitterly from backwards classes entering in Vidhan Sabha.

It should be mentioned here that Bal Gangadhar Tilak, speaking at a mammoth public meeting held at Sholapur in Maharashtra, vehemently opposed backward classes in the matter and in reply to their demand, Tilak[25], the leader of trio extremist group said:

> मैं नहीं समझता कि तेल निकालने वाले तेली, तम्बाकू विक्रेता आदि गैर ब्राह्मण और पिछड़ी जाति के लोग विधान सभा में क्यों जाना चाहते हैं।

Tilak[26] considered:

> उन वर्गों का कार्य है आदेशों और कानूनों को स्वीकार करना न कि कानून बनाने की आशंका रखना।

After Tilak, Gandhi was the second who expressed the same feeling and after 96 years, the Congress also followed suit.

When the then Chief Minister of Gujarat, Narendra Modi, was declared as a Prime Ministerial candidate of the BJP for the first time in the history of India in Lok Sabha elections held in 2014, it was a challenge for the Congress. Since then all political parties, including the Congress, had been perturbed by Modi's election strategy. They even passed sarcastic remarks several times against Modi and his caste Modh-Ghanchi, a sub-group of the Teli community, which is counted among OBCs. The original Hindi proverb, '*Kahan Raja Bhoj aur Khan Gangu Teli*' and is frequently used in north India to emphasize the incomparable statures of the two extremes. One such scarcastic remark was, 'चाय वाला क्या देश का प्रधानमंत्री बनेगा'।

Print media of India immediately carried reports. But a humiliating and casteist comment on Modi was made by Mani Shankar Iyer – a Cambridge educated, Congress leader and former Cabinet Minister in Congress Ministry at the Centre. According to print media, including *The Times of India*, which published the comment: if Modi so desires, the Congress may give a small place in AICC office, New Delhi, to instal his tea shop to serve the people. In his own words:

'In the 21st century Narendra Modi, will never became the PM ... But if he wants to distribute tea here (at the Congress Headquarter), we will find a place for him'. (*The Times of India*, Sunday, Jaipur, 15 November 2015)

This shows the level of frustration of the party and its leaders. Iyer sparked a controversy by saying all this. His comments have evoked sharp reaction.

These views convey bad message against the Congress. The Congress leadership's silence could send a wrong indication to the people. People of this country do not expect such language from Congress leaders. What has changed and what has not in Dalits-Congress relationship over the last century?

This is caste prejudice and evident in profusion. Certainly, it was ill conceived and motivated on part of reputed Congress person of Mani Shankar Iyar's stature. If Hinduism has internalized all other religions it is the evils of caste and ills of their hatred and prejudices towards the low castes as Hindus.

After political parties, it was now the turn of the best Indian academicians in Britain's top universities[27] like London School of Economics, Cambridge, Oxford, SOAS and King's College that issued a letter opposing Narendra Modi as the next Indian Prime Minister.

According to the *The Times of India*[28], Jaipur, Thursday, 24 April 2014, in an open letter issued on Tuesday, 75 academics led by Professor Chetan Bhatt and Gautam Appa of LSE attacked the BJP leader saying, the idea of Modi in power fills us with dread. They warned that a Modi victory would 'likely mean greater moral policing, especially of women, increased censorship and vigilantism and more tensions with India's neighbours'.

While Tilak opposed the representation, the Congress spearheaded an agitation to boycott the Vidhan Sabha to pressurize the British Government to get their demand accepted for Swaraj. In 1919[29], the Congress across the country launched campaign in different provinces and processions were taken out, with a slogan 'विधानसभाओं में कौन लोग जायेंगे?' After slogan, followers shouted[30] in a scarastic way 'केवल नाई, मोची, कुम्हार और झाडू लगाने वाले भंगी।'

The conditions that prevailed at that time were such that Congress never wanted to see them in Vidhan Sabha. According to Congress:[31] 'उन्हें दास ही बने रहना चाहिए'।

Harijan Nivas

During the British rule many times from 12-4-1915 to 30-1-1948, Gandhi visited Delhi for various activities and causes, such as:

(i) To attend the Congress Working Committee's meetings
(ii) To launch Non-Cooperation movement
(iii) To attend War Conference
(iv) To see Viceroy regarding ROWLET Act and Hunter Committee Report etc.
(v) To see Viceroy and to attend Inter Asian Conference.

During this period, Gandhi generally stayed with his own persons/friends[32] namely P.S. Rudra's residence at Kashmiri Gate, Dr M.A. Ansari's residence at Ansari Road, Shri Vittal Bhai Patel's residence, Seth Laxmi Narain Gadodia's residence at Chandni Chowk, Ghanshyam Das Birla's residence, etc. The frequent visit to Delhi in the 20th Century and dependence of Gandhi on his friends being great followers could not, therefore, afford to cause inconvenience to his friends. Thus, on 2 January 1935[33], the foundation stone of 'Harijan Nivas' in Delhi was laid down by Gandhi at Kings way road near Dhaka Gaon and later on double-storey building was constructed for Gandhi's stay. It should, however, be noted that later Udyogshala Guest House and offices were added. Gandhi received the benefit of stay. According to Brij Krishan Chandiwala, it should be noted that from 29 December 1934 to 10 November 1938 whenever Gandhi came to Delhi, he stayed in Harijan Nivas. For instance, on 4 August 1937[34] Gandhi met Lord Linlithgow at Harijan Nivas.

As a result of frequent visits of Gandhi to Delhi for formal politics and services in the field of Harijan Welfare, campaign against Untouchability, redemption of Bhangis, there had been a change in Harijan Nivas. Because of the increased Harijan reform activities, Harijan Nivas was converted into headquarters of Harijan Sewak Sangh.

Harijan Sevak Sangh

The Poona Pact signed on 24 September 1932, raised both Gandhi and Ambedkar's socio-political stack sky high. Just as his political career was reaching its zenith, the spotlight shifted on his efforts to campaign against untouchability.

Then a public meeting of Hindus was held on 30 September[35] in Bombay under the presidentship of Pandit Madan Mohan Malaviya and the following resolution was passed.

This public meeting of Hindus resolved that an All India Anti-Untouchability League, with its headquarters at Delhi and branches in different provincial centres, be established for the purpose of carrying on propaganda against untouchability and that for this purpose the following steps be taken:[36]

(i) All public wells, roads, schools, etc. be declared open to the depressed classes.

(ii) All public temples be opened for members of the depressed classes.

(iii) This meeting appoints Seth G.D. Birla as President and Amritlal V. Thakkar as General Secretary to take all necessary steps to organize the League and to bring about the fulfilment of its objects.

'The All India Anti Untouchability League was Gandhi's project. It was inspired by him and was the direct outcome of the Poona Pact. The first thing Gandhi did was to change its name. In a press message issued on 9 December 1932, Gandhi told the public that the organization would henceforth be known as Servants of the Untouchables Society. This name also did not appear to Gandhi as the best.

Ultimately he decided to give it a new name. He called it the 'Harijan Sevak Sangh', which means a society of those engaged in the service to the untouchables.[37] ...'

In the following pages, the author has endeavoured to place before the readers, thoughts and views of Gandhi and Ambedkar in their own words quoted verbatim.

'Dr. Ambedkar considered the Harijan Sevak Sangh as a Charitable organisation only in name and its real aim was to ensure the untouchables to make them camp followers of the Hindu and the Congress and to scotch any movement aimed at freeing the untouchables from social, religious and economic domination by the Hindus. The object of the Congress and the Harijan Sevak Sangh, Ambedkar said, was to kill the untouchables with kindness. With regard to the work of the Harijan Sevak Sangh, Ambedkar said in his writings and speeches, 'The Harijan Sevak Sangh' is spoken of as a memorial to Gandhi's labours in the cause of the untouchables. What are the achievements of the Sangh.'[38]

'The Sangh is an All India organization. It has a Central Board. Then there are Provincial Boards and under the Provincial Boards there are District and Local Committees. The financial resources of the Sangh are mainly drawn from the collections made on an All India tour specially undertaken for the purpose by Mr Gandhi between November 1933 and July 1934. The total amount collected on this tour comes to about eight lakh of rupees and is known as the Gandhiji Purse fund and forms the principal reserve for the Sangh to draw upon. The rest of the resources are made of annual donations.[39]

'India is a vast continent with 6,96,831 villages as per the Census Report of 1931. The untouchables are spread out all throughout these villages. There is no village without its untouchables. The Sangh is in exhausted condition. Its affairs in fact would have been wound up on account of its bankruptcy. If the Sangh is still existing, it is not because its endeavours are sustained by Hindu charity directed to the uplift of the untouchables. It exists because the Congress governments which are now established in the different provinces have come to the rescue of the Sangh. They have handed over to the Sangh certain social welfare work which former governments carried out through government departments or government officials with the money grants. Thus, the Sangh is now living on government funds. As an institution maintained by the Hindus with the help of Hindu charity for the untouchables, the Sangh simply does not exist'.[40]

'The Sangh is largely directed by the caste Hindus. There are very few untouchables who have any voice in directing the activities of the Sangh. I have no connection with the Sangh. But when the Sangh was started, I was invited to join. I had a great desire to cooperate with the Hindus for the removal of untouchability. But immediately after the Sangh was established, I had to go to London to attend the Round Table Conference and therefore, I posted a letter to General Secretary of the Sangh, Mr Thakkar, on the 14 of November 1932 on Board the ship, 'M. Victoria'.[41]

The following is the full text of the letter:[42]

In my opinion there can be two distinct methods of approaching the task of uplifting the depressed classes. There is a school which proceeds on the assumption that the fate of the Individual belonging to the depressed classes is bound up with his personal conduct. If he is suffering from want and misery it is because he must be vicious and sinful. Starting from this hypothesis, this school of social workers concentrates all its efforts and its resources on fostering personal virtue by adopting a programme which includes items such as temperance, gymnasium, cooperation, libraries, schools etc. which are calculated to make the individual a better and virtuous individual. In my opinion there is also another method of approach to this problem. It starts with the hypothesis that the fate of the individual is governed by his environment and the circumstances he is obliged to live under, and if an individual is suffering from want and misery, it is because his environment is not propitious'.

This letter was not even acknowledged by the Secretary. That not a single suggestion of mine was accepted goes without saying. Even my suggestion that the workers of the Sangh should be drawn largely from the untouchables themselves was not accepted. Indeed when the attention of Gandhi was drawn to the fact that the Harijan Sevak Sangh had become the hive of mercenary Hindus, he defended it on the ground which are clever, if not honest. He said to the deputation of the untouchables, 'The welfare work of the untouchables is a penance which the Hindus have to do for the sin of untouchability'. The money that has been collected has been contributed by the Hindus. From both points of view, the Hindus alone must run the Sangh. Neither the ethics nor right would justify untouchables in claiming a seat on the Board of the Sangh.[43]

Not only all my proposals were rejected by Gandhi and his advisers, but in framing the constitution of the Sangh, aims and objects were adopted which were quite opposed to those which had been suggested.[44]

It is surprising that Gandhi who threatened to fast unto death against separate electorates on the ground that it involved segregation of the untouchables should himself sanction a line of activity which perpetuates this segregation. In undertaking to render this social services to the untouchables, Mr Gandhi and his Sangh should have forgotten what the untouchables want. What the untouchables want is not education, but the right to be admitted to common schools. The untouchables do not want Medical Aid, what they want is the right to be admitted to the general dispensary on equal terms. The untouchable does not want water. What he wants is the right to draw water from a common well. The untouchables do not want their suffering to be relieved. They want their personality to be respected and their stigma removed. Once their stigma is removed their suffering will go. This the Harijan Sevak Sangh does not seems to have realized. The Sangh is said to be the friend of the untouchables and the orthodox Hindu the enemy of the untouchables.

One fails to understand what the friend has done which the enemy would not do. The orthodox Hindus insist that the untouchables shall have separate wells, schools, separate dispensaries and separate wells. The Sangh says, they shall be done. Except the fact the orthodox Hindu believes in untouchability and Harijan Sevak Sangh does not, what difference in practice is there between the friend and the foe? Under both the untouchable is condemned to separate schools, separate hostels and separate wells. If this is so, it is difficult to understand why Gandhi and the Harijan Sevak Sangh should pick up a quarrel with the orthodox Hindu, if he and his Sangh are not prepared to force the issue. Whether the Hindu Shastras recognize untouchability or not is only an academic quarrel between Gandhi and the orthodox Hindu. It can do no practical good. 'On the contrary, I am prepared to say that it had done positive harm to the untouchables. In the first place it has created enmity between the untouchables and the orthodox Hindus. Before Gandhi picked up this needless quarrel the relations between the untouchables and the Hindus were non-social. The quarrel has made them anti-social. Secondly, if there was no such quarrel, if instead of untouchability being made the issue – which Gandhi does not intend to fight it out – an appeal was made to the orthodox Hindu to remove the suffering of the untouchables, many orthodox Hindu I know would have come forward to help to remove the sufferings. Gandhi has reaped the glory for having established the Sangh. But the Sangh has neither sought to remove untouchability nor has it helped to alleviate the sufferings of the untouchables.[45]

'Why has the Sangh failed? My answer is quite definite. 'I say the Sangh has failed because of its wrong politics'.[46]

'It has been often said that the Harijan Sevak Sangh is a political organization. Gandhi has always resented such an allegation and repudiated it as being false. The General Secretary of the Sangh has also protested against it. To quote his words: 'The Sangh, though a sequal of a political pact, has no politics'.[47]

> I do not see any reason for the resentment of Mr Gandhi nor for the protests of his Secretary. I wish very much that the Sangh was a political organization. The untouchables have obtained a share of political power. But power which is not conscious of itself is no power. Again power which is not organized is no power. The Harijan Sevak Sangh would have been of great use if it had helped the untouchables to organise independent political parties to fight the election and make their political power effective. Nor can I accept the statement of Mr Gandhi and his Secretary that the Sangh has no politics. On the contrary I insist that not only the Sangh had a definite line of politics but the line of politics is wrong because it is prejudicial to the cause of the untouchables.[48]

Since Gandhi does not admit that the Sangh has politics, one must go to the circumstances for proof. Circumstantial proof is always better than oral testimony because as is well said man may lie but circumstances cannot. In this connection, I want to rely upon a clause in the Constitution of the Sangh as a piece of evidence in support of my contention. The clause relates to the means to be adopted by the Sanghs, for removing Untouchability and for securing equal rights to the untouchables along with the caste Hindus.[49]

Satyagrah or passive resistance has been found by Gandhi as a form of resistance which is morally beyond cavil. Why does not Gandhiji ask the Sangh to launch Satyagrah by the untouchables against the caste Hindus for the abolition of the injustice against the untouchables. He asked the people of India to offer Satyagraha against British imperialism. Why does he not want to use the same means against the caste Hindus in the interests of the untouchables?[50]

'What is the answer of Mr Gandhi to this question? The only answer I can see is that it comes in the way of his politics. Mr Gandhi must remain at the head of the nation. I wonder if life would be worthwhile to him if for some reason he ceased to be at the head of nation. He is, I think, the most ambitious politician. I know, he regards as his rivals those whom he calls as friends. To be at the head of the nation means that he must preserve the integrity of the Congress. The Congress is 99 per cent composed the Hindus. How can Gandhiji succeed in maintaining the integrity of the Congress if he were to direct the Sangh to carry on Satyagraha against the Hindus for the sake of the untouchables. The Hindus would leave the Congress and the Congress would disrupt. This is detrimental to the interests of Mr Gandhi. This is the explanation why Mr Gandhi and the Sangh have adopted peaceful persuasion as the only means of removing untouchability. It is a means which is least likely to hurt the Hindus and the Congress. Not only in big matter but even in small matters, the Sangh is careful to see that the Hindus are not hurt or annoyed. I am told that in distributing scholarships for instance, the Sangh makes inquiries into the political affiliations of the applicant and if it is found that the applicant belongs to a community which is against the Congress or Hindus, he gets no aid from funds of Sangh.[51]

'Why has Mr Gandhi failed? According to me, there are three reasons which have brought about this failure. The first reason is the Hindus to whom he makes his appeal for the removal of untouchability do not respond. Why is this so? It is a common experience that the words a man uses and the effect they produce are not always commensurate. What he says has its momentum, indefinitely multiplied or reduced to nullity, by the impression that the hearer for good reason or bad happens to have formed of the spirit of the speaker. This gives a clue to know why Mr Gandhi's sermons on untouchability have completely failed to move the Hindus, why people hear his after-prayer sermons for a few minutes and then more on to the comic opera and why there is nothing more to it. The fault is not entirely of the Hindu public. The fault is of Mr Gandhi himself. Mr Gandhi has built up his reputation of being a Mahatma on his being a spiritual teacher. Whatever may be his intention, Mr Gandhi is looked upon as an apostle of Swaraj. His anti-untouchability campaign is looked upon as a fad if not a side show. That is why the Hindus respond to his political biddings but never to his social or religious preaching. The momentum of his anti-untouchability campaign must therefore remain a nullity. Mr Gandhi is a political shoemaker. He must stick to his political task. He thought he could take up the task of solving the social question. That was a mistake. A politician is not the man for it. That is why the hope held out to the untouchables that Mr Gandhi's sermons will do the trick has failed.[52]

'The second reason is that Mr Gandhi does not wish to antagonize the Hindus even if such antagonism was necessary to carry out his anti untouchability programme. A few instances will illustrate Mr Gandhi mentality'.[53]

'Most of Mr Gandhi's friends give credit to him, for sincerity and earnestness for the cause of the untouchables and expect the untouchables to believe in it on the mere ground that Mr Gandhi is the one man who keeps on constantly preaching to the Hindus the necessity of removing untouchability. They have lost sight of the old proverb that an ounce of practice is worth a ton of preaching and have never cared to ask Mr Gandhi to explain why does he not cease to preach to the Hindus the necessity of removing untouchability and launch a campaign of satyagraha or start a fast, if they would ask for such an explanation they would know why Mr Gandhi merely contents himself with sermons on untouchability'.[54]

'The third reason is that Mr Gandhi does not want the untouchables to organize and be strong. For he fears that they might thereby become independent of the Hindus and weaken the ranks of the Hindus. This is best illustrated by the activities of the Harijan Sevak Sangh. The whole object of the Sangh is to create a slave mentality amongst the untouchables towards their Hindu masters. Examine the Sangh from any angle one may like and the creation of slave mentality will appear to be its dominant purposes.[55]

'The Harijan Sevak Sangh for its petty services has collected a swarm of grateful untouchables who are employed to preach that Mr Gandhi and the Hindus are the saviours of the untouchables. Daniel O' Connel, the Irish leader, once said that no man can be grateful at the cost of his honour, no woman can be grateful at the cost of her chastity and no country can be grateful at the cost of its liberty. The untouchables are too simple minded to know that the cost of the services which the Harijan Sevak Sangh offers to render is loss of independence. This is exactly what Mr Gandhi wants'.[56]

'The worst part of the activities of the Harijan Sevak Sangh is the help rendered to the untouchable students kept in the hostels maintained by the Sangh. These untouchable students remind me of Bhishma and Kacha, two prominent characters which figure in the Mahabharata. Bhishma proclaimed with great show that the Pandavas were right and the Kauravas wrong. Yet when it came to a war between the two, he fought on the side of the Kauravas and against the Pandvas. When asked to justify his conduct, he was not ashamed to say that he fought for the Kauravas because they fed him. Kacha belonged to the community of the Devas who were engaged in a war against the Rakshasa. The spiritual head of the Rakshasas know a mantra (incantation) by which he could revive a dead Rakshasa. The Devas were losing the battle since their head did not know the mantra and could not revive their dead. The Devas planned to send Kacha to the head of the Rakshasas, with instructions somehow to learn the mantra and come back. Kacha in the beginning could not succeed. Ultimately he entered into an agreement with Devayani, the daughter of the spiritual head of the Rakshasas, that if she helped him to acquire the mantra he would be prepared to marry her. Devyani succeeded in fulfilling her part of the contract. But Kacha refused to perform his part alleging that the interests of his community were more important than his promise to her.[57]

'Take a fourth illustration. The Sangh is run by the caste Hindus. There are some untouchables who have demanded that institution should be handed over to the untouchables and should be run by them. Others have demanded that the untouchables should have representation on the Governing Board. Gandhi had flatly refused to do either on two very ingenious grounds which no man with the greatest cunning could improve. Mr Gandhi's first argument is that the Harijan Sevak Sangh is an act of penance on the part of the Hindus for the sin of observing untouchability. It is they who must do the penance. Therefore the untouchables can have no place in running the Sangh. Secondly Gandhi says the money collected by him is given by the Hindus and not by the untouchables and as the money is not of the untouchables, the untouchables have no right to be on the Governing Body. The refusal of Gandhi may be tolerated but his arguments are most insulting and a respectable untouchable will be forgiven if he refuses to have anything to do with the Sangh. One should have thought that the Harijan

Sevak Sangh was a trust and the untouchables its beneficiaries. Any trio in law would admit that the beneficiaries have every right to know the aims and objects of the Trust, its funds and whether the objects are properly carried out or not. The beneficiaries even have the right to have the trustees removed for breach of trust. On that basis it would be impossible to deny the claim of the untouchables for representation on the Managing Board. Evidently Gandhi does not wish to accept this position. A self-respecting untouchable who has no desire to cringe and who does not believe in staking the future of the untouchables on philanthropy of the strangers cannot have any quarrel with Gandhi. He is quite prepared to say that if meanness is a virtue then Gandhi's logic is superb and Gandhi is welcome to the benefit of it. Only he must not blame the untouchables if they boycott the Sangh'.[58]

'These however could not be the real reasons for not allowing the untouchables to run the Sangh. The real reasons are different. In the first place, if the Sangh was handed over to the untouchables, Mr Gandhi and the Congress will have no means of control over the untouchables. The untouchable will cease to be dependent of the Hindus. In the second place, the untouchables having become independent will cease to be grateful to the Hindus. These consequences will be quite contrary to the aim and object, which have led Mr Gandhi to establish the Sangh. He wants to create among the untouchables what is known among Indian Christians as the mission compound mentality. That is why Mr Gandhi does not wish to hand over the Sangh to the control and management of the untouchables? Is this consistent with a genuine desire for the emancipation of untouchables? Can Gandhi be called a liberator of the untouchables? Does this not show that Gandhi is more anxious to tighten the tie which binds the untouchables to the apron strings of the Hindus than to free them from the thralldom of the Hindus?[59]

These are the reasons why Mr Gandhi's anti-Untouchability campaign has failed.[60]

Gandhi and Low Castes

What is almost never acknowledged is that Gandhi worried less about Bhangis than untouchables. Gandhi had no sympathy for this most neglected section of society or for their welfare. Writing in *Hind Swaraj*, Gandhi feared:[61]

'If the Shudras (Low castes) leave their ancestral profession and take up others, ambition will rouse in them and their peace of mind will be spoiled. Even their family peace will be disturbed.

Gandhi should be criticized personally or politically? He continued his indifferent attitude towards untouchables. Like many caste Hindus, he eagerly supported caste system. For the first time in 1927 writing in *Young India, Gandhi*[62] supported caste system by referring to:

'According to Hindu belief, he who practices a profession which does not belong to him by birth, does violence to himself and becomes a degraded being by not living upto the varna (caste) of his birth'.

Gandhi[63] described his vision for caste system in India as:

'To abolish caste is to demolish Hinduism'.

Further, Gandhi[64] asserted that:

'I call myself a Sanatan man one who firmly believes in the caste system'.

A few months earlier to Independence, on 3 June 1947 Gandhi[65] again reiterated in his paper *Harijan*:

> 'I believe in Varnashrama (caste system) which is the law of life. The Law of Varna (color and/or caste) is nothing but law of conservation of energy. Why should my son not be scavenger if I am one?'

As Gandhi Congress grew larger and larger, the untouchables were pushed further and further to the margins. In any case his attitude to the untouchables was not marked by a genuineness for their upliftment and empowerment. He wanted them to remain within Hindu gripping command. As architect of the Poona Pact, his evil design denying political power to the untouchables and tribal communities, has been codified. Gandhi was virulently against the untouchables for holding any elective office. For instance, Dr Narayan Bhaskar Khare, who after winning a majority as Congress leader in central provinces and Berar, became its Chief Minister in 1937 with few ministers of whom one was Rameshwar Agnibhoj, an untouchable. Chief Minister (who was then called upon as the PM) from 1937–1938, Gandhi[66] was angry with this move and so he publically castigated Khare's action saying:

> 'He was opposed to the creation of such high ambition among persons belonging to the Scheduled Castes'.

In 1942, the All India Conference of Untouchables, which adopted resolutions of political demands for the untouchables, was attended by Gandhi. The untouchables who attended the conference solicited the view of the Mahatma, and if he would advise the Congress and the leaders of the various majority parties in the legislatures in the provinces to nominate the Cabinet members from among the Scheduled Caste members'. The reply of Gandhi was clear and unequivocal:

> 'I cannot. The principle is dangerous. Protection of its neglected classes should not be carried to an extreme which will harm the country. A cabinet minister should be a topmost man commanding universal confidence. A person after he has secured a seat in an elected body should depend on his intrinsic merit and popularity to secure covetted positions. (Emphasis added)'

Ambedkar Overshadowed

In the country's history for the first time, what is important is that after 66 years and more than 100 Constitutional amendments, at the commencement of winter session of the Parliament, on Thursday, 26 November 2015, the Parliament's debate commemorated the Constitution Day on the 125 the anniversary of Dr B.R. Ambedkar. Seemed an inspiring way of celebrating Dr B.R. Ambedkar's rich contribution to the national life.

Needless to say, one can blame today Congress's betrayal culture. Since Independence, the Congress had been in power at the Centre for nearly 48 years but 'Constitutional Day' was never celebrated during their tenure. It is a pity that in past Constitution Day was never celebrated by previous governments too. It was a cardinal mistake and PM Narendra Modi showed gratefulness in acknowledging true worth of Ambedkar. Celebrating 26 November as Constitution Day must be the beginning of much larger efforts to fulfill Ambedkar's vision in all its aspects.

On Tuesday, 1 December 2015 in a nearly hourlong speech in upper House (Rajya Sabha) with citation from Dr B.R. Ambedkar, Jawaharlal Nehru, Max Mueller, Kabir etc. PM Narendra Modi said:

> 'Ambedkar endured indifference, mockery and reluctant acceptance. When pressure came from the ground, the country is praising his Constitution. Good things should be acknowledged again and again'.

Stressing that constitution was both a legal and social document, Modi said, 'We have to live up to it. Faith in Constitution takes us out of daily verbal duel' (tu-tu, main-main), he said: That the downtrodden need love, compassion and camaraderie. ('Modi in Major Outreach to Congress ...' in *The Times of India*, Jaipur, Wednesday, 2 December 2015)

Swapan Das Gupta, a political commentator, thus wrote in *Sunday Times of India*, Jaipur, 29 November 2015 under caption 'Right And Wrong':

> There are individuals in history whose true worth is acknowledged post humously. Bhim Rao Ambedkar was such a man. Despite his varied contributions he was overshadowed in his lifetime, first by Mahatma Gandhi and subsequently by Jawaharlal Nehru. But country has made amends and the parliamntary debate commemorating Constitution Day seems an inspired way of celebrating his rich contribution to national life.

On 125th birth anniversary of Dr B.R. Ambedkar, Christophe Jaffrelot, a Senior Research Fellow at CERI – Sciences PO/CNRs, Paris, Professor of Indian Politics and Sociology at King's India Institute, London, and non-resident scholar at Carnegie endowment for international peace, wrote an article in *The Indian Express* (Jaipur, Thursday, 14 April 2016) described diverse kinds of activities of Ambedkar with regard to publicizing the miserable conditions of the untouchables in the British India and measures for the betterment of the untouchables which angered the Congressmen and leaders of the freedom movement further. Opposing Mahatma Gandhi's decision in August 1942 to launch the Quit India movement, Ambedkar declared that the 'patriotic duty of all Indians' was rather to prevent such movement from creating 'anarchy and chaos which would unquestionably help and facilitate the subjugation of the country by Japan'.

In the 2016 article, 'Ambedkar against Nationalism: For him Human Dignity Mattered More', Christophe Jaffrelot, Professor of Indian politics and sociology, has observed:

'During world war II, Ambedkar continued to collaborate with the colonial power in exchange for concessions to Dalits and the working class at large. In July 1941, he joined the Defence Advisory Committee that had been set up by the Viceroy to involve Indian leaders in the war efforts and to give to this forced participation of India in the conflict a greater legitimacy. In 1942, he entered in the Executive Council of the Viceroy as Labour member. In this capacity, he worked relentlessly to develop social legislation. One of the most significant bills that he managed to have passed was the Indian Trade Unions (Amendment) Bill, making compulsory the recognition of a trade union in every enterprise under certain conditions. He also introduced the payment of wages (Amendment) Bill and numberous factories (Amendment) Bills which were all passed. In fact, many of the Labour Laws independent India was to elaborate upon after 1947 were initiated by Ambedkar under the British. He also obtained a larger recruitment of Dalits in the Army and in particular, the reinstatement of Mahar Battalion'.

As indicated in Round Table Conference, 1930, the Indian untouchables suffered socio-economic deprivation and also faced discrimination. These arguments suggest the kind of strategies Ambedkar had in mind.

Similarly, Upendra Bakshi, an expert on Constitution affairs, the former Vice-Chancellor of University of South Gujarat and Delhi and now Professor of Law in University of Warwick, wrote recently in his article. 'How not to Recall an Icon' (*The Indian Express*, Jaipur, Monday, 18 April 2016). Bakshi observed:

'Although India has at last produced a Dalit bourgeoisie, it has yet to produce a post colonial intellectual like Ambedkar, who felt haunted (to borrow the words of Jacques Lacan) by the "Schizoid paranoid ... murmur" of a million "anonymous persecutors". But he developed the ability and the courage to ask questions about the ubiquitous injustice of social, political and economic orderings. A restless and dynamic politician, reformer, crusader and thinker, Ambedkar wished to "annihilate the caste system", restore the title deeds of humanity to untouchables and to liberate the India from "Dalit-hunting" rape, arson, stripping and parading, plunder, killing and massacre of untouchables'.

SDGs (Sustainable Development Goals)

India's permanent representative to the UN Syed Akbaruddin recently announced on Twitter: 'Babasaheb's birth anniversary to be observed at UN for the first time with focus on combatting inequalities to achieve SDGS'. A recent news published by *The Times of India*, Jaipur, Tuesday, 12 April 2016 explained:

'India's permanent mission, in association with the Kalpana Saroj Foundation and Foundation for Human Horizon, will commemorate the 125th birth anniversary of the Dalit leader on 13 April at UN headquarters in New York – showcasing the Universal Approval of Priuncipal architect of India's Constitution, who fought caste injustice'.

Again on 13 April 2016, the editorial, 'War for Ambedkar' in *The Times of India,* a leading Indian newspaper, explained:

'Indeed, from being an icon solely of Dalit parties in yester year, Ambedkar's legacy is enjoying a revival with the political parties across India's ideological spectrum fighting to appropriate it. And now, with inequality a rising concern and cause for political turnmoil in western countries, Ambedkar's appeal was reached Western shores as well. Prime Minister Narendra Modi is scheduled to travel to Ambedkar's birth place in Mhow, MP to observe Social Harmony Day'.

Similarly, on Thursday, 14 April 2016, *Hindustan Times* another leading newspaper, published from New Delhi, writes on the editorial page, 'A Celebration for Votes', wherein the editor observed that parties are vying with each other to appropriate Ambedkar, but the plight of the Dalits remains.

The editor further wrote:

> 'In April, Prime Minister Narendra Modi will address two rallies on B.R. Ambedkar, whose 125th birth anniversary is today and highlight issues related to villages and farmers ... It has also nudged the United Nations to observe the anniversary for the first time with a focus on combatting inequalities to achieve the Sustainable Development Goals. Other parties are not behind in race to woo Dalit voters'.

Ambedkar, the farmer of the Constitution of India was a champion and messiah of weaker sections of society. But he did not get the kind of homage and recognition for his contribution in nation-building which he truly deserved; especially when compared to the leaders of other countries like Abraham Lincon of America, Lenin of the then USSR (now Russia), Mao-Zedong of China, Sukarno of Indonesia and Nelson Mandela of South Africa received what they deserved from their people/countries respectively.

Further, it is clear from the following speech, when Prime Minister Narendra Modi addressed to BJP Parliamentary Party meeting in New Delhi on 16 March 2017.

The Times of India (Friday, 17 March, 2017) of Jaipur, carried the following story:

> Ambedkar is yet to get what he deserved, Modi said, echoing BJP's charge that Congress regimes promoted members of the Gandhi-Nehru Family at the cost of other stalwarts. He also said the government will introduce a coin on April 14 to mark the 125th anniversary of the leading framer of the Constitution.

Gandhi and Bhangi

Gandhiji wanted to see a "Bhangi" as the head of the state. He said that he did not want to be reborn, but if at all there is a rebirth he should be reborn as Bhangi , the lowest among the Harijans.[67] Gandhiji said:[68]

> 'I have long since considered myself to be a Bhangi in my speech, in my action and above all in my mind and spirit ... Indeed I hold it an honour to be among the despised Harijans and among them with Bhangis'.

'While in Delhi, Gandhiji insisted on living in the Bhangi colony where all the dignitaries, British or Indian, had to go and meet him and where many momentous meetings of the Working Committee of the Congress were held.'[69]

During the last day of his life, Gandhiji[70] declared:

> 'I would rejoice to think that we had a sweeper girl of a stout heart incorruptible and of crystal purity to, be our first President assisted in the discharge of her duties by a person like Jawahar Lal Nehru'.

'Bhangi Beti' as India's President – Gandhi

After India achieved her Independence, a few questions were tossed at Gandhi: Who will be the President of Republic of India? Would you keep a big English man on the post? If not Englishman then Pandit Jawaharlal Nehru because he is highly qualified person and have foreign experiences? Gandhi replied:[71]

> 'इसके उत्तर में मैं कहना चाहता हूं कि भारतीय प्रजातंत्र की प्रेसीडेंट एक भंगी लड़की बनेगी, यदि कोई पाक और बहादुर लड़की मुझे मिल गई। प्रेसीडेंट बहुत पढ़ लिखा ही हो और उसे कई भाषाओं का ज्ञान हो, यह कोई जरूरी नहीं है। किसी बड़े विद्वान ब्राह्मण या किसी क्षत्रिय को प्रेसीडेंट बनाकर हम दुनिया को अपना घमंड दिलाना नहीं चाहते।
>
> एक हरिजन लड़की को उस पर बिठाकर हमें अपना आत्मिक बल दिखाना चाहते हैं। हमें संसार को यह बताना है कि यहां न कोई उच्च है, न नीच है। परन्तु वह लड़की दिल की और 'शरीर की साफ होनी चाहिए। उसमें किसी प्रकार का मेल न हो' यदि लड़की हो तो सीता जैसी पवित्र हो और उसकी आंखों में तेज बरसता हो। सीताजी में इतना तेज था कि उन्हें रावण छू नहीं सकता था। यह तो एक ऐतिहासिक कथा है परन्तु इसका अर्थ यह है कि जिसमें इतनी पवित्रता हो उसे कोई छूने का साहस नहीं कर सकता। ऐसी लड़की यदि मुझे मिल गई तो वह हमारी पहली प्रेसीडेंट बनने वाली है। हम सब उसको सलामी देंगे और इस प्रकार एक नई बात दाखिल करके दुनियां के सामने एक मिसाल रखेंगे।
>
> आखिर कोई हिन्दुस्तान की बागडोर तो उसे संभालनी है नहीं। उसका एक सचिव मंडल रहेगा और वह जैसी सलाह देता जायेगा उसी के अनुसार वह काम करेगी। उसे केवल अपने दस्तखत ही करने होंगे वह कितनी बड़ी नैतिक बात है जो मैंने आज आपको बता दी। हिन्दुस्तान में रहने वाले सब लोग, चाहे वे सवर्ण हिन्दू हों या मुसलमान या अन्य कोई कोम, एक आवाज से यही कहें कि जिस किसी को प्रेसीडेंट बनाया जायेगा हम सब उसको सलामी देंगे। यही सच्चा नैतिक बल है और बाकी सब मिथ्या है। यदि मेरी कल्पना की लड़की हमारी प्रेसीडेंट बनी तो मैं भी खादिम बनकर उसका काम करूंगा और सरकार से अपने आने तक के लिए भी पैसा नहीं मांगूंगा। जवाहरलाल जी, सरदार पटेल और राजेन्द्र बाबू आदि को भी मैं उसके सचिव मंडल में भेजकर उसके नौकर बना दूंगा।'

Of course, it was a good move. Instead, Bhangis got Gandhi the dreamer, the conciliator but man with no plan. He came up with no new ideas or at least ideas that sounded new. We will say to the world, 'प्रेसीडेंट भंगी की बेटी बनेगी', that was more than a slogan. It was Gandhi who surprised every body. It was Gandhi, the coiner of catchy new labels 'प्रेसीडेंट भंगी की बेटी बनेगी'. If he (Gandhi) was so wishful of getting a 'Bhangi Beti' as India's President, why he did not do efforts to look for one within the Indian fold. Was it tactical or he in reality not want to see 'प्रेसीडेंट भंगी की बेटी बनेगी'. The expectations of Bhangis on the issue of the 'प्रेसीडेंट भंगी की बेटी बनेगी?' had been raised sky high and nothing had moved on it during Gandhi's era. It indicates Gandhi's inability to deliver on his own commitment. Thus, long years ago, Gandhi thundered by saying 'प्रेसीडेंट भंगी की बेटी बनेगी'. But the spirit of Gandhi seems to have been almost buried by the Congress.

I made a few points which I thought, I should discuss and perhaps elaborate on.

For me, whether Gandhi was good or bad, it is not as important as whether it was better than what went before it. Gandhi did not come forward for redemption of Bhangis. Bhangis were relieved when Ambedkar and Gandhi finally protected them from the excesses of caste Hindus (who still squat on untouchables).

From the writings and clarifications made by Gandhi through the columns of *Harijan* and *Young India*, it is beyond doubt that Gandhi wanted redemption of Bhangis. When we look at Gandhi as an intrepid warrior for socio-economic liberation of the lowliest, especially the Bhangis, there is no doubt that a politician like Gandhi showed more sympathy than anyone else to make Bhangi a public issue and to get their support. He knew that mere lip sympathy will not bring transformation in the status and conditions of the Bhangis, but he seems to be deliberately gaining support for his political gain. Gandhi probably wanted to play the role of a shepherd who would steer the Bhangis, who were still so ignorant that it was easy to play on their sentiments. There cannot be an uglier form of politics. Therefore his 'words', for instances consider myself (Gandhi) to be Bhangi in my speech, in my action and above all in my mind and spirit'[72], are questionable.

Further, the spirit that Gandhi displayed in a philosophical manner is not visible in his functioning. Again, in his own words,[73] 'he (Gandhi) wanted to see a Bhangi as head of the state' but no Bhangi or Dalit in the country has ever become the 'head of the State'. This makes it clear that Gandhi Congress has failed on Gandhi's parameters of Bhangi as head of the state.

As a 'Father of the Nation, it was his duty to act tough. But Gandhi has completely failed to have a control on the Congress and, therefore, Gandhi himself is accountable for this failure.

The fact is that Bhangis remained where they were and that is why, it is not very different today because of the mentality of the Congress and the BJP. The fault is in our Heroes.

According to Poona Pact (1932), Gandhi established the Harijan Sevak Sangh (HSS). Its main aim/object was the propagation of removal of untouchability programmes across the country. Gandhi used several strategies, such as agitation against untouchability, launching of socio-educational reform movement amongst the untouchables and uniting all untouchable castes/communities. He wooed untouchables in general and Bhangis in particular for their support for Gandhi's agitation.

Another significant strategy that was adopted by Ambedkar was to leave permanent and collective withdrawal of untouchables from menial occupations. At this point, more than seven decades had passed since Ambedkar took the initiative to give a slogan regarding liberation of Bhangis. Ambedkar said that 'Bhangi Jharoo Choro'[74] (Bhangi leave the Broom). This slogan is not heard much these days. Now, Ambedkar slogan assumed significant proportion and created awakening. As Ambedkar agitation gained momentum amongst the Bhangis, Gandhi perceived the danger to the Congress. The main concern of Gandhi Congress now shifted to Bhangis. Gandhi had earned a reputation of being a saviour of Bhangis and an opponent of Ambedkar's activities.

Not only did the Congress combat the militancy of Safai Karamcharis Trade Union, but the guardians of established, order also went after the Balmiki cultural and social groups as well as after many political formations floated by Ambedkar and his followers.

Similarly, Vijay Prashad states:[75]

> 'Balmiki politics came under the hegemony of the Congress and of the Hindutva factions from 1950 and Balmikis found themselves in a position of subservience to the petty satraps in Congress organisation and to the class of Municipal administrators'.

Gandhi amongst the Bhangis

During 1930s, Gandhi visited several untouchable Bastis/colonies in Delhi and he found conditions of life in them 'to be abhorrent'.[76] After his preliminary visit in 1930, Gandhi described the untouchable Bastis through his powerful writings and speeches in 1937. He described thus:[77]

> 'Untouchable colonies as the worst of any I had seen and he urged the tax payers, to wake up and make their city fathers realise their duty'.

Looking towards most miserable conditions of the untouchable Bastis in different parts of Delhi, Brij Krishan Chandiwala and G.D. Birla toured Delhi. The drive for Gandhi's comfortable stay in an untouchable Basti took a positive turn when Chandiwala and Birla 'decided to locate Gandhi in the most recent colony which is today located on Mandir Marg'.

Quoting Pyarelal, a famous Gandhian writer, Vijay Prashad[78] in Untouchable Freedom played an important role in improving the pitiable conditions of the Bhangis in Delhi.

> 'Eight hundred people lived in hundred rooms and shared two water taps and thirteen ramshackle latrines. The tenements looked like minature Black holes, with as many as ten people sharing a room. How could they possibly live their with decency God alone knew'.

He further wrote:[79]

> 'Shortly before Gandhi moved into the colony, volunteers from the Swayam Sevak Dal, from Shriram's Delhi Cotton Mills, from the Congress and from the DMC tried to improve the horrendous living conditions. They repaired the latrines, put the taps in working order and erected huts, tents and shamianas to give the colony an appearance of a camp. The temporary structures, housed reception rooms, a secretariat, a guest suite, a field kitchen and an eating shed. How devastatingly representative of our mud-hut civilization and categorically different from the massive stone, built Imperial Secretariat and Viceregal Palace of Imperial Rulers'.

Aruna Asaf Ali,[80] another Congress leader and also closed associate of Gandhi wrote:

> 'But to a foreigner this camp is just a phoney, Headquarters of a revolutionary organization about to take responsibility for the state.'

Pyarelal[81] again wrote:

> 'He (Gandhi) himself stayed in two rooms beside the Valmiki temple which stood about 50 meters from the tenements. This was a political gesture, not an instance of the glorification of poverty, for the openly declared that the actual homes of the dalits appeared worse than the worst prison cell, he had experienced in India and South Africa'.

At his first prayer, meeting in the Colony on 31 March 1946, Gandhi[82] said that he prayed that the day should come when he would be able to stay in the houses of the Harijans themselves and partake of the food they would serve.

Pyarelal[83] made a statement on Gandhi:

> 'As of now, he (Gandhi) could not live in the filth in which they (Bhangis) lived. Gandhi, like Nehru, was scrupulously historicist in his account of the squalor in Dalit hamlets'.

The Unknown Face of Gandhi Exhibited in Public Domain

Similarly, we get another idea of how untouchables in general and Bhangis in particular across the country were relegated to the background with the growth of Ambedkar movement, from the accounts of A.K. Biswas:[84]

> 'The hero of the national movement was prefabbed in workshops of skilled manipulators and committed workmen away from public view only to charm and deceive people by creating a mirage around him for mass consumption. The gainers and beneficiaries have much to lose if the hallow crafted by immense mischief and manipulation is blasted. Nation of billions should be ashamed of such mean designs'.

> 'The secret though exposed, but the Mahatma's sham of love for the Bhangi is a gigantic tragedy. This is over emphasized everywhere. His antipathy against an untouchable, even though meritorious and adequately qualified, holding an elective or high office, however, exploded over Rameshwar Agnibhoj, who was included in the Cabinet formed by Dr. Narayan Bhaskar Khare, chief minister (then called Prime Minister) of Central Provinces & Berar from August 1937 ... July 1938. A graduate, Agnibhoj was a well known freedom fighter and patriot. Gandhi publicly admonished Khare for his action, saying, he 'was opposed to the creation of such high ambitions among persons belonging to the Scheduled Castes'. A chastised Khare dissolved his Council of Ministers and fell in line to please the inveterate dictator in no time! Because he hated ambition in untouchables. Deception as a cultural heritage has been bequeathed for every Indian to follow without qualms and much less retribution to treat untouchables across the subcontinent, ambition in untouchables is bad. It is good to the hearts of others'.

Why not a National Day for Deception

Bhangis, in particular, were highly impressed by Gandhi's views but like many scholars, A.K. Biswas too differed from Gandhi on questions of Bhangis. Criticizing bitterly Gandhi's views towards untouchables, Biswas, in his article of 2016, said:[85]

> 'Adolf Hitler, one of the most hated men in human history, uttered an eternal truth: 'The great masses of people will more easily fall victims to a big lie than to a small one. Especially, if it is repeated over and over'. The masses are to be fooled in the name of religion and patriotism and those who do so are the biggest beneficiaries of their pretentious moves and designs. The victims of deception and perfidy – the great masses – cannot conceive, much less demolish, them because the cheats are defended and protected by strong walls raised by their powerful devotees and state

authorities. This is the unfortunate experience of India for ages. It will continue for many more decades. Illiteracy has to be perpetuated for the benefit of the charlatan and deceiver.

The enemies of the nation struck the innocent and ignorant masses long ago. One of the trendsetters was a tall man, revered as a saint and apostle of non-violence – so called father of the nation. It is unfortunate to name such a man of history responsible for befooling the lowliest, the most under-privileged and accursed souls on earth.

See the level and scale of his hypocrisy. 'The Sudra, who only serves (the higher castes) as a matter of religious duty and who will never own any property, who indeed has not even ambition to own anything, is deserving of thousands obeisance. The very gods will shower down flowers on him. This squarely fits into Hitler's afore mentioned prescription and prognostication! None questioned him. Placed on a high pedestal, he is beyond reach of the common man. He went unchallenged. Any attempt to accost him will be shouted down. Questioning him or his wisdom is viewed as blasphemy, an inevitable sign of slavery of thoughts. He has left even the malicious Manu miles behind in putting a glow on the chain of slavery for the Sudra!! A known enemy with an open sword in hand is better than a deceitful angel reciting scriptures.'

None harmed the Bhangi more than the Mahatma, worshipped almost as an avatar.

Valmiki Mandir[86]

During British India, at the end of the road leading to Panch Kuian Road, a group of Bhangi families was residing. The Bhangis Basti was popularly known as Harijan colony. There is around 150 ft. long and 100 ft. wide area of four walls. In the centre of the four walls, the local Bhangis established the temple of Valmiki Rishi, the first author of Sanskrit *Ramayana* for worship. On both sides, right and left, there were two rooms. The room located to the left side, measuring around 15–20 ft. long and 10–12 ft wide, was later for the first time marked for Gandhi's stay in 1946. Although Gandhi used the temple for Prarthna, Gandhi followers, supporters and the Congress workers were allowed to set up tents in Valmiki Mandir to stay and they participated in the evening prayer. Besides, thousands of men, women and children assembled here. It should, however, be noted that another room was used as 'kitchen'.

The foregoing account shows that Gandhi and his supporters made constant efforts to win the Bhangis over to his side by disassociating them from Ambedkar. Gandhi tried to give them importance and Gandhi's impact among the Bhangis increased. The poor and innocent Bhangis, under Gandhi's influence supported the Congress since then. This enabled the Bhangis to strengthen the ties with the Congress, about which the author has already discussed in other chapters.

In April 1946, Gandhi decided to remain in Valmiki Mandir during the summer. The Cabinet Mission[87], under the leadership of Pathiki Lawrence, the Secretary, Government of India, Sir Stafford Cripps and A.V. Alexander during the same period had already arrived in India and a meeting was held at Valmiki

Mandir between Gandhi and the members of the Cabinet Mission. On 1 May 1946, with the increase of summer, Gandhi left the Valmiki Mandir and went to Simla. Here Gandhi stayed till May 26. Next day (i.e. 27 May 1946) again Gandhi moved to Masuri and continued to stay there till 8 June. On 9 June, Gandhi returned back to Valmiki Mandir, New Delhi, from Masuri. On his return, Gandhi stayed at Valmiki Mandir up to 28 June and then left for Poona.

Many foreign and Indian dignitaries wanted the support of Gandhi in the country for various socio-political activities and causes. It was for this reason that several meetings of the VIPs with Gandhi were arranged at Valmiki Mandir. For instance on 5 July 1947, Lady Mountbatten[88] visited Valmiki Mandir in order to meet Gandhi. It was for the first time in the Indian history that a Viceroy's wife came here. Soon Valmiki Mandir gained all India fame as eminent dignitaries from distant places reached there.

A hundred secret files relating to Subhash Chandra Bose were made public by PM Narendra Modi on the 119th birth anniversary of the Freedom fighter on 23 January 2016 do throw new light on Gandhi's stay in a Bhangi Basti, saying Bose had indeed died in an air crash in Taipei on 18 August 1945.

There seems to be no scope for doubt that Col. Habibur Rahman met Gandhi in Bhangi Basti in New Delhi. The Times of India was the first to report on 24 January 2016. A quick glance at what 100 files declassified on Subhash Chandra Bose's birthday have thrown up on the three most vexing issues on Netaji's life and disappearance. Out of three, an important one runs as follows: When Col. Habibur Rahman, who accompanied Netaji in the plane from Saigon, was released from prison, he visited Mahatma Gandhi in Bhangi Basti in New Delhi, had a detailed discussion and was able to place before Gandhiji, one of the most significant facts of the Netaji's life. As a result of Habibur Rahman's efforts and specific course of action by Gandhiji, the matter came up before the public. At that time Amiya Nath Bose was present in the room when Habibur Rahman spoke to Gandhi about the alleged air crash at Taihoku airport on 18 August 1945. After Habibur Rahman left the place, Gandhi met journalists who were waiting to interview Gandhiji. He told them, 'Habib is carrying out his leader's order. I do not believe that Subhash died in any air crash'. ('What's Hot in the Bose files' in Sunday *Times of India*, Jaipur, 24 January 2016, p. 10)

Thus, Gandhi's brief period of seven-times stay at Valmiki Mandir in 16 months from 1 April 1946 came to an end on 30 July 1947.

The leadership of the Congress, in this phase, was in the hands of Gandhi who had entered politics in 1919–20. He participated in the National movement and courted arrest during the national movement. Gandhi in his individual capacity also remained the leader of the Congress party and started coming to Delhi from 1915 onwards. During the later years of national movement, Gandhi visited Delhi many times and also met Viceroy for Hunter Committee Report and other causes. After India achieved Independence, Gandhi continued to visit Delhi. Thus, in 1915, he started visiting Delhi and by January 1948, he had visited Delhi 80 times. On 30 January 1948, he was shot dead at Birla Bhavan, New Delhi.

Sixty Eight Years of Independence, No Change for the Bhangis

What does it mean to be Bhangis in India then?

Let us first look at what it meant 69 years ago, meaning more than two generations ago. It was the last period with several and serious socio-economic and religious restrictions and disabilities imposed on untouchables castes in general and Bhangis in particular. The life of Bhangis was worst than animals. The Bhangis then meant 'lowest among low', 'untouchable among untouchables'. The Bhangi families were engaged in most dirtiest work and removing night-soil. What was the scenario then, two generation on? Here are seven of my casual observations:

i. There was social distance with Bhangis but there is now a mix that was not visible earlier. The Bhangis a few decades ago were not physically touched. This has changed. Even if only a little.

ii. When the author visited Valmiki Mandir from Jaipur on 31 July 2015, a few months ago he did not encounter a single Bhangi in Valmiki Bhangi colony, who could narrate about Gandhi's stay at the Mandir. Gandhi's closest associate Mahadev Desai, an eminent writer who wrote about Gandhi in his book '*From day-to-day, Gandhi*', has not written a single line about it. This is very surprising. Thus unusual much remains to be written, particularly on Gandhi-Bhangi relations and interaction.

iii. Religion remains as important as it has always been. There is also an unquestioning acceptance of rituals. The present Mahant of Valmiki Mandir says the mental set-up of orthodox Hindus has not changed so far. When author asked him about any written literature, his response was that no scholar has written about it. The author hesitates to say it is worse because nobody paid attention to it.

iv. Visit of VIPs to Valmiki Mandir has become common. Most of the Prime Ministers of India, such as Indira Gandhi, P.V. Narsimharao, Rajiv Gandhi and Narendra Modi have visited it, which is a good thing. And most of them were comfortable there, showing how easy this move is. The Bhangis still feel cheated by the political parties.

v. Many economic aspects have changed. Many social facets have not changed. Above all is the caste Hindus attitude towards Bhangis. The Bhangis are still treated in a way, that would be unacceptable in any civilized society.

vi. Bhangis – the most marginalized, backward and neglected community in India – the night-soil remover, expected from Gandhi, the well known figure in Indian politics, to play the part of the decider. Going by Gandhi's scheme of socio-political engineering, Gandhi failed to prove himself as the saviour of Bhangis. There was no interaction. His professed love for redemption of Bhangis was political hoax, Gandhi's concocted[89] desire. 'If I am destined not to gain redemption in this very birth, it is my aspiration to be born as a Bhangi in my next birth' was a fool proof evidence of his pretense. The government's welfare and support measures over several years have been stuttering along suffering from caste prejudices and misplaced priorities. Even after 68 years of Independence, manual scavenging is a reality and is still practised across the country.

vii. Despite the peculiar character of stigma and persecution they bear, they were not provided any separate Constitutional safeguard. Instead they were fitted into existing category of SCs in ways which have left much to be desired. Further, despite inclusion in official category, members of Bhangi caste have found it particularly difficult to get a government job of their category.

Many have formed associations based on community identities. Numerous official committees, commissions and Acts have addressed the plight of this marginalized community. The latest act among these is 'Legislation on Abolition of Scavenging, passed by Parliament in 1993.

A major concern of many people of Bhangi community is the lingering stigma of manual scavenging. In many parts of India, the poor Bhangis still remove the night-soil. Organizations such as the Akhil Bharatia Safai Mazdoor Congress, which has been formed by a number of educated members of community, are rare as not many are convinced of its worth to come out in the open and support their less fortunate community members. For this shabby state of affairs more than 40 years rule of the Congress is blamed.

Sarojini Naidu's Frank Assessment of the Father of Nation

The last Governor General Lord Mount batten was sent to India with a single agenda – transfer of power to Indian hands. A series of events occurred during this period and they were directly over the issues of untouchables and untouchability. This was a manifestation of the man now anointed as the Father of Indian Nation. Some of the Congress leaders began to question the efficacy of Gandhi. Sarojini Naidu, who was a noted poetess, good orator, freedom fighter and also a closest associate of Gandhi during the freedom movement, had removed the mask that Gandhi wore. She gave her frank assessment of the Father of the Nation.

Soon after his arrival in Delhi, Lord Mountbatten asked one of the Gandhi's associates, Sarojini Naidu, whether in view of the determined poverty in which Gandhi chose to live, the Congress party really could protect him?

The irreparable poetess Sarojini Naidu trilled:[90]

> 'Ah' she laughed. You and Gandhi may imagine that when he walks down that Calcutta station platform looking for a suitably crowded third class carriage that he is alone, or when he is in his hut in the untouchables' colony he's unprotected. What he does not know is that there are a dozen of our people dressed as untouchables walking behind him crowding into that carriage.'

Gandhi's Living with Bhangis in a Bhangi Basti: A Reality or Myth

Among the various socio-political issues faced by Gandhi then, one was redemption of the Bhangis. On 11 January 1912, speaking about redemption of the Bhangis, Gandhi wished[91] 'to serve the Bhangis in number of ways'. He further said:[92] 'I do wish the upliftment of the Bhangis'. Consequently, Gandhi chose one way. The way was living with Bhangis in a Bhangi Basti. The living venue was Bhangi Basti, Panch Kuia Road, New Delhi.

The idea of living with Bhangis was no doubt good and distinct. Not only Gandhi supporters but also the Congress supported Gandhi. In the Congress party, there were in majority *kisan, mazdoor,* labourers and workers and almost all members were poor people. Besides, there were also some big businessmen like Tata, Birla etc. Birla as a businessman continues to be the main supporter of Gandhi. He also supported the Congress, being a leading progressive party.

Drive against untouchability took a new turn when Gandhi started living amongst the Bhangis in Panch Kuain Bhangi Basti, New Delhi. It is said that Gandhi brought about a new socio-political and cultural awakening among the Bhangis of Delhi by staying with them. The English press also played an important role in publicizing Gandhi's activities among the Bhangis in Delhi.

It was noted earlier that living with Bhangis was a good idea but not at the cost of poor party funds. For instance, Sarojini Naidu narrated the entire sequence of events in her assessment. She alleged that the Congress came to an understanding in which the Congress spent a lot of money to show that Gandhi was living in a most miserable conditions. During the later years of Gandhi's leadership even upper caste Hindus, social workers were asked to accompany him as if they were real Bhangis. The demonstration was a ploy to mislead the Bhangis and people, so they stayed with him. Why Gandhi supporters or the Congress *netas* had never talked about it? Has Gandhi not befooled people? The Gandhi Congress remained a mute spectator.

Thus, Gandhi made constant efforts to win the Bhangis and other untouchables on his Congress side by disassociating them from Ambedkar. Instead of working as untouchables' protector, Gandhi as a recognized leader was not expected to work in such a way. It proves that Congress fully supported Gandhi, which was surprising to the common man. Common man was not against the redemption of the Bhangis but they wished Gandhi to act accordingly.

In another instance narrated by Sarojini Naidu,[93] she explained:

> 'When he (Gandhi) moved into Bhangi colony in New Delhi ... a score of congress workers again unscrupulously clothed as Harijans were sent to live in the novels around his'.

She concluded:[94]

> 'My dear Lord Louis, you will never know how much it has cost the Congress party to keep the old man in poverty.'

Sarojini Naidu's assessment on Gandhi conveyed a message that there was a difference in practice and perception of Mahatma Gandhi. It is now clear that Gandhi did not intend to walk the path of political morality. There is a need to maintain probity in the public life. Now where did Gandhi showed his greatness? It did not last long and Gandhi was exposed. Gandhi's artificial love for the Bhangis showed us how easily Bhangis, the simple and honest people, could accept Gandhi as their saviour. Not on political reasons, Gandhi's supporters should tender apology on serious ethical impropriety charges. Political credibility is essential and politicians like Gandhi must live up to the trust placed in him by the untouchables in general and Bhangis in particular.

Gandhi may be the Father of the Nation in the country, but his hypocrisy towards untouchables makes him one of the smallest. The Bhangi *netas*, workers and social activists are in the state of shock and dismay when down-trodden of India came to know this reality. For thousands of Bhangis, the plight continue even after 68 years of Independence.

Thus, for the first time, the manifestation of the Father of the Nation emerged in the fourth and fifth decades of the 20th century, piercing through 28-years-old orthodox iron curtain. Gandhi was not interested in the welfare of untouchables. On the contrary, he stressed on hypocrisy.

The recent events make it clear that Gandhi was befooling the untouchables and that Gandhi still enjoys respect among them. This was politically motivated. Such a negative attitude weakened the issue. Living as Bhangi in a Bhangi Basti was not so simple, as Gandhi did. Negative approach cannot deliver good fruits. The focus should have been on affirmative action. Bhangis were by no means an isolated instance, but part of a wider attempt by Gandhi Congress to seize direct control over untouchables as a whole.

Why there was not a semblance of protest by the Indian academicians, intelligentsia and its educated? Why Gandhi was not condemned? It was because the matter was related to the untouchables, i.e. lowest of the low. It did not attract the attention of the elite class.

Why the Congress remained silent all these years? Like the Congress, many others ignored the fact too. Some intellectuals remained critical in their personal assessment, but even they chose silence as better part of valour. Has political sycophancy decreased? Did most political parties have healthy traditions of dissent and debate? Now Gandhi's true followers should come forward on the issue. Why they are ashamed of being followers of Gandhi. If they do so they would earn enormous goodwill for the Congress and would become a vote bank for at least a generation and helping the Congress win election. Such a move would also make the Congress on side of untouchables and tribal communities.

Have 'Anti Untouchability Act' and 'Reservation' improved Quality of Bhangis Life?[95]

Seventy years ago when India achieved her Independence and, on 26 January 1950, adopted the Constitution of India, it then abolished the untouchability Constitutionally. The Constitution priority was ending the centuries of socio-religious discrimination and to remove the cultural blot of the nation too. It was presumed then that the wind of socio-religious and political change would sweep the untouchability from the country.

Over the last seven decades, it has become clear that untouchability is still practised untouchables in general and Bhangis in particular, keeping them away from schools, temples, shops, etc. The questions of removal of untouchability from Hinduism did not come up for the first time in 1947. It was a recurring phenomenon as noted earlier. In 18th and 19th centuries, the contact with the Western liberal ideology gave a more vigorous and concrete shape to the struggle. Mahatma Jyotibha Phule in Maharashtra, Sri Narayana Guru in Kerala and E.V. Ramaswamy Naikar in Madras (now Chennai) represent this stage of struggle. But all these leaders had a glaring limitation- they could not encounter the caste system in its totality. But Ambedkar surprisingly countered the caste system in its totality.

In the five State assembly elections of 2017 (Punjab, Goa, Uttar Pradesh, Uttarakhand and Manipur) after seven full decades, the prevalence of untouchability rose again. Alok Sharma, a correspondent of leading English daily paper, published a news from Iglas, Hathras, UP, regarding untouchability in *The Times of India*, Jaipur, Wednesday 8 February 2017. The paper also played an important role in publicizing the conditions of Bhangis (also known as Valmiki in UP) . The paper carried the following story:

Dalit Nominee Sits on Floor, Carries Own Cup; MP's Son Fighting on BJP Ticket in Jat-Dominated Reserved Seat says he Accepts Casteism

Iglas (Hathras): A Dalit BJP candidate here not only sits on the floor when he goes canvassing to the homes of upper caste voters, he never forgets to carry a steel glass along to drink tea. Here's why: A Dalit using a cup at an upper caste home would make the utensil 'impure'. This is an age when ending casteism is the stated mission of all parties.

Amit Shah, national president of the party, Rajvir Diler represents, recently participated in a sit-down lunch, 'sah bhoj' with Dalits across Uttar Pradesh to drive home his party's social equality message. It's not difficult to understand why Diler, BJP nominee from Iglas, is averse to breaking the caste shackles, unlike fellow Dalits elsewhere. Iglas is a reserved seat, a three-hour ride from Delhi, less than 300 km away.

It is dominated by Jat voters, about 90,000 of them. They decide the winner. So while other Dalit candidates have too show respect to upper caste voters, he takes things to the extreme, Diler calls his ways of sitting on the floor and using his own glass his '*paramparagat aadat*' (family custom).

And the '*paramparagat aadat*' is followed at every step. Metres from the panchayat office, Diler in his late 40s, repeatedly touches the feet of Mohan Singh, Jat pradhan from Tochhigarh, who is years younger to him. '*Main aapke pair padhta hun, mujhe meri galti to batao. Main ek goon ka chowkidar bannna chahta hun, vidhayak nahin* (I beg of you, please tell me my fault. I'd rather be a watchman than an MLA, if you are angry with me)', he exhorts Mohan. But the pradhan, who controls about 4,500 Jat votes, tells him things are different this time. Ajit Singh's RLD, a party that Jats identify with, too has fielded a Dalit.

Diler is candid in justifying his desire to remain shackled in casteism. '*Main ek bhangi ka beta hun. Mere pita bhi yahin karte thhey. Main apni maan maryada khatm nahin kar sakta. Zamana chahe badalta rahe* (I am the son of a Valmiki, I can not break away from tradition. Let the world change, I won't), he says.

He pulls out his steel glass from his pocket when asked, if it is true that he doesn't drink tea in cups provided by the upper castes.

Valmika is the lowest among Dalits in the caste hierarchy and Diler inherited the so-called tradition from his father Kisen Lal, five-term MLA and one time MP.

Diler's supporters say people of all castes love him for his desire to remain steeped in discriminatory casteist practices.

The caste hierarchy is evident in the black Bolero that Diler uses. While he sits with the driver in the front seat, the most comfortable middle seats go to Jagdish Prasad, a Brahmin, and Robin Chaudhary, a Jat. In the two cramped last-row seats are Amit Valmiki and Mukesh Kumar Baghel, who also belong to the most backward caste.

Facing almost similar humiliation for selling his kidney in different situation, Mahesh Valmiki, from Alwar, Rajasthan, and also a second-year student of mining at IIT – BHU, wanted to sell his kidney to repay his study loan, but upper castes refused to take Valmiki organ, reported The Times of India, (Jaipur, Saturday, 23 January 2016). The paper carried the following story:

IIT Pupil Tries to Sell Kidney to Repay Loan, But No Takers for Dalit Organ, Drops Out to Earn Living as a Sweeper

Agra: Thrust into an uncomfortable debate about casteism by the alleged suicide of a Dalit PhD scholar in Hyderabad, Indians will find themselves further red-faced by the story of an aspiring engineer from IIT-BHU making ends meet as a sweeper.

Mahesh Balmiki, a second-year student of mining, mulled some desperate measures to pay off a ₹ 2.7 lakh loan he had taken for his studies. 'There was a lot of pressure. Due to my prolonged illness, I had to incur expenses for my treatment and could not give back the loan I took for my studies', he told ToI.

Short of options, Mahesh even began a search for a buyer for one of his kidneys. But, he later told some friends, in the thriving black market for kidneys, people first asked the donor's caste.

Mahesh added, 'I visited around five hospitals in Varanasi and Alwar. The doctors there informed me that no one would take my kidney as I am a Dalit'.

It proved a dead-end for Mahesh, and the 19-year-old, whom some teachers describe as 'very bright' had to leave his studies midway and take up a sweeper's job back at his village in Rajasthan's Alwar, for just ₹ 4,000 a month. Tired and frustrated, he often spoke with his friends about ending his life. Sensing trouble, a few of his friends approached Magsaysay award winning activist Sandeep Pandey, who took to Mahesh's cause immediately and approached the BHU alumni for funds to pay off his loan. He succeeded and just a few days ago, paid off Mahesh's loan. But Mahesh whose father is paralysed and mother earns her living as a domestic help in several houses, still works as a cleaner to survive.

The brightest among his parents' three sons, Mahesh scored 85 per cent in Class X. Despite working part time as a cleaner during his exams and frequent bouts of illnesses, he still managed 70 per cent in class XII. Better results were in store for the diligent teen who did exceedingly well in the IIT entrance test and got a seat at BHU.

'I have no other option than to clean and sweep', he said. For him, Pandey, a former contractual teacher at BHU, literally came as a god send. 'Sandeep sir helped me get rid of the loan through funds he collected from former IIT-BHU students. I have paid everything back. I believe there are hundreds like Rohith Vemula (the University of Hyderabad PhD Scholar) studying at prestigious institutions in our country. Some are forced to end their lives. A few lucky ones get people like Sandeep sir,' he said.

In both cases, Bhangis are humiliated and harassed ruthlessly. Every day they (Bhangis) are going through these voluminous harassment, humiliation and atrocities. These atrocities are multiplying with each passing day. What is going on? These incidents highlight the most pitiable plight of the poor and voiceless Bhangis are far away from protection of their fundamental rights.

Over the years many landmark judgments have been pronounced on protection of fundamental rights of untouchables in general and Bhangis in particular brought forth through the Parliament and Apex Courts. But the government has failed in providing Justice.

Notes

1. For more details, see particularly Sheshrao Chavan, *Gandhi and Ambedkar: Saviours of Untouchables*, Mumbai, Bharatiya Vidya Bhavan, 2001. p. 69.
2. Ibid., p. 81.
3. Ibid.
4. Ibid., p. 86.
5. Ibid., p. 88.
6. Ibid., p. 88–89.
7. Ibid., p. 95.
8. Ibid.
9. Ibid., p. 108.
10. Ibid., p. 103.
11. Ibid.
12. Ibid.
13. Mohandas Naimishrai, *Bhartiya Dalit Aandolan ka Itihas–3*, New Delhi, Radhakrish Publication, 2013, p. 414.
14. Ibid., Vol. 1, p. 414.
15. Ibid., Vol. 1, p. 415.
16. Ibid.
17. Ibid.
18. Ibid.
19. Ibid., Vol. 1, p. 416.
20. Ibid.
21. Ibid., Vol. 2, p. 153.
22. Ibid., Vol. 3, p. 417

23. Ibid., Vol. 2, p. 149.
24. Ibid., Vol. 3, p. 384.
25. Ibid.
26. Ibid.
27. For more details, see particularly 'Dons from Britain's Top Varsities Oppose Modi a next PM' in *The Times of India*, Jaipur, Thursday, 24 April 2014.
28. Ibid.
29. Mohandas Naimishrai, ibid., 2013, p. 384
30. Ibid., p. 384.
31. Ibid., p. 385.
32. According to Brij Krishan Chandiwala, Gandhi first came to Delhi in 1915 for formal politics and causes. His last visit to Delhi was on 30 January 1948. During 1915–1948, Gandhi visited several times and stayed at Delhi at different places with different persons. For more details, see particularly ब्रजकृष्ण चांदीवाला, गांधीजी दिल्ली कब-कब आए और कहां-कहां ठहरे, इन गांधीजी की दिल्ली डायरी, खण्ड-3, पृ. 644–647.
33. ब्रजकृष्ण चांदीवाला, दिल्ली की खोज: अठारह दिल्लियों की कहानी, दिल्ली, प्रकाशन विभाग, सूचना और प्रसारण मंत्रालय, भारत सरकार, 1965, पृ. 312.
34. Ibid., p. 318.
35. Sheshrao Chavan 2001, ibid., p. 134.
36. Ibid., p. 134.
37. Ibid., p. 81.
38. Ibid., p. 141–142.
39. Ibid., p. 142.
40. Ibid.
41. Ibid., p. 144.
42. Ibid.
43. Ibid., p. 149.
44. Ibid.
45. Ibid., p. 151–152.
46. Ibid., p. 152.
47. Ibid.
48. Ibid.
49. Ibid., p. 152–53
50. Ibid., p. 154.
51. Ibid.
52. Ibid., p. 155–156.
53. Ibid, p. 156.
54. Ibid.
55. Ibid.
56. Ibid., p. 157.
57. Ibid., p.157–158.
58. Ibid., p. 158–159.
59. Ibid., p. 159.
60. Ibid.

61. Hind Swaraj quoted by A.K. Biswas.
62. Young India, 11–14, 1927 quoted by A.K. Biswas.
63. Varnasharma quoted by A.K. Biswas.
64. Dharma Manthan, p. 4, quoted by A.K. Biswas.
65. Harijan, 3.6.1947 quoted by A.K. Biswas.
66. विश्वास का पंपलेट देखे quoted by A.K. Biswas.
67. Sheshrao Chavan, 2001, p. 249.
68. Ibid., p. 249.
69. Ibid.
70. Ibid., p. 255.
71. देखें, ब्रजकृष्ण चांदीवाला, 'प्रेसीडेंट भंगी की बेटी बनेगी' इन गांधी जी की दिल्ली डायरी, खण्ड-3, पृ. 178–179.
72. Sheshrao Chavan, 2001, ibid., p. 249.
73. Ibid., p. 249.
74. Vijay Prashad, Untouchable Freedom: A Social History of a Dalit Community, New Delhi: Oxford University Press, 2000, p. 168.
75. Ibid., p. 168.
76. Ibid., p. 137.
77. Ibid.
78. Ibid.
79. Ibid.
80. Ibid., p. 138.
81. Ibid.
82. Ibid.
83. Ibid.
84. For more details, sec, A.K. Biswas, Why not a National day for Deception. Un published article, a copy with author.
85. Ibid.
86. विस्तृत जानकारी के लिए देखें, ब्रजकृष्ण चांदीवाला, 'वाल्मीकि मंदिर' इन दिल्ली की खोज, अठारह दिल्लियों की कहानी, दिल्ली, प्रकाशन विभाग, सूचना और प्रसारण मंत्रालय, भारत सरकार, 1965, पृ. 320–322.
87. Ibid., p. 321.
88. bid., p. 322.
89. Mahadev H. Desai, From Day to Day, Gandhi. Vol. V, p. 334.
90. Dominique Lapierre and Larry Colins, *Freedom at Midnight*, New Delhi: Vikas Publishing House, 2012, Footnote at p. 151.
91. Mahadev H. Desai, ibid., p. 334.
92. Ibid., p. 334.
93. Dominique Lapierre and Larry Collins, *Freedom at Midnight*, ibid. 2012, p. 151.
94. Ibid., p. 151.
95. दीनाभान, '60 साल की आजादी में वाल्मीकि जातियों को कुछ भी नहीं मिला' हरकिशन संतोषी, (स.) दलितों के दलित, नई दिल्ली: सस्ता साहित्य मंडल, 2009, पृ. 82, यह भी देखें, भाषासिंह, अदृश्य भारत: मैला ढोने के बाजबजाते यथार्थ से मुठभेड, नई दिल्ली: पेंगुइन बुक्स, 2012.

11

Emergence of the Bhangis as a Force to Ambedkar's Ideology

In this chapter I shall analyse the genesis, growth, internal dynamism and social and cultural consequences of Ambedkar agitation amongst the Dalits in general and Bhangis in particular. An examination of the position of the Dalits in the traditional social structure reveals the range and magnitude of diverse kinds of relative deprivation. The presence of deprivation itself will not give rise to a movement. Hence, I shall analyse the conditions under which Dalits began to receive the deprivation and the nature of leadership that made them realise that some thing could be done to improve the situation. The ideology of movement was mainly formulated by Dr B.R. Ambedkar. He transformed the outlook of Dalits by giving them a programme of action for their uplift and encouraged the founding of Scheduled Castes Federation (SCF). A number of regional and local associations emerged with the intention of carrying out various programmes and spreading the message of Ambedkar. Ambedkarites systematically worked for greater politicization of Dalits and spearheaded the movements focussing on one issue after another, the fight against untouchability, the right of admission to public schools, entry into temples, roads, recruitment to government jobs and political representation.

Besides the Dalit movement headed by Ambedkar, there were several agitations of which one was based on divergent ideological differences, such as the Gandhian ideology. The former introduced a wedge in the movement while the latter gave rise to splinter Dalit movements. A strong attack on Gandhi and on the Congress movement was led by Ambedkar. As a result of all this, the movement as a whole brought about transformative socio-political and cultural changes.

By any standard, the Gandhi-Ambedkar relationship is a fascinating story. Many, including this writer, have looked at it and many more will do so in future. The Ambedkar-Gandhi debate is vital part of that relationship and an important subject in itself.

Ambedkar was not a part of any organization when he arrived in India in 1920. But he was, perhaps, the only untouchable intellectual at that time with a conscious goal of involving all untouchable castes. Adivasis and other weaker sections of society in political agitation, the first person striving to enlist people from outside his or her linguistic/cultural region and, perhaps, the first person who was determined to fight against atrocities of caste Hindus. As for this plunging into the socio-political movement, it might be fair to say that in 1920, he created a political movement into which he and others plunged head long.

Let's examine this claim using evidence from published materials. Writing in 1996 Bhagwan Das the Dalit author of 'बाबा साहेब भीमराव अम्बेडकर और भंगी जातियां' reported:[1]

> 'अछूतों की बहुत सी जातियों परैया, पल्लन, माला, मदिया, नमो शुद्र, चाण्डाल महार, मांग, चाम्भार, कोली, मेहतर, डोम, धोबी, पासी, जुलाहा, भंगी आदि जातियों से लोग ऊपर आने लगे थे और उनकी शिक्षा, प्रोग्राम आंदोलन और व्यक्तित्व से प्रभावित होने लगे थे।'

Bhangis were the major sufferers. Ambedkar wanted to bring all untouchables together. The 'stitching together' notion was apt for Ambedkar.

This created enthusiasm among the Bhangis which made them realize that the leadership of Ambedkar was essential to get rid of caste Hindu atrocities and, therefore, decided to work along with Ambedkar. Bhangis were more harassed, tortured, murdered and humiliated. Not only this, Bhangis were prevented from using wells and refused admission in schools. This was the manifestation of deep-rooted hatred of caste Hindus because they (Bhangis) removed night-soil. The Bhangis were now attracted in bulk across the country including good deal of their support. Bhagwan Das was well aware of all this. According to him:[2]

> 'भंगी जातियों के लोग भी इससे अछूते नहीं रहे। अन्य जातियों के मुकाबले में वे सबसे अधिक घृणा के शिकार थे क्योंकि उनका काम गंदगी से जुड़ा हुआ था। बहुत सी अछूत और शूद्र जातियां भी उन्हें अछूत मानती थी और घृणा करती थी। उधर भंगी जातियों ने मार्क्स से भी बहुत पहले जन आन्दोलन के महत्व को समझा और अपनाया था। जब कभी समय मिला बगावत भी की। धर्म परिवर्तन और अपना एक स्वतंत्र धर्म उनकी विशेषता रही थी। उत्तर भारत में उनमें से सबसे अधिक संख्या में लोग मुसलमान, सिख और ईसाई बने थे तथा सत्ता में ऊंचे स्थानों पर भी पहुंचे थे। परन्तु हिन्दू नेताओं ने उनकी कमजोरियों को अपने धर्म और चतुराई का भरपूर प्रयोग उनकी जागृति को रोकने उनके संगठन को तोड़ने तथा उन्हें बाबा साहेब अम्बेडकर से दूर ले जाने में किया। पंजाब में 1937 में हुए पहले चुनाव में चौधरी बन्सी लाला कामयाब हुए और विधायक बने। उन्हें हिन्दुओं का समर्थन प्राप्त था परन्तु वे डॉ. अम्बेडकर के विरोधी नहीं थे। श्री चुन्नीलाल थापर, बालमुकुंद, भागमल पागल, र : र शुभ बाबू, फकीरचंद नाहर, चौधरी संतराम आदि बाबा साहेब अम्बेडकर से प्रभावित हुए और उनके नेतृत्व में काम किया। फिरोजपुर के हरवंत सिंह काफी समय अम्बेडकरी आंदोलन से जुड़े थे। मिहां सिंह गिल पैप्सू में शिड्यूल्य कास्टस फैडरेशन के उम्मीदार रहे और पहले मंत्री बने। हिमाचल प्रदेश उस समय पंजाब का हिस्सा था। शिमला में तेलूराम बैदवान एकमात्र कर्मठ लीडर था जो 1935 से लेकर लगभग पचास वर्ष तक बाबा साहेब के मिशन को पूरा करने में ईमानदारी और वफादारी से जुड़े रहे स्वयं अपना कुछ नहीं बनाया और निस्वार्थ ढंग से बिना जातिगत भेदभाव के दलितों की सेवा करता रहा। बैदवान साहेब एक या दो बार शिमला म्युनिसपल कमेटी के सभासद भी चुने गए। वे शिडयूल्ड कास्टस फैडरेशन तथा रिपब्लिकन पार्टी के प्रधान रहे। उनके नेतृत्व, चरित्र और सम्पूर्णता

से प्रभावित होकर बहुत से बाल्मीकि, चमार और कोली जाति में जन्में नौजवान अम्बेडकर आंदोलन से जुड़े। हिमाचल में तेलूराम बैदवान के बाद अम्बेडकर आंदोलन का काम अम्बेडकर मिशन संस्था जिन्दा रखे हुए है। लेखराम और उनके सहयोगी ईश्वर दास अम्बेडकर मिशन द्वारा बाबा साहेब के मिशन को फैलाने का काम कर रहे हैं। भंगी जाति (डोमार) में जन्में दूसरे प्रसिद्ध व्यक्ति नागपुर के भूतपूर्व मेयर श्री रामरत्न जानोरकर हैं जो लगभग 50 वर्षों से बाबा साहेब अम्बेडकर की पार्टी तथा फर्म से जुड़े हैं। वे शिडयूल्ड कास्टस फैडरेशन, रिपब्लिकन पार्टी तथा बौद्ध आंदोलन में महत्वपूर्ण भूमिका अदा करते रहे हैं। उनकी तरह का कट्टर ईमानदार और वफादार अम्बेडकरवादी कम ही देखने को मिलता है।

उत्तर भारत में लेखकों तथा कवियों में पंजाब कवि गुरदास राम आलम बाबा साहेब के विचारों और व्यक्तित्व से बहुत प्रभावित हुए। उनकी कविताओं के कई संग्रह छप चुके हैं। जालन्धर की कान्फ्रेन्स में 'आलीम' साहेब ने अपनी नजम 'अछूत' पढ़ी जो बाबा साहेब ने बहुत पसंद की।

जालन्धर के भागमल 'पागल' की कविताओं पर भी अम्बेडकरी असर साफ दिखता है। भंगी जाति में जन्में दूसरे लेखक और शायर बाबू फकीर चंद नाहर (लुधियाना) थे जो अछूत गजट पत्रिका के संपादक भी थे। उनकी पत्रिका के पहले अंक में छपी कविता 'रहने दो हमे अछूत बने हिन्दू हमें बनवा न' बहुत समय तक पढ़ने और सुनने वालों को झंझोड़ती रही।'

Before Independence, Shankar Rao migrated from Indore and settled down in Lucknow. Here he worked among his caste fellows (Bhangis) and united them. He also asked them to address untouchability and caste injustice and also propagated the socio-political message of Ambedkar. Bhagwan Das[3] elaborates his point with a historical anecdote:

'इन्दौर से जाकर लखनऊ में बसे शंकरराव उर्फ शंकर राव दामोदर गांगर्ड़े बाबा साहेब अम्बेडकर के आन्दोलन में हिस्सा लेते रहे। वे बहुत सुलझे हुए जोशीले नौजवान थे। सज्जन सिंह विशनार जो फैडरेशन छोड़कर कांग्रेस में चले गए और मध्य प्रदेश में मंत्री बने उनके सहयोगी और साथी थे। शंकर राव ने अपना पूरा समय भंगी जातियों में जागृति और संगठन पैदा करने में लगाया। वे एक बार उत्तर प्रदेश में विधान परिषद के सदस्य भी बने। भंगियों को ब्याज पर पैसा देकर गुलाम बनाने वालों की गुलामी से मुक्त कराने में जो काम उन्होंने किया वह उत्तर प्रदेश में उनसे पहले और उनके बाद किसी ने नहीं किया। साहूकारों के गुंडो ने महानगर स्थित उनके घर पर मिलने का बहाना करके उनके बदन में 5 गोलियां दागी और हमेशा के लिए उन्हें खामोश कर दिया। लखनऊ में ही धानुक जाति में जन्में बाबू महादेव प्रसाद ने इस सदी के तीसरे दशक में एमएएलएलबी पास किया और लखनऊ नगरपालिका में शिक्षा विभाग में सुपरिन्टैन्डैन्ट के पद से रिटायर हुए। बाबा साहेब ने जब वे लेबर मैंबर थे बाबू महादेव प्रसाद को एक ऊंचे पद पर नियुक्त किया था परन्तु वह किसी कारण लखनऊ नहीं छोड़ पाए। वे एक विद्वान तथा साहित्य से प्रेम करने वाले उच्च चरित्र के व्यक्ति थे। उन्होंने बाबा साहेब के आंदोलन को बहुत खामोश तरीके से बढ़ाया और दलितों में जागृति पैदा की।

कानपुर मजदूर आंदोलन का गढ़ था और शिडयूल्ड कास्टस फैडरेशन का भी मजबूत कैम्प था। चमार, भंगी, खटीक, पासी, कोली सभी जातियां मिल कर काम करती थी। आहिस्ता-आहिस्ता लोग टूटते गए और स्वार्थवश ही उन पार्टियों में चले गए जो अछूतों के संगठन की विरोधी थी। आज धानुक जाति में जन्मे श्री केनाथ बौद्ध उपासक संघ के झंडे तले अन्य बौद्धों के साथ मिलकर बाबा साहेब के मिशन को आगे बढ़ाने में लगे हैं।

बाबा साहेब अम्बेडकर 1942-1946 में वाईसराय काउंसल में लेबर मैम्बर रहे। दिल्ली में बाल्मीकि जाति के बहुत से लोग उनके सम्पर्क में आए। बाबा साहेब ने पंचकुई रोड स्थित कॉलोनी में से

चुनकर अच्छे लोगों को सफाई कर्मचारी यूनियन स्थापित करने की सलाह दी और उनकी सहायता भी की। इसका नाम म्यूनिसिपल कामगार संघ रखा गया। बाद में गांधीजी और कांग्रेस के समर्थकों ने संस्था के लैटर हैड पर से बाबा साहेब का नाम भी मिटा दिया। गांधीजी ने जब रहने के लिए भंगी बस्ती में प्रवेश किया तो इस संस्था के लोगों ने उनका कड़ा विरोध किया था परन्तु 1947 के बाद कांग्रेसी हरिजनों का प्रभाव बढ़ता चला गया और नई पीढ़ी के लोग बाबा साहेब से दूर होते चले गये।

Dalit literature has recorded Bhangi's remarkable role in spreading Ambedkar Mission. Nobody took it seriously since Gandhi Congress stalwarts themselves were engaged in sabotaging Ambedkar campaign. But, says Bhagwan Das, a prominent writer, the Bhangis active involvement has created fear among the Congressmen. When Babasaheb Ambedkar began his activism in the 1920s, Bhangis played a vital role in spreading his philosophy, writes Bhagwan Das. Slowly, all those who were spreading Ambedkar's message began to explore broader social themes. After providing valuable information of Ambedkar' s mission, Bhagwan Das says:[4]

'परन्तु भंगी कॉलोनी के बाहर लोग बाबा साहेब के मिशन का प्रचार प्रसर करते रहे। श्री गंगी लाला, अमीन चन्द द्राविड, तथा भगवान सरूप अम्बेडकरी आंदोलन से जुडे रहे। गंगीलाल जी ने बोद्ध धर्म ग्रहण किया और भिक्षु बने। धर्म प्रचार तो वे करते ही थे परन्तु जाति तोड़ों की शिक्षा पर अमल करते हुए उन्होंने अपने बच्चों के विवाह जाति और प्रदेश के बंधनों को तोड़कर किए। दिल्ली में ही बाल्मीकि जाति में जन्मा एक और नौजवान ब्रह्मजीत 1947 के पश्चात उभरा और पिछले 44 वर्षों से बाबा साहेब के मिशन में काम कर रहा है। वह ट्रेड यूनियर लीडर था फिर बौद्ध धर्म ग्रहण करने के बाद कुछ समय के लिए श्रामणेर (भिक्षु) बना। आज भी वह रिपब्लिकन पार्टी का कर्मठ कार्यकर्ता है। एक और नौजवान जो राष्ट्रपति भवन में सफाई कर्मचारी का काम करता था बाबा साहेब से प्रेरणा लेकर पढ़ने लगा। बीए पास किया और एलएलबी में दाखिला लिया। अम्बेडकर मिशन तथा बौद्ध उपासक संघ में काम करता रहा। वह एक अच्छा और कट्टर बौद्ध है उसने अमली तौर पर जाति व्यवस्था को तोड़ा और बच्चों के अन्तरजातीय विवाह किए।'

After Independence in 1947, Pramod Kumar, born in Aligarh in Bhangi family, left Aligarh and came to Delhi. Here, he joined the Ambedkar Mission and Bodh Upasak Sangh. Bhagwan Das, author of बाबा साहेब अम्बेडकर और भंगी जातियां, points out this fact in the debate. The author also argues that Bhangis dedication remain unmatched at that time.[5]

'आज की पीढ़ी में अलीगढ़ की बाल्मीकि जाति में जन्में प्रमोद कुमार अलीगढ़ से एमए, एमफिल करके दिल्ली आए और अम्बेडकर मिशन तथा बौद्ध उपासक संघ में काम करते रहे हैं दलित सौलिडैरटी में वे विशेष स्थान रखते हैं। वे बौद्ध धर्म अनुयाई हैं और 'शिक्षित बनो, संगठित बनो' के काम को झुग्गी झोपड़ियों में अमली जामा पहना रहे हैं। दिल्ली सरकार ने उनके काम को सराहा है और पुरस्कार भी दिया है। वे भी दलित सोलिडेरेटी की कार्यकारिणी समिति के भी सदस्य हैं। इनके अतिरिक्त बाल्मीकि जाति में जन्मे कई नौजवान जैसे नफे सिंह, मास्टर त्रिलोकचन्द, वीर सिंह, देवीदास वैंस, मेहरचन्द अछूत ज्ञानिन्दर कल्याण (अम्बेडकर मिशन हरियाणा) श्री स.प. राय, श्री विजय प्रकाश, श्रीमती अनुसूईया 'अनु' कई क्षेत्रों में काम कर रहे हैं और बाबा साहेब के मिशन को बाल्मीकि तथा अन्य जातियों में फैला रहे हैं।'

'पंजाब में बाल्मीकि जाति में जन्मे श्री रामचन्द संगर कई अम्बेडकरी संस्थाओं से जुड़े हैं और बौद्ध धर्म प्रचार का काम भी करते हैं। पंजाब में अम्बेडकरी आंदोलन में उनका खास स्थान है।'

Every one knows that in eastern region of Uttar Pradesh, Hellas are found in bulk. From pre-Indpendence to post-Independence, several Hellas were staunch supporters of Ambedkar and accepted Buddhism. Thus, Bhagwan Das again points out:[6]

> 'हेला जाति पूर्वी उत्तर प्रदेश में काफी संख्या में पाई जाती है। स्वतंत्रता के पहले से कान्सटीटूएंट असेम्बली से लेकर भंगी जातियों में से हेला जाति में जन्मे भगवान दीन, 1957 में नारायण दीन सांसद चुनकर आए। परन्तु उन्होंने बाबा साहब से कुछ अधिक असर नहीं लिया। परन्तु हेला जाति में जन्में इलाहाबाद निवासी रामसंजीवन राम न केवल बाबा साहेब अम्बेडकर के अनुयायी है बल्कि एक अच्छे बौद्ध भी हैं। वे बौद्ध धर्म प्रचार का कार्य प्रदेश के इस भाग में बड़े जोश और श्रद्धा से कर रहे हैं। उन्होंने हेला जाति पर एक खोजपूर्ण पुस्तक भी लिखी है। बनारस और इलाहाबाद में भंगी जाति में जन्मे श्री कलहन जी कल्याण चन्द जी के नाम से प्रसिद्ध हुए राज्य सभा तक पहुंचे। उन्होंने जवान उम्र में बाबा साहेब द्वारा चलाया 'समता सैनिक दल' तथा 'शिडयूल्ड कास्टस फैडरेशन में काम किया परन्तु बाद में वे कांग्रेस में चले गए। इसी प्रकार बद्री प्रसाद जी जो बाद में बदरी प्रसाद वाल्मीकानन्द के नाम से प्रसिद्ध हुए बाबा साहेब अम्बेडकर के विचारों से प्रभावित हुए और समता सैनिक दल और शिडल्यूड कास्टस फैडरेशन में काम करते रहे। परन्तु 1948 के बाद अम्बेडकरी आन्दोलन छोड़कर वे शिक्षा को बढ़ावा देने में लगे और बाल्मीकि धर्म प्रचार में मरते दम तक काम करते रहे।'

This work seeks to analyse or assess Ambedkar's influence on Bhangis, though I hope this might add to our understanding of it. While touching upon the Ambedkar-Bhangi relationship, the analyse that relationship.

It was around 1980s that Bhangi activism found new voices in writers like Om Prakash Valmiki, Sushila Takbhore and many others, including this author. These writers had played a great role in the changing society.

Some of Bhagwan Das's remarkable descriptions have resulted in spreading Ambedkar Mission. Bhagwan Das has been an Ambedkar scholar. The narration in 'बाबा साहेब भीमराव अम्बेडकर और भंगी जातियां' constitute the text's most valuable information incidents. These incidents provide its readers a glimpse of the true relationship between the two. To assert this relationship Bhagwan Das discusses some well-educated Bhangis. For instance[7]:

> 'भंगी जातियों में जन्में प्रसिद्ध अध्यापकों में उस्मानिया यूनिवर्सिटी (आंध्र प्रदेश) के डॉ. जयकिशन बाबा साहेब अम्बेडकर की शिक्षा से बहुत प्रभावित हैं और उन्होंने दलितों में शिक्षा को बढ़ाने का काम हाथ में लिया है। वे दलित सोलिडैरिटी के मान्य सदस्य भी हैं। वे कॉलेज में हिन्दी पढ़ाते है। परन्तु मजदूर और गरीब बस्तियों में शिक्षा का प्रचार-प्रसार करने में अपना समय, शक्ति और धन लगाते हैं। उन्हें किताबें पढ़ने तथा पढ़ाने का बहुत शौक है।
>
> इसी प्रकार गुजरात के डॉ. रमेश चन्द्र 'हाथ में झाडू माथे मेलू' के लेखक अम्बेडकरी संस्थाओं या बौद्ध धर्म से नहीं जुड़ें हैं परन्तु बाबा साहेब के विचारों से प्रभावित हुए और इस वर्ग की जीवन पद्धति तथा जीवन स्तर में परिवर्तन चाहते हैं। भारत के अन्य प्रान्तों में रहने वाले दलित नौजवान किताब लिखने में उनकी पुस्तक से प्रेरणा ले सकते हैं।
>
> भारत में भंगी जातियों में जन्मे लेखको में दो प्रसिद्ध नाम उभरकर सामने आते हैं जो बाबा साहेब के व्यक्तित्व, विद्वता तथा शिक्षा से प्रभावित होकर और प्रेरणा लेकर साहित्य सृजन के मैदान में उतरे हैं। इनमें उत्तरी भारत में ओमप्रकाश बाल्मीकि एक प्रसिद्ध लेखक हैं जो कहानियां कविताएं आदि लिखते रहे हैं। हाल ही में उन्होंने अपनी आत्मकथा 'जूठन' लिखी है। अछूत जातियों में कई लोग जाति सूचक

नाम या दुमछल्ले लगाकर छुपते फिरते हैं। परन्तु ओम प्रकाश बाल्मीकि एक साहसी नौजवान हैं जो हीनता के भाव के शिकार लोगों में आत्म विश्वास तथा आत्मसम्मान की भावना जगाना चाहते हैं।

दूसरा व्यक्ति डॉ. सुशीला टाकभौरे हैं जो मध्य प्रदेश की भंगी जाति में जन्मी और नागपुर के एक कॉलेज में पढ़ाती हैं। उनके लेखों से पता चलता है कि बाबासाहेब अम्बेडकर से वे किस हद तक प्रभावित हैं। कविताओं के अतिरिक्त सुशीला जी ने बहुत अच्छे लेख तथा नारी जाति पर एक बहुत अच्छी पुस्तक 'हिन्दी साहित्य के इतिहास में नारी' लिखी है। हिमाचल की एक साहित्यिक संस्था ने उन्हें पुरस्कार देने का फैसला किया है। उनके लेखो में गंभीरता गहराई और मजबूती देखने को मिलती है। उनको शिक्षा दिलाने तथा मार्गदर्शन करने में उनके पति श्री सुन्दर लाल टाकभौरे तथा नागपुर के राजनीतिक एवं सामाजिक वातावरण का बड़ा योगदान है।

कई धार्मिक नेता चमत्कारों या भगवान के नाम पर आध्यात्मिक या नैतिक शिक्षा के जरिए परिवर्तन लाने की कोशिश करते हैं। राजनीतिक नेता सत्ता प्राप्त करके कानून और शासन के जरिए परिवर्तन लाना चहाते हैं परन्तु लेखक, विचारक, कवि, बुद्धिवादी लोग शांत तरीके से देर तक रहने वाले टिकाऊ परिवर्तन लाने का काम करते हैं। वे मन को बदलते हैं क्योंकि मन ही व्यवहार को प्रभावित करता है।

The best assessment of the outcome of Ambedkar-Bhangis relationship has been made by Bhagwan Das in his book. Virtue of Ambedkar-Bhangi relation has become more relevant in this fast-paced world. The scholars, researchers and others should heed and take measures in the right earnest.

In his other writings on Bhangis, Bhagwan Das outlines the Ambedkar policies for Bhangis and the potential of Ambedkar-Bhangis political and social partnership, Bhagwan Das emphasized again the need to revive the relationship between the two.

Till 1947, Ambedkar-Bhangis relationship was maintained in socio-political realm. But since 1956, things began to change rapidly and Bhangis started to drift towards the Congress. The Congress was seen as the saviour of the Dalits in general and Bhangis in particular. The Congress-Bhangis relationship seemed even more solid with the Congress' socio-economic commitment.

In 1970, the idea of construction of hostel for the Bhangi boys as a weapon for promoting education among them, first came to mind of J.P. Singh[8] (henceforth called Singh) when he was studying at D.N. inter College, Meerut. At that time he was student of Class XI (Science) and living in a rented room with Dhanpal at Mohalla Jantiwada Kher Nagar, Meerut.

A woman manual scavenger who met her livelihood by removing human excreta from dry latrin in a nearby basti called 'Kumharon-ki-Basti' in Meerut district. The woman face obscured with duptta perched on head and wrapped around shoulder. Bad smell of human excreta was intolerable. This attracted the attention of Singh. He wanted to move from Jantiwada Kher Nagar to some where else and after a few months Singh shifted to Kumar Ashram, located at Kelashpuri, Meerut.

Singh toured all over Meerut and visited Bhangi bastis located in Meerut city such as Bhagwatpura, Purva Shekhlal, Rajban, etc. to see the socio-educational conditions of untouchable among untouchables. He noticed that literacy among the Bhangis is negligible because of social discrimination. Most of the children left the schools after passing VI, VII and VIII standards. While living in Kumar Ashram, he used to think how to provide them a good social environment.

The inhuman conditions of the Bhangis ignited the mind of Bhangi youth, Singh towards the efforts to overcome their socio-educational disabilities and this led frustration in him. Singh began to question the efficacy of Hinduism and thought of an alternative, namely Ambedkar teachings for overcoming their social – religious deprivation. Singh favoured education – a view supported by Bhangis and others.

Singh was active as socio-educational reformer in 1994. He believed that progress in education is the basis for upward social mobility and keeping this in mind encouraged the organization of caste sammelan and meetings. On 12 July 1994 Singh had formed a Valmiki Shiksha Prashar Samiti at Meerut with the object to encourage the poor Bhangis so that they may send their children to schools.

The drive for education took a positive turn when Singh established Valmiki Shiksha Prashar Samiti in 1994. Born on 1 December 1954 in Jawaharpur Mevla village situated 6 miles from district Bagpat, UP, his father Dabli Ram, a poor Bhangi was working as a traditional worker in Calcutta (now Kolkata). He never received former education in schools. However, he learnt Urdu, Bangali, English and Hindi from Maulvi, Englishman, etc. However, it may be noted in this connection that Dabli Ram used to write letter in Urdu, Hindi and Bangli, etc.

Singh brought about a new socio-educational awakening among the Bhangis of Meerut by providing hostel accommodation, food, stationary, newspapers, pens and pencils.

Since the early phase of education campaign was associated with the leadership of Singh, it is necessary to assess his contribution to education movement. In 1975, Singh passed his BSc degree examination from Meerut University and had the honour of being the first Bhangi post graduate in three subjects, viz. History, Political Science and Sociology. In 1974 he joined LIC as Assistant at Meerut. In 1981, he had applied for the test to qualify in UP Administrative Services and he was declared successful. He joined as Sales Tax Officer at Gajiabad Checkpost, Uttar Pradesh where he rose from the position of Sales Tax Officer to that of Additional Commissioner of Sales Tax in Uttar Pradesh government and retired in November 2014. He believed, like Ambedkar that education is more essential and hence Bhangis by educating themselves in modern education, could attain the height that some upper caste hindus has achieved.

Singh attempted to transform the common people and uplift the Bhangis by propagating the teachings of Ambedkar. Untouchables elsewhere became followers and supporters of Ambedkar to gain access to modern education, government employment and higher social status. On 14 April 2011 it was mainly due to his efforts that the name of Samiti was changed from Valmiki Shiksha Prashar Samiti to Ambedkar Samaj Shiksha Prasar Samiti, Meerut Uttar

Pradesh. It was mainly because Bhangis and other down trodden need no other education but Ambedkar education based on equality and justice.

Spreading of education in Meerut dates back to 1994 with sincere efforts of Singh. Due to his encouragement and patronage, Ram piyari – widow of Om Prakash Valmiki, donated 2200 sq. ft (nearly 2.5 *bigha*) land at Dantal Jatoli Road, Shradhpuri, Kankarkheda, Meerut in 2000 to construct a own community Hostel in the memory of Om Prakash Valmiki – a hero of Indo-Pak War 1971. He was serving in Indian Navy. It should be mentioned here that according to Singh – President of Ambedkar Samaj Shiksha Prashar Samiti, the then market value of the donated land was estimated to be around ₹ 11 lakh.

In an attempt to build a community hostel, Singh in pursuit of his efforts started the construction work in 2002. Therefore, by 2005, it had six rooms. In order to make the social changes effective Singh realized the importance of having an inaugural ceremony. Thus under the Shyamlal's Chairmanship, rooms were inaugurated by the Bhagwan Das – an eminent Supreme Court Advocate.

The most significant event during inauguration ceremony was laying the foundation stone of more rooms at hostel premises in 2006, by Bhagwan Das and Shyamlal. The assembled people were happy with this move and so they thanked Singh and his team.

In the past one decade, large number of new rooms were constructed. Therefore, by 2016 the Ambedkar Shiksha Prashar Samiti has 32 rooms in the hostel. It is significant that this community hostel was named after Om Prakash Valmiki and whose objective is propagating Ambedkar's teachings. It is regarded as the beacon light of new knowledge and moon light in the dark. It is also significant that teachings are centered around the Ambedkar. Thus the hostel supported the object of Ambedkar socio-educational philosophy. Through the hostel the message of Ambedkar spread all over Meerut and even reached the village level.

Singh was active as socio-educational reformer in 1994 and continued even today. During the period of about 23 years, the changes which he shered are remarkable. Besides, running hostel, Singh also organized so far nine to ten regional seminars in which university professors, readers, college lecturers, bureaucrates, eminent Dalit writers, social activists, volunetters, poets and social workers participated to discuss the internal and external factor responsible for their backwardness and maintained that the reformation of Bhangis are necessary for the upliftment of the Bhangi masses. The scholars made direct attack on caste system. Since caste is associated with traditional occupation, they advocated that Bhangis should give up their traditional occupation of removing night soil. They believed that progress in employment and education is the basis for upward social mobility.

We have noted above Singh's attempts to hold seminar to seek redress with regard to backwardness of Bhangis inspite of protective discrimination. Between 1994 and 2016 several seminars were held. Singh's organization exchange ideas and experiences on issues related to education, traditional occupation, socio-economic backwardness, social welfare, etc. for instance:

'सफाई कार्य करने वाली जातियों के उत्थान में डा. अडम्बेडकर की भूमिका'

'सफाई पेशे से जुड़ी जातियों का आपसी ध्रुवीकरण : कितना सामयिक और कितना मजबूरी'

'शोषित व स्वच्छकार समाज के युवक व युवतियों को रोजगार परख शिक्षा की ओर अग्रसर करने विषयक'

A few eminent scholars and bureaucrates were highly influenced by Singh's academic activities and programmes, notably – Bhagwan Das – an eminent Supreme Court lawyer, New Delhi; Shyam lal, former Vice Chancellor of three State Universities; Dharmpal Peehal, Hyderabad; Kosal Panwar, Delhi; Sheikhar, DIG, Jail Meerut, writer Om Prakash Valmiki, Dehradun, etc.

As the president of Samiti, Singh did much to expand accommodation facilities. Therefore, by 2016, hostel has 25 hostellers in all. It has 18 Bhangi, 1 Chamar, 2 Jatav, 1 Dom, 1 Raut. Besides, SCs, there are few OBC boys: 1 Yadav and 1 Teli. Singh took initiative in providing books, food, pens and pencils, newspapers etc.

It may be noted that hostel in mate are studying different subjects, such as PG in History and Geography, BTech, BCom, BA, LLB, BEd, and inter. A few students are studying in VI to X standard. The academic programme initiated by Singh in 1994 such as building of common hostel for SC and OBC students, abolishing social discrimination and encouraging inter-dining between SC and OBC and popularizing the Ambedkar teachings formulated by him.

A marble statue of Om Prakash Valmiki was installed on 9 December 2006 at the hostel premises and inaugurated by Bhagwan Das and Shyam lal. At the time of sammelan and meetings men, women and the volunteers offer prayer to Om Prakash Valmiki.

By the 2008, hostel's publicity and influence was wide spread and some enlightened men of Meerut realized that it is Singh who has been providing hostel facilities free of cost to our boys. They also said that we should be thankful to Singh for this great work. Singh takes an active interest in collecting funds/donation for construction of rooms, conference/meeting hall, library centre etc.

Singh not only interested in collecting the funds but he, as the President of Samiti made a general appeal for becoming a life member of samiti by paying ₹ 5,000. In one of his pamphlet, he appealed to common men to pay ₹ 100 per month or Pay ₹ 1 per day to samiti as donation. Besides, Samiti has got printed coupon of ₹ 100, 500 and 1,000 and those who were interested in the growth of education can obtain from President. However, it may be noted that Singh, as the President of Samiti, regularly support financially from his pension towards hostel and educational programmes. This is the zeal with which Singh spearheaded the educational campaign, mobilizing public opinion among the Bhangis and other untouchables.

Another notable supporter and follower of Ambedkar, who is associated with the activities and programmes of Ambedkar Movement in Delhi and Uttar Pradesh is Surajpal Chouhan. Surajpal Chouhan[9] did his matriculation in 1974 from the Central Board of Secondary Education (CBSE) and passed BA in 1978 from Delhi University.

Coming from a poor Bhangi family, Chouhan had applied for the test to qualify as junior assistant in 1978 and he was declared successful.

He joined as junior assistant in STC office of India, New Delhi, from where he rose from the position of junior assistant to that of Chief Administrative Manager. In his earlier days as junior assistant, he was harassed, tortured and humiliated being a untouchable Bhangi. He had the courage to face all this. He had the skills of writing stories, essays, poems, and brought about the awakening for concentrated action with intention of redressing them. This formed the basis of Ambedkar movement. Om Prakash Valmiki, Surajpal Chouhan and Sushila Takbhore are the first Bhangi Ambedkarite writers who have shown an intellectual ability in writing stories, essays, poems, etc. This attracted the attention of Hindi Pandit of Brahmins, Kayasthas, Yadav and other castes.

Chouhan took a special interest in the publication of Ambedkar literature and the envisaged the need to bring out some selected works of all Valmiki Ambedkarite writers in order to reach the masses. Thus, in 2017 he published the famous book entitled *Valmiki Ambedkarite Samaj ke Kathakaron ki Charchit Stories* for social and political awakening, which are published with a view to propogating the message of Ambedkar.

As such other writers and intellectuals also tried to give an internal message for a pro-Ambedkar inclusive stand, and send out a message to Congress. He considered literature essential which would educate the people. In 2008, he was honoured by the then President of India Pratibha Devi Singh Patil with 'Subramanium Bharti Award' at Rashtrapati Bhavan. The award carries ₹ 1 Lakh cash.

In October 2016,[10] some educated Bhangi youths (all Graduate and Post-gradudate) realized the importance of having a vachnalay. Thus, they opened an Vachnalay called as 'Valmiki Ambedkar Pustkalay' at Chharra, a small town in Aligarh, District of Uttar Pradesh for spreading and promoting Ambedkar's views amongst the Bhangis. Padam Kumar, Samar Deep, Pinki, Bobi Chouhan and Kuldeep Chouhan assumed the leadership to fight the injustice done to the Bhangis in the fields of education and government employments. This is the first set of events which sparked off a literary movement. These educated youths have literary interest.

This Vachnalay did evoke good response from some well established organizations. For instance, 'Ramnika Foundation' located in New Delhi, the Capital of India around 126 km from Aligarh, donated a large number of books, Magazines etc. to the Vachnalay, so that educated youths could know more and more about Ambedkar's views, works and teachings etc. which are enjoyed by other scheduled castes who became Ambedkar followers and supporters.

Ramnika Gupta hails from the then undivided Bihar, who owns 'Ramnika Foundation' in Vazir Nagar, Kotla Mubarakpur, New Delhi has been publisher and editor of a monthly Hindi magazine *Yuddhrata Aama Aadmi*. Besides, the foundation has published a number of books on socio-economic and educational conditions of the scheduled castes and scheduled tribes in particular and weaker sections of society in general.

It should be mentioned here that according to Surajpal Chouhan – a well known Vakmiki author, the current market value of the donated books, is estimated to be around ₹ 30,000. Surajpal Chouhan also donated books.

In the same year (2016), the youths collected the donation from their caste fellows and they installed a statue of Ambedkar at Vachnalay premises. People come here to study of Ambedkar's work and to propogate Ambedkar's teachings. This is the zeal with which these youths spearheaded the literary campaign, mobilizing public opinion amongst the Bhangi massess.

We get an idea of how the Valmikis of Delhi and Haryana came under Ambedkar influence from the account of Kailash Chandra Chouhan.[11] Kailash Chandra Chouhan, editor of *Kadam*, a quarterly Hindi magazine, published from New Delhi, visited Sirsa district in Haryana to know from Valmikis about Ambedkar. With all these preparation the stage was set for tour to began in May 2016. He travelled by bus from New Delhi towards Sirsa, 263 Km from Delhi and reached Sirsa bus stand. From here he hired a ricksha and reached Chadigadia, a Valmiki Basti. Here, Chouhan met O.P. Anthoni, Chouhan stayed here for a while. Anthoni arranged break fast for him. In Sirsa, there are four Valmiki bastis: Chadigadia Mohalla, Lakhi Talab, Thed and Loku Mohalla. In all there are 18,000 to 20,000 Valmikis residents. He also visited all Bastis in order to know the people's views about Ambedkar.

Here he met Ravipal, a Valmiki and newspaper publisher and owner. Ravipal publishes a paper called 'Apna Chenal': while paper propogate Ambedkar's views and teachings among the caste fellows, he considered supporting of Ambedkar idealogy as useful to the self respect of Haryana Valmikis. Chouhan was pleased to know from Ravipal's sister – Jyotibala that they do not worship Hindu God and Goddesses.

In 2010 in Mirchpur village in Sirsa district in an attempt to supress the Valmikis, the upper caste Bahubali set fire 18 Valmikis houses and few were killed. More than 150 families left the village for ever. Why it happened, asked Chouhan. Prahlad Meghnath, a painter by profession replied, because we were never supporters of Ambedkar. Ambedkar rightly said, Be educatged, Be united and struggle, he further added.

In Sirsa, there is a Ambedkar Bhavan, initiative to build a Bhavan came from Jatavs/Chamars. It should be noted here that Jatavs/Chamars, however has gained the support of Valmikis at local level. We get an idea of how the Valmikis at Ambedkar chowk near Sirsa bus stand installed a Ambedkar statue, with the growth of Ambedkar influence from the account of Chouhan. It is note worthy that initiative to install Ambedkar statue came from Valmikis. Valmikis, however has gained the support of Jatavs/Chamars.

On the occasion of 125th birth anniversary of Dr. Ambedkar, 'Bharatiya Samaj Nirman Sangh' (BSNS), New Delhi, decided to celebrate the 125th anniversary in 125 Valmikis Bastis of Delhi. Delhi people know that Valmikis do not assemble in the name of Ambedkar and also not ready to listen about him. They are against Ambedkar. We have not yet made efforts to bring them in our fold who are against Ambedkar. However, leaders of BSNS wanted to celebrate the Ambedkar Jyanti as it would add prestige to Ambedkar movement. Leaders, social workers and volunteers assembled at Valmikis bastis and addressed the gathering, extoling the virtue of Ambedkar. Thus, BSNS succeeded in celebrating birth anniversary of Ambedkar in 130 bastis, The celebration of Ambedkar Jyanti had many important consequences on Ambedkar movement, as a whole and on Valmikis in particular. BSNS expressed the hope that Valmikis would advance towards socio-political goal which Ambedkar had placed before them (*Kadam*, 4(16) Feburary-April 2017, pp. 89–94). They were also pleased to find many educated men among Valmikis. Thus, BSNS created a socio-political awakening among the people.

The illiterate, literate and educated among the Valmikis, however, support Ambedkar and they do not bother about the Congress. Although they support the Congress. Thus, the long period of several decades when Bhangis associated itself with Congress came slowly and slowly towards an end.

The foregoing account shows that growth of Ambedkar influence in Delhi and Haryana introduced a split in Congress base as Valmikis are divided, the educated Bhangis supporting the Ambedkar campaign and the illiterate and poor supporting the Congress and others. The schism is based on divergent ideologies.

Dharmpal Peehal[12] born on 20th August, 1953 in Hyderabad, the then undivided Andhra Pradesh (now in Telangana) in a poor Bhangi family. His father was Banwarilal Peehal and his mother's name was Bharpai Devi. His father was a man with progressive ideas. In 1976, Peehal passed B.Sc. degree examination from the Usmania University, Hyderabad and had the honour of being the first Bhangi Science Graduate. Although Peehal had qualified in B.Sc., he obtained Master's degree (Hindi Literature) in 1979 from the same University. He too did his MPhil and PhD from Hyderabad University, Hyderabad in 1986 and eventually joined Giriraj Government Degree college Nijamabad, Andhra Pradesh in 1984 to 1989 as Lecturer in Hindi. From the beginning Peehal had literary interest and hence in 1989 he was selected as a Senior Lecturer in Department of Hindi, Usmania University, Hyderabad. In 1991 he became reader and was promoted to the post of Professor in 1999 in the same department and in 2007 Peehal became Head, Department of Hindi, Usmania University, Hyderabad. In 2013 Peehal became Dean, Faculty of Arts and eventually retired in the same year (2013).

During his student days Peehal was directly inspired by the Ambedkar and was associated with the activities of Ambedkar's agitation in Andhra Pradesh.

In order to make socio-religious changes effective, Peehal realised the importance of spreading and propagating the Ambedkar's views, works and teachings amongst the dalits in general and Bhangis in particular. Thus, he founded several socio-educational and religious organisations in Andhra

Pradesh and Delhi; 'प्रबुद्ध भारत संघ दिल्ली', 'समता साहित्य समिति, हैदराबाद', आंध्र प्रदेश वाल्मीकि समाज प्रगति संघ, 'भारतीय बौद्ध महासभा, आन्ध्र प्रदेश, बुद्ध जयंती उत्सव समिति, हैदराबाद'

Peehal not only enouraged Ambedkar's views and teachings amongst the Bhangis but also Budhist philosophy. Attempts were made to change traditional religious beliefs and practices, but these attempts failed and could not become a movement.

It is only with propogation of Ambedkar's socio-religious and political philosophy, Peehal believed in Buddhism. Thus, Peehal served the cause of Bhangis in two ways. First, worked as a champion of Ambedkar's view and secondly he published several essays, poems and books for spreading and propogating Ambedkar's views for the progress of the community. He was also honoured by different organizations.

It should be mentioned here that during Seventh decade of twentieth century, Himat Ram Jodha[13] (henceforth called Jodha) a Meghwal by caste spearheaded an agitation which was fairly, wide spread in Jodhpur. He is considered to be initiator of Ambedkar Movement in Jodhpur.

In 1966 after passing middle school, Rajanlal Jawa got admission in Government Mahilabagh Higher Secondary School, Jodhpur. He tried to pass Matriculation twice in 1967 and 1968, but in vain and eventually, he went to Madhya Pradesh and passed Higher Secondary in 1970, he returned to Jodhpur and admitted in JNV University, Jodhpur. In course of his student days he came in contact with Bhanwar lal Pandit (Bhangi) who was staunch follower and supporter of Ambedkar and was considered to be the first Bhangi converted Buddhist and pracharak of Ambedkar views. According to Rajanlal Jawa it was Bhanwar lal Pandit who influenced him much by Ambedkar teachings and views and gave him a few books to read. Thus, Rajan Lal Jawa became staunch follower of Ambedkar and participated all programmes and activities oriented towards social transformation. His involvement in Ambedkar programmes effected his academic career. In 1970 and 1971 he appeared in first year T.D.C. exam, but failed. He left the University. In 1971–72 he was appointed as casual labour in Central Arid Zone Research Institute. Here he came in contact with H.R. Jodha. In 1975, he was made permanent class IV employee in CAZRI.

It should be mentioned here that H.R. Jodha had formed a union called 'Scheduled Castes Upliftment Union' (SCUU) and made several representations to Director, CAZRI to secure social justice for SCs and STs employees. Jodha and his supporters including Rajanlal Jawa staged dharna, protest, hunger strike and demonstration.

In 1977, Rajanlal Jawa was promoted as Technical Assistant, but transferred to Borunda – a range management and soil conservation area (RM and SC) of CAZRI, 105 km from Jodhpur. Rajanlal Jawa was a dedicated Ambedkarite and continued in social activities. He was mainly responsible for propagating and promoting Ambedkar views, works etc. in neighbouring towns namely Bhopalgarh, Peepar City and Bilara. It was because of Rajanlal Jawa's active role his annual confidential report was spoiled by his superior and eventually he was transferred to another RM and SC Area of CAZRI namely Samdari – a small village in desert Barmer district of Western Rajasthan. The conditions that were prevailing at that time were such that scheduled castes people were not celebrating Ambedkar Jyanti. In 1985 the idea of celebrating Ambedkar Jyanti conceived for the first time by Rajanlal Jawa, with the help of local people and social activists. In an attempt to celebrate Ambedkar Jyanti, Rajanlal Jawa visited the neighbouring towns namely : Barmer and Balotra. A few months later at two more places, Barmer and Balotra, Ambedkar Jyanti was organized. Thus, the dalits in increasing numbers participated in Ambedkar Jyanti. This was the zeal with which Rajan lal Jawa spearheaded the agitation, mobilizing public opinion amongst the dalits.

In 1987, Rajanlal Jawa was transferred to Central Arid Zone Research Institute (CAZRI), Jodhpur and he retired as T-5, officer in 2011. Since 1970 till today he kind of work, he did are remarkable.

As stated above, there was a great social worker of Jodhpur. Coming from a poor Meghwal family of progressive man, Jodha took his initiative in starting socio-religious establishment, such as 'Bodh Vihar'. In order to make the socio-religious changes effective, H.R. Jodha along with Prof. Kanhailal Khawas, Chen Prasad Pandit, Rajanlal Jawa and Daulal Changra realized the importance of having Bodh Vihar and a category of celiberated Monks, Priests, Missionaries and a separate library cell. Thus, the first Bodh Vihar and liberary cell established by Jodha and his colleages in 1968 was at Masuria, Jodhpur. In this Bodh Vihar, there was a dalit Bodh Sanyasi devoted to the stay of Bodh and Ambedkar's work and to the training of Ambedkar followers who will propagate Ambedkar's teachings.

In 1972, H.R. Jodha and his team established a branch of the Buddhist society of India for Ambedkar followers in Jodhpur and spread the message of Lord Buddha. A small committee came into existence in 1990 to manage the Bodh Vihar at Masuria, Jodhpur which Jodha and his team had build in 1968. The main object of the Bodh Vihar was to promote and to encourage socio-religious education among the down trodden. Rajanlal Jawa became the Secretary.

In addition to socio-religious activities, the office bearer of Bodh Vihar achieved significant gains by 1990. They had popularized the Bodh Vihar through inviting eminent Bodh Bhikksu to deliver the lecture. For instance, in 1992 on occasion of Budh Purnima P. Samravi Diwan, the proponent of Buddhist in Thailand came and delivered the lecture. Likewise, on different occasions, such as Dham Diksha Divas, Ashok Vijay Dasmi a few Buddhist Bhikksus monks, missionaries, etc. from Bodh Gaya, Bihar, Japan, visited the Bodh Vihar, Jodhpur in order to deliver the lectures. Bhante Gyan Jagat, the Chairman of Management Committee came from Bodh Gaya, Bihar. After few years of active involvement in propagating Ambedkar views among masses, Buddhist Society of India in 2001 nominated Rajanlal Jawa as District President of Buddhist Society of India, Jodhpur. When Rajanlal Jawa was the District President of Buddhist Society of India then different eminent personalities like spiritual leader Dalai Lama was invited to Jodhpur. In 2002, Rajanlal Jawa took part in Buddhist Sammelan held at Ajmer.

A Diksha Sammelan at Ghantaghar, Jodhpur was organised nearly 40 years ago (1977) by Buddhist Society of India, Jodhpur. The aim of Sammelan was to bring the downtrodden in the Buddhist fold. L.R. Bali, a well-known Ambedkarite leader came from Jalandhar, Punjab and Bhante Shant Raksak from Delhi presided over the function. In an attempt to support the sammelan, a large number of men, women, children and volunteers assembled here. The success of the sammelan was the result of continued support under the leadership of H.R. Jodha, Prof. Kanhailal Khawas, Chen Prasad Pandit, Rajanlal Jawa and Daulal Changra.

Besides, Rajanlal Jawa took a special interest in establishing Dr. Ambedkar Kala Kendra, to propagate Ambedkar teachings through Music, Bhajan, Songs, Poems etc.

It is significant to note here that between 1990 to 2011 most of the associations just as the Dalit Sahitya Academy, Delhi whose main objective is propagating Ambedkar teachings honoured Rajan Lal Jawa.

Gaining confidence by his success in the socio-religious field, Rajanlal Jawa concentrated his efforts on books and essays writing, making it a part of Ambedkar movement. As a writer, he published five books. These are:

i. डा. भीमराव अम्बेडकर, संक्षिप्त जीवनी, (भाग प्रथम - 1989, भाग द्वितीय - 2004)
ii. भीम गीत माला (भाग प्रथम-1990)
iii. भीम गीत माला
iv. भगवान बुद्ध के प्रेरक प्रसंग (2012)
v. राजस्थान के दलित साहित्यकार (2016)

Mohanlal Joad[14] born on 14 April 1949 in a Udaimandar Bhangi Basti, Jodhpur. His father, Puna Ram, a poor Bhangi was working as a Safai Karamchari in the then Jodhpur Nagar Palika (now Nagar Nigam, Jodhpur). His mother's name was Jadav. Mohanlal Joad received his primary and middle education in Udaimandar Harijan School, Jodhpur. In 1965, he passed higher secondary education from Mahilabagh Higher Secondary School, Jodhpur.

The drive for higher education took a positive turn when Government of Rajasthan established Jodhpur University, Jodhpur in 1962. Apart from upper castes, untouchables also took admission to receive modern education. In 1966 Mohanlal Joad took admission in Jodhpur University. He did his BA in the year 1969 and MA (Political Science) in 1972. While he was studying for his MA in Jodhpur University, he came in contact with professor (Dr). Laxman Singh Rathore (later Rathore became Vice Chancellor of Jodhpur University) who was then a most popular teacher among the students. Mohanlal Joad was a poor Bhangi student and not interested in carrying his higher study. So he appeared for bank exam in 1969 and declared successful. He joined State Bank of Bikaner and Jaipur (now in April 2017 merged in State Bank of India) as a clerk in 1969 too and after few years, in 1980, became Branch Manager and continued for several years.

One of the most significant incident of Mohanlal Joad, occurred during his school days. Once Madhur Mathur a lady Hindi teacher went on leave. In absence of her Magadutt: Shrimali – a Sanskrit Brahmin teacher engaged the class. Orthodox Brahmin considered the Bhangis as most degraded untouchables. Shrimali asked certain questions to Mohanlal Joad. In response to Shrimali's call, although Mohanlal Joad answered most of the questions, he did not reply to a few questions. Irked with Mohanlal Joad, Magadutt Shrimali started beating him with stick mercilessly. As a result, Mohanlal's shoulder was fractured. It gave wide publicity to incident. The Bhangis also protested against Shrimali. Thus, since his childhood Joad was directly affected by the inequalities and status of untouchability.

Madhur Mathur was a very popular teacher among students. When she returned back and came to know about this incident, she was shocked. She was a progressive teacher who loved good students. She gave Mohanlal Joad, a small book entitled 'डा. अम्बेडकर की जीवनी' to read. Mohanlal Joad took keen interest in reading the book and came to know of Ambedkar's struggle for untouchables in India. This was the turning point in his life. Having read Ambedkar's writings, Joad turned his attention to write about Ambedkar. Thus, in 2002 Mohanlal Joad wrote and published his first book entitled 'महान विभूति बाबा साहिब डा. भीमराव अम्बेडकर'. Another book entitled 'डा. भीमराव अम्बेडकर ने धर्म परिवर्तन क्यों किया' came out in 2009. Gaining confidence by his success in publication of books he published a few more books, such as 'संविधान शिल्पी डा. भीमराव अम्बेडकर (2017)' etc.

Notes

1. भगवान दास, बाबा साहेब भीमराव अम्बेडकर और भंगी जातियां, लखनऊ, दलित टुडे प्रकाशन, 1998, पृ. 56.
2. Ibid., p. 56–57.
3. Ibid., p. 57–58.
4. Ibid., p. 58.
5. Ibid., p. 58–59.
6. Ibid., p. 59–60.
7. Ibid., p. 60–61.
8. For more details, see, particularly letter, pamphlet etc. dated 24-4-2017 by J.P. Singh – The president, Ambedkar Samaj Siksha Prashar Samiti, Meerut, Uttar Pradesh. Telephonic talk with J.P. Singh in April and May 2007.
9. See, particularly, 5 page letter plus enclosure dated 19-4-2017 from Suraj pal Chouhan, Talk with Suroj Pal Chauhan, April, 2017.
10. Ibid.
11. विस्तृत जानकारी हेतु देखे, कैलाशचंद चौहान, 'हरियाणा के सिरसा शहर में वाल्मीकि समाज और बाबा साहेब फरवरी-अप्रैल, 2017, पृ. 89–94. यह भी देखे, 'रिपोर्ट: अम्बेडकर फुले की 125वीं जयंती पर भारतीय समाज निर्माण संघ द्वारा वाल्मीकि बस्तियों में 125 जागरूकता कार्यक्रम का आयोजन', कदम, 2017, वही पृ. 92–95.

12. धर्मपाल पीहल, 'हैदराबाद की मेहतर जाति और उसका इतिहास' कदम, 2017 वहीं पृ. 29–35. दूरभाष पर धर्मपाल पीहल से बातचीत मई 2017.
13. Fore genesis and growth of Ambedkar Movement in Western Rajasthan, Particularly in Jodhpur, See, 15 page letter from Prashant Kandare regarding Rajanlal Jawa. dated 25-4-2017.
14. See Mohanlal Joad's letter dated 10 January 2017.

Index